THE LANDS OF
CHARM AND CRUELTY

Stan Sesser has written extensively on Southeast Asia for the
New Yorker and has reported for the *Wall Street Journal*. He
has also taught at the Graduate School of Journalism at the
University of California in Berkeley, the city where he lives.

THE LANDS OF
CHARM AND CRUELTY

Travels in Southeast Asia

Stan Sesser

PICADOR

First published 1993 as a Borzoi Book by Alfred A. Knopf, Inc., New York
and simultaneously in Canada by Random House of Canada Limited, Toronto

First published in Great Britain 1994 by Picador
a division of Pan Macmillan Publishers Limited
Cavaye Place, London SW10 9PG
and Basingstoke

Associated companies throughout the world

ISBN 0 330 33387 9

3 5 7 9 8 6 4 2

A CIP catalogue record for this book is available from
the British Library

Printed and bound in Great Britain by
Cox & Wyman Ltd, Reading, Berkshire

*To Bob Gottlieb,
who had the courage to take a chance,
and to Sasha Sesser-Ginzberg.
I hope she will grow up to see
Southeast Asia as the lands
of charm and freedom.*

CONTENTS

INTRODUCTION

———

ONE SUNDAY MORNING in the fall of 1990, in a communal dwelling called a longhouse located deep in the rain forest of Borneo, soft music slowly woke me well before dawn. I was lying wrapped in the mosquito net on a rough wood-plank floor, with no mat or blanket and only my towel as a pillow. My body ached from the hard floor, but I quickly forgot the discomfort as I listened to hauntingly beautiful choral singing; in such a remote spot, it seemed to possess an otherworldly quality. Looking for the source, I got up and walked along the veranda that connected the rooms of the longhouse. In one of the rooms, all the families of this tiny settlement called Long Leng had gathered. They were sitting cross-legged on the floor singing Christian hymns, set to melodies of their Penan culture.

The inhabitants of Long Leng are among the nine thousand Penan left on the island of Borneo, which lies in the South China Sea between Malaysia and Indonesia. Several hundred Penan still lead the nomadic lives of hunter-gatherers, one of the last such people left on earth. To visit the Penan is to get a glimpse of a civilization that, in today's world, I would consider enlightened rather than backward. The Penan don't know the meaning of greed; the men who are the most skilled hunters with the blow-pipe share their food with everyone else. The community looms so important that all the members choose to live in the longhouse, since building a private home would represent a selfish act. Respect for the environment is paramount, and the Penan teach their children how to preserve the rain forest for future generations.

I was only the second Westerner to have visited Long Leng; some of the inhabitants vaguely recalled an Australian coming a few years before on a charitable mission. The experience, from the ethereal music to the spectacular setting, should have been idyllic. Long Leng lies in a lushly forested bowl ablaze with flowers, alongside a rapidly flowing river. The visitor enters another world, one of loincloths and poison darts and strange traditions like trying to avoid the light of the sun. Despite some trappings of Christianity left by missionaries, the Penan culture is poles apart from anything in the West. The Penan have no concept of days or dates, or even the passage of time as we know it. To them a long journey, no matter what its duration in hours, will be any trip that is hard, with lots of sun and not very good hunting.

Yet I was to leave Long Leng more devastated than uplifted, for I had also witnessed the Penan's participation in a seemingly hopeless battle. This was a confrontation with a very different civilization—one of rapacious politicians, of businessmen out for a quick gain no matter what the consequences, of Japanese companies willing to destroy a rain forest to feed Japan's insatiable demand for tropical hardwoods. Long Leng itself was an oasis, but the rain forest surrounding it had already vanished, with nothing but scrub growth remaining. The Penan hunters found few animals left, and the rivers, polluted by the logging operations, no longer provided fish. These unique people were both hungry and dispirited, and their way of life appeared doomed.

Much about Long Leng represents in a microcosm my experiences elsewhere in Southeast Asia. The rain forests of Borneo are but one of the many features that make Southeast Asia perhaps the most intriguing part of the world: nations of beautiful people who warmly welcome a visitor, of ancient cultural traditions that still thrive, of great religious monuments and works of art. But Southeast Asia is also a place of tyranny and repression, where governments dismiss democracy and human rights as indulgences of the West, and view the most severe environmental degradation as a small price to pay for economic growth. The constant tension between the charm and the cruelty of life in Southeast Asia lured me as a journalist, and left me with memories of both fond encounters and endless tragedies.

I became fascinated with Southeast Asia during two trips to Burma as a tourist in 1985 and 1986. Burma reflects the dichotomy between charm and cruelty in a way that mesmerizes many Western visitors: the most gracious people and the most repressive government; a rich and beautiful land overwhelmed by poverty; a highly literate society enslaved by superstition. Rangoon, little changed over the decades, is a city that gives a glimpse of the Asia of fifty years ago. Pagan, about four hundred miles north of Rangoon, is filled with so many hundreds of ancient Buddhist monuments that a farmer literally can't plow a field without having to detour around one.

On my first visit, some chance encounters during a rainstorm in Mandalay, the center of Buddhism and intellectual life in Burma, left me with a friend whose help would prove invaluable when I returned to the country to write about it four years later. I had taken shelter in a teahouse and quickly fell into conversation with a tall, mustachioed Burmese who shook the water off his umbrella, walked over to my table, and announced in English, "It's raining cats and dogs." He filled his speech with an astonishing rapid-fire string of American idioms; when I asked him why he was doing this, he replied without hesitation, "To keep up with the Joneses."

This particular teahouse functioned as a gathering place for young Burmese intellectuals, who competed with each other to show off their knowledge of American English. After the first man left, Myint Thame, a journalist who earned $250 a year writing for a Burmese magazine, came up and proudly asked me about "Rambo-mania." But he quickly admitted he was a rank novice in the school of idioms, and he asked me to bring a dictionary of idioms on my next trip. This I did the following year, when we traveled together for a week. During that week I got my first insight into the darker side of life in Burma. Each time we checked into a hotel, a policeman knocked on the door within minutes demanding an explanation of what a Burmese was doing in the company of an American; an American, in the government's view, could spread dangerously subversive ideas, like that of democracy. I pretended to be outraged, demanding to see their superiors and threatening to call the American embassy, and that generally scared them away.

In August and September of 1988, the Burmese people staged massive democracy demonstrations, which ended in disaster when the army slaughtered hundreds of demonstrators. I had seen the enchantment of Burma, and now I wanted to return to write about the tyranny. In April 1989, the Burmese government allowed seven reporters into the country. I was one of them, and Myint Thame agreed to act as my interpreter.

During my years of reporting in the United States, I took for granted the idea that a reporter should not get personally involved in an article but should instead dispassionately gather all the facts. But Southeast Asia, with its underside of heavy-handed repression, leads to situations that require a very different set of rules. In Burma, where I began writing about Asia, the credo of personal detachment lasted exactly five days.

On the sixth day, military intelligence agents pulled in Myint Thame for questioning. They acted while I was interviewing members of the military junta, who referred to themselves by the wonderfully evil-sounding name of "the SLORC" (State Law and Order Restoration Committee). Since it would have been too dangerous to bring him with me to the interview, I had suggested to Myint Thame that he take the afternoon off. But military intelligence had other plans for him. That evening, on the way to dinner, he told me about the interrogation. "They asked me for the names of people you talked to," he said. "I told them that you were mainly interested in visiting the markets, that you loved Burmese cooking and wanted to see what food was on sale."

Myint Thame made light of the interrogation, but I was worried. If the military had taken action even before I had left the country, what might happen after my departure? I realized that if it were at all possible, the Burmese government must learn immediately that a powerful foreign country was watching out for Myint Thame. I went to a pay phone and rang the American ambassador, Burton Levin, at his home, assuming that his phone was tapped and hoping I could talk in a stilted enough manner to lead him to deduce my motive. Levin, whose forceful advocacy of democracy in Burma made for a distinguished chapter in the history of American diplomacy, caught on immediately. "This is an outrage," he said, assuring me he'd take a personal interest in Myint Thame's fate. "I've never heard of anything so stupid," he said. "How can they hope for investment if they interrogate Burmese after foreigners talk to them?" Then, speaking slowly and distinctly, he stated, "And I want whoever is listening to this conversation to report it to your superiors *immediately*!" Apparently the strategy succeeded, because I later heard that Myint Thame was left alone.

So in writing about Burma, I had to abandon my usual role as the detached observer. After all, I was describing a government that shoots down its dissenting students in cold blood— and chooses to do so on days of the month divisible by nine, because the country's dictator, General Ne Win, believes that this number poses perils to him that he must overcome. Instead, I tried to replace the concept of detachment with one of fairness, by giving the government the opportunity to defend itself. My attempt to get a government official to speak with me was about as strange an episode as anything I encountered in Southeast Asia, a part of the world where the bizarre is commonplace. The government in no way would acknowledge my presence in the country, and soldiers with bayonets frustrated my efforts to enter government buildings. But when I phoned the main number of the Foreign Ministry and asked for someone who spoke English, a mysterious man who refused to identify himself came on the phone to say he knew everything about me. Interviews with the foreign minister and members of the SLORC followed.

Nowhere in my travels to some of the remotest spots in Southeast Asia did the contrast between charm and cruelty emerge so clearly as on the Ho Chi Minh Trail in Laos. This mountainous area bordering Vietnam offers striking views of a pastoral setting: little villages with houses of bamboo and thatch on stilts, water buffalo working the fields, mountain tribesmen dressed in colorful clothes selling their handicrafts. Yet these people's lives had been ravaged by the American bombing of Laos during the Vietnam War. Although this bombing completely failed in its objective of disrupting North Vietnamese supply lines, it succeeded in killing and wounding many Laotians, leveling every house in the area, and driving the people—guilty only of the misfortune of having lived in the area—to a life of near-starvation while they hid in the jungle.

Now an American had returned, and remarkably I found myself being greeted with overwhelming warmth and hospitality by the villagers, even by those who had been maimed by American bombs. A village chief put me up in his house and refused to accept compensation; local officials arranged a banquet concluding with the rare delicacy of a can of Spam, and a woman who lost a leg to the bombing told me her story with warm smiles and without a trace of rancor. In the spirit of swords into plowshares, the villagers had turned bomb craters into fish ponds, lining the edge of the craters with decorative rows of spent artillery shells.

In theory, Singapore should have been different from the other countries in this book. Because it is an economic power-house with universal employment, one might expect Singapore to reveal a new side of Southeast Asia, a record of prosperity and accomplishment unmarked by suffering. But the curse of Southeast Asia—the oppression inevitably intertwined with a country's allure—appeared as poignantly in Singapore as any-where. Some tourists dismiss this booming island nation, with its endless shopping malls filled with boutiques, as worth no more than a boring overnight stop. But they have missed the fascination of the place, because Singapore also represents a living laboratory that shows what can be achieved by competent government, a sign to the rest of the world that cities need not plunge into the abyss of crime, pollution, and decay. On a continent where corruption, filth, and poverty are the norms, Singapore is honest, clean, and prosperous. From telephones to subway trains, everything works with impressive efficiency. Walk down any street in Singapore—the pavement will be spotless, the air clean—and you can be sure that you will see no begging, no homelessness, and no one badly dressed. Everyone receives excellent medical care; the prosperity extends so deeply that four out of five families own their home.

Yet this same government rules over its people with an aston-ishing disregard for basic human rights. The government deter-mines what books and magazines Singaporeans can read, what television programs and movies they can watch, what artists they can see or hear perform. And above all, the government ruthlessly stamps out any sign of dissent, distrusting even the social-welfare functions of church groups. Big Brother in Singa-pore is always watching, including a special squad to ferret out those men who fail to flush urinals in public bathrooms.

The uniqueness of Singapore allowed me to devise a Sunday

outing that combined both the pleasures and the pathos in a single day. A friend and I took a cable car to Sentosa Island, a beautiful theme park with beaches, miles of trails, an old fort, and buildings devoted to exhibits ranging from butterflies to historic photographs. We started touring the island on the monorail, and then I made an extra stop. I got off at Fort Siloso and walked to the nearby guardhouse to introduce myself to Chia Thye Poh, the prisoner in the theme park. Arrested in 1966 because he refused to back down from his vocal advocacy of democracy and human rights, never charged with a crime, and never brought into court, Chia has now been a prisoner for more than a quarter of a century. Since he refuses to appear on television and read a "confession," he has suffered one indignity after another, beginning with solitary confinement and ending with exile to Sentosa, where he is required to spend every night as the park's only resident. The irony of putting a political prisoner in a theme park is apparently lost on Singapore's leaders, whose considerable qualities don't include a sense of humor.

The explanation for the charm of Southeast Asia is easy to come by. Each country has deep cultural roots going back centuries. Buddhism, the predominant religion, teaches peace and contentment. The mores of social interaction are strict, demanding politeness and consideration for every situation. Westerners can look with awe upon a family structure in which children not yet of school age conscientiously tend their younger brothers and sisters, while adults always care for their elderly parents, no matter how sick the parents might be. In Burma, when I told Myint Thame about Westerners putting parents in nursing homes, he was genuinely shocked. "When you get old," he immediately told me, "I want you to come to Burma to live. We'll take care of you."

While a visitor can easily understand the charm, a far more difficult question is why in these nations the themes of tyranny, authoritarianism, and repression appear again and again. I can only begin to grope for an answer, by citing three common threads that I have seen running through the countries.

The first is the legacy of a colonial past. The contempt that the British and French felt for so many of the dark-skinned peoples under their domination—a contempt satirized brilliantly in George Orwell's novel *Burmese Days*—led to rule by fiat and the absence of trained civil servants who could step in to run the country. The British thought so little of Burmans, the ethnic majority in Burma, that they brought with them Indians to staff middle-level government positions; the French had the same attitude toward Laos and Cambodia, and filled the civil service of both countries with Vietnamese. Sarawak, the Malaysian state on the island of Borneo that is being logged with such intensity, didn't even reach the level of colonial rule until 1946. From 1841 to World War II, it was under the control of a British adventurer and his descendants, who governed it as a personal fiefdom.

Moreover, the colonial powers frequently set artificial national boundaries to include ethnic groups hostile to the majority population. British-created Burma encompassed not only the Burmans of the central plain but Karens, Shans, Chins, and other minorities who were fighting relentlessly for their independence. The nation of Laos included dozens of mountain tribes, like the Hmong, who hated the lowland Lao, and who eventually ended up as victims of the Vietnam War. Given these factors from the colonial past—the absence of democratic traditions, the lack of expertise in running a nation, and the potential for ethnic conflicts—these countries were ripe for authoritarian rule when the chance for freedom came to Southeast Asia after World War II.

The second thread in the pattern of repression appeared when the colonial experience ended. The United States, Britain, France, and other major powers saw the nations of Southeast Asia not as a fertile field for the planting of the seeds of democracy and human rights, but as pawns in the struggle between East and West. The concept of democracy too often gave way to the question of whether the dictator in power was "our dictator or theirs." During the Vietnam War, the United States relentlessly bombed both Laos and Cambodia, and successfully destablized their governments. In Laos, the CIA coddled the right-wing generals attempting to undermine the neutralist government of Prince Souvanna Phouma; in Cambodia, an American-sponsored right-wing coup in 1970 overthrew Prince Sihanouk. With Western support and encouragement, these two leaders could have promoted democratic reforms. Instead, the American machinations paved the way for Communist takeovers in 1975 and for the mass murders by the Khmer Rouge in Cambodia.

Britain's policies were less cataclysmic but equally cynical. In 1963 the British ceded control of Sarawak and Sabah on the island of Borneo, merging them into Malaysia. It was an effort to add enough non-Chinese to Malaysia's population to make certain that the country would remain under the domination of the Malays. (The British feared that the Chinese were sympathetic to Communist China.) The move delivered the natives of the Sarawak rain forest, and their vast timber resources, into the hands of the Malays, who proceeded to exploit them without British interference. And in the 1960s, when Britain and the United States discovered that Lee Kuan Yew was not a Communist after all but was aligning Singapore with the West, neither country attempted to moderate his authoritarian tendencies.

Finally, the pattern of repression in Southeast Asia owes much to the fact that, as Singapore's leaders frequently point out, Asia is not the West. Anyone writing a history of Southeast Asia would have difficulty finding enough material for even a short chapter on the development of democratic traditions. Instead, it is a history of rule by tyrannical kings, domination by foreign powers, and relentless persecutions. A peasant in an Asian village yearns for stability and economic well-being, to be let alone to feed his family. Democracy and human rights become abstract concepts that have little relevance or meaning. Even when a country like Singapore fully emerges into the modern world, most of its citizens are still preoccupied with holding on to their material gains, and they are quite willing to forgive the government its human rights abuses.

This means that democracy and freedom as we know it in the West can come to Southeast Asia only through a long and arduous process. When I write about the United Nations' efforts to hold free elections in Cambodia, I point out the difficulty, if not the futility, of imposing an American-style election on a country that has never known free expression, a free press, or a secret ballot, a nation with primitive communications and a road system that is in shambles. Democracy for Cambodia is an effort that should start with economic development and with the establishment of schools and universities. Instead, Cambodians, many of them illiterate, are being exposed to a Western-style election campaign from another world. The achievement of real democracy demands that the United States, Japan, and other wealthy nations make a long-term commitment of money and people. But so far, such a commitment has been available to Southeast Asia only for war, not for peace.

In the spring of 1990, I went to the Ho Chi Minh Trail in Laos and saw the effects of American bombing. When this bombing ended in 1973, the United States had dropped 2 million tons of bombs on that country, with an average of one planeload of bombs every eight minutes around the clock for nine years. The cost exceeded $7 billion, or more than $2 million a day.

In the winter of 1991, I sat in the Phnom Penh office of Bjorn Johansson, who was planning the United Nations effort to repatriate 330,000 Cambodian refugees from the Thai border. These refugees were another product of the Vietnam War, when the American bombing of Cambodia in 1969 began the process of destabilization that, six years later, led to the Khmer Rouge takeover. Johansson was worried about raising the $110 million needed for the repatriation. It was a pittance compared with American efforts to undermine Cambodia two decades earlier, he conceded. "We should remember that there's always plenty of money to make war, but when it comes to peace, funding dries up quickly."

The charm of Southeast Asia conveyed in this book somehow always seems countered by the cruelty, and numbingly sad incidents appear, too. They range from the Burmese, who lost their savings because General Ne Win wanted new banknotes with denominations divisible by nine, to the Borneo natives, who fell victim to the Japanese insistence that plywood be made from the finest tropical hardwood logs. Perhaps saddest of all is the role played by the United States, Britain, France, and other Western democracies. In Southeast Asia, which has known little but tyranny and repression, the actions of the West seem to have compounded the problem rather than helping to resolve it.

In books of this sort, it's appropriate to say a few words about the glamorous life of the foreign correspondent, the excitement of visiting remote lands. Since Laos is about as remote as any place can be, I'll start by describing my arrival in the capital, Vientiane. The "excitement" began that day, a Sunday afternoon, when I discovered one of the sleepiest cities on earth. There were no cars on the streets, no shops or markets open, nothing but the broiling tropical sun reflecting its rays off the pavement. I hadn't yet heard about the Australian-built swimming pool, where all the Westerners congregate on weekends, so I spent my first day taking a long nap.

Early Monday morning I rushed over to the Foreign Ministry, which had issued my visa and, as required in all Communist countries, would assign me an official guide. The building was completely deserted; it turned out that Laotian government workers got paid so little, most of them spent their days at other jobs. So I went to the American embassy, where I had a bit of luck; my guide, a young man named Bounneme, had left a message that he would be in contact with me.

Although Laos was rushing headlong down the road toward capitalism, I had the misfortune to get as a guide one of the last idealistic Marxists left in the country. Bounneme was a pleasant enough fellow, but he insisted that everything be done by the book. That meant typing new letters to every government official I wanted to interview, even though I had already sent such letters from the United States. He explained that the letters would then go to a secretarial pool, which would translate them into Lao. A messenger would carry them to the relevant ministries, where, presumably, lower-level officials would consider them and take them up with their bosses. This arrangement had one major drawback: there were no secretaries, messengers, or lower-level officials, since people rarely showed up for work. Each day I pleaded with Bounneme to contact the ministers directly, and each day he shook his head sadly and told me that they were "very busy men." After about ten days of this, some interviews actually started getting scheduled; I accepted this as a miracle and didn't want to jinx it by asking what had happened.

Meanwhile, Bounneme agreed to my request that we visit the Ho Chi Minh Trail. But since that would involve flying to the southern city of Savannakhet and then taking a four-wheel-drive truck, he told me that the Central Committee of Savannakhet Province would have to make the arrangements. He duly wired them about our plans, and a couple of days later we left for the airport.

At the Savannakhet air terminal, Bounneme looked around for the people who would be meeting us. No one had come. We had to hire a tuk-tuk, an open-air motorized three-wheel vehicle, and unceremoniously backfire our way into the city to the Central Committee headquarters. It was clear from our indifferent reception that I was expected to grease some palms, but Bounneme wouldn't hear of it. "The Central Committee has been properly informed, and they will find a vehicle," he insisted. The Savannakhet party officials were in no hurry, however. They insisted we take a room in a fleabag hotel and wait for our truck. I was specifically instructed not to leave the room; they worried that an American walking around Savannakhet would get into some sort of trouble, and they would be held responsible.

Eight hours later, the truck arrived. Bounneme and I were to go to the Ho Chi Minh Trail in the company of not only a driver and a security guard, but also officials of both the administrative and information sections of the Central Committee. I was expected to pay for all of them. (The "security guard," armed with nothing but a camera, was perhaps five feet, two inches tall and weighed no more than 120 pounds.) As soon as the truck took off, frowns turned to smiles. For everyone on board but me, it was to be a paid vacation.

Once I had accepted the fact that the unhurried life of Laos was not about to bend for a reporter, the charms of the country proved to be captivating. My feelings about Burma, a nation I had come to love from my previous two visits, ended up exactly the opposite. The cumulative effects of people afraid to speak, of soldiers waving bayonets at me, of dinners that had to be gulped down to beat the curfew took their toll. Rangoon contained exactly six hotel rooms that weren't seedy—the cottages on the shore of Kandawgyi Lake. I had one of them, but my stay at the hotel was clouded by the paranoia that came from feeling constantly watched. The door of my cottage had a flimsy lock that could be defeated simply by turning the knob hard, and I often saw evidence of my things having been gone through. Whenever I got into the shower, the room boy would open the cottage door, walk into the bathroom, and stand there watching me until I screamed at him to leave. (His motives were unclear; he kept talking about his girlfriend and asking me for presents for her.) One day I sat him down and offered to pay him more than he was getting from the government as a spy, but he denied everything. On the streets of Rangoon, I would see arrests of those the government deemed to be political opponents; once I witnessed an entire truckload of soldiers stop to snatch away a single terrified-looking student. When I got back to Bangkok, the pollution, noise, and chaos never looked so good.

When I'm asked about the perils of reporting from remote places in Southeast Asia, my standard reply is that the most dangerous thing I have ever done was to cross a street in Bangkok. Those who have visited Bangkok would immediately understand that this isn't a joke. Thais who get behind the wheel feel suddenly liberated from the rigid rules that govern every other form of social behavior in their country. They drive on the wrong side of the street and glory in daredevil maneuvers, while pedestrians become objects of scorn, since many of them are people who can't afford cars themselves.

Only once did I feel a threat as acute as Bangkok's traffic, and that occurred in the jungle of Borneo. The danger certainly wasn't from the people of the rain forest; although their ancestors a century ago had been headhunters, the natives are now unusually kind and gentle, and I couldn't help thinking that a little of the ancestral militance would have gone a long way in dealing with the loggers. Nor was it snakes dropping from tree branches, a sort of event that happens only in movies. Instead, the problem involved slippery logs. The Borneo natives consider a slimy log to be an ideal bridge for fording a creek; they don't even bother planing it on top to flatten the surface. They had an unshakable grip, whether with bare feet or rubber shower sandals; I, wearing expensive running shoes, couldn't remain upright for two consecutive steps.

Finally, a word about the practice of journalism in Southeast Asia. Throughout this region, governments consider local journalists to be tools of the state, and none of the countries I've written about has anything approaching a free press. Only in Malaysia will an occasional bit of dissent appear, but even there reporters find themselves severely restricted. I once attended a press conference in Penang, an island that is one of Malaysia's more prosperous and enlightened areas. At this press conference, environmentalists criticized a proposal to turn Penang Hill from a national park into a development of apartment houses and hotels, thereby imperiling the local water supply and depriving residents and tourists of a scenic gem. The press conference drew about twenty reporters, but not a word of it appeared in Malaysia's newspapers the next morning. One reporter admitted to me that he was there as a show of solidarity with the environmentalists, that he wasn't even going to bother writing an article because he knew his newspaper wouldn't print it.

This for Southeast Asia is a display of relative freedom. In Burma and Laos, and in Cambodia before the U.N. arrived—as well as in the technologically advanced communications hub of the region, Singapore—such a press conference by environmentalists could never even be held.

Governments of this sort frequently try to avoid coverage by foreign publications. Their simplest method is to deny visas to reporters, a practice that Laos and Cambodia used to employ with regularity. Even though these two countries have recently liberalized their visa policies, they haven't changed their bureaucratic ways. In Cambodia, I went through the same excruciating experience as I had in Laos with Bounneme, submitting endless interview requests to the Foreign Ministry's press department, then waiting and waiting. When I finally got some interviews, they were often a waste of time, sometimes comically so. In Laos, the vice-minister of agriculture took an agonizing forty-two minutes to answer my first question, glaring at me fiercely if he saw me stop taking notes. In Cambodia, the vice-minister of finance explained away the presence of so many recent-model BMWs and Mercedes-Benzes on the streets of Phnom Penh by stating that the cars in Cambodia are secondhand and in other countries would be "put into the furnace."

Until April 1989, Burma granted almost no visas to journalists. But because the government wasn't alert enough to obtain a membership booklet from the Foreign Correspondents' Club of Thailand, newly assigned reporters to Southeast Asia each were able to enter Burma one time by posing as a tourist; as soon as their articles appeared, they went on a blacklist. I didn't have to adopt this subterfuge, because in 1989 someone got the idea that if Burma were to admit reporters and tell them the "truth," the journalists would obediently write favorable articles. Three months later, when the government saw the results in print, they slammed the door shut again.

Singapore, although wide open to Western businessmen and tourists, bans reporters from publications it doesn't favor. This routinely includes anyone from the *Asian Wall Street Journal* or the *Far Eastern Economic Review*, two publications of Dow Jones & Co. that several years ago printed articles that offended Singaporean officials. I received a very different sort of reception, however, from Lee Kuan Yew, who has run Singapore with a firm hand since independence from Britain in 1959. Lee granted me two interviews totaling almost three hours, and instead of evading tough questions in the manner of leaders around the world, he responded to everything directly and frankly. Since Lee possesses an awesome intellect, the interviews turned into an exciting verbal sparring match.

At the end of the second interview, I talked to Lee about his reputation for shouting down reporters and cutting interviews short. Since I had experienced none of this, I asked him whether he was mellowing with age. Lee's reply revealed another interesting facet of this remarkable man. In an era when political leaders are usually no deeper than a sound bite, Lee had taken the time to read a twenty-thousand-word article merely to check out a visiting journalist. "If I know someone is out to get me, I'll get them first," Lee told me. "But I read your article on Laos, and I knew you couldn't have written that unless you had entered the country with an open mind. So I assumed you were open-minded about Singapore, too."

When the Singapore piece finally appeared in *The New Yorker*, I assumed I would become persona non grata. I thought that the article was fair, commenting favorably on the government's brilliant economic management and the envious material gains this had brought about. But it was also critical on human rights abuses—the sort of criticism the government doesn't accept readily.

A month after the article appeared, I received a letter from Francis Seow, Singapore's most famous dissident, who is in exile in the United States. "You might be flattered to hear," Seow wrote, "that your article was quoted with approval by both the government and the opposition. Brig.-Gen. Lee Hsien Loong [the deputy prime minister and son of Lee Kuan Yew] held it up in parliament as indicative of how much Singapore is admired in the West, especially in America. On the other hand, J. B. Jeyaretnam [the leader of the opposition] reproduced parts of it in the Workers' Party organ, *The Hammer*, as symptomatic of the many ills of Singapore's government and its leaders." I later saw an account of the younger Lee's speech to parliament. "Stan Sesser . . . is not an admirer of Singapore, right?" he stated. "He is a liberal. This is a liberal magazine. . . . But he has to acknowledge the facts." I've been subject to a lot of accusations over the years, but having to acknowledge the facts is one that I will gratefully accept.

The Lands of
Charm and Cruelty

SINGAPORE
The Prisoner in the Theme Park

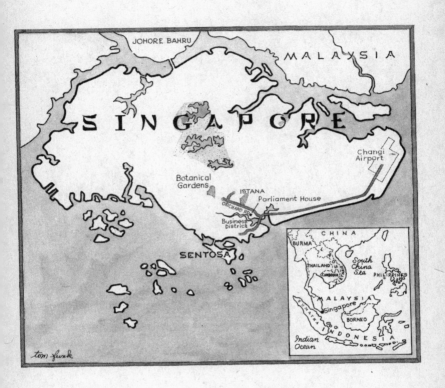

A POLITICAL SCIENTIST who visits Singapore would regard the island nation as fascinating, since its authoritarian government functions in many ways like that of a Communist state yet is dedicated wholeheartedly to the pursuit of capitalism. An economist would consider Singapore instructive, because there is no better example of a country that has gone from poverty to riches through good economic management. A sociologist looking at rules and regulations would call Singapore unique in the world. But more casual visitors might characterize Singapore differently, often by using the word "dull." Friends in the United States who had been to Singapore used this word and looked at me sympathetically when I told them that I was going there for a month. The taxi driver taking me from the airport to my hotel also used it, and added that "no tourist should spend more than two days in Singapore—one day shopping and the other sightseeing." When I met the prime minister's press secretary, he smiled in an embarrassed way and said, "You must find Singapore dull."

That Singapore can be so interesting beneath the surface and at the same time appear to be so dull is just one of its many paradoxes. Approximately 240 square miles, with 2.7 million residents, Singapore has bulldozed almost all its past, tearing down colorful ethnic neighborhoods and replacing them with office towers and high-rise apartment blocks that go on mile after mile—an endless horizon of uniform drabness. The tourist district bisected by Orchard Road, one of Singapore's main streets, offers another numbing sort of repetition: multistory indoor shopping malls filled with stylish boutiques, malls by the dozen, and boutiques by the thousand, evoking the image of a prosperous American suburb that has run amok. The weather is certainly dull: the average temperature varies by only one degree centigrade from the hottest to the coldest months, and the oppressive humidity never lets up. Then there are the Singaporeans themselves. People stand in interminable lines waiting for a taxi instead of going out on the street to hail one, because the latter act is frowned upon by the authorities. Joggers routinely stop at Don't Walk signs—even on Sunday mornings, when there isn't a car in sight. The government tells Singaporeans what books and magazines they can read, what movies they can see, and what television programs they can watch, and the result is a cultural desert in a nation so wealthy that it could easily be a showcase for the arts. Residents of Singapore pursue but one activity with passion—a passion so great that it sometimes seems to constitute recreation as well as vocation. This is the making of money.

Lee Kuan Yew, who since Singapore gained its independence from Britain, in 1959, has presided over the nation in much the way a strict father might rear what he feels are errant children, dismisses with contempt the notion that a dull, soulless city has replaced the excitement of the teeming ethnic communities that populated the island three decades ago. (Singapore is 75 percent Chinese, 14 percent Malay, and 7 percent Indian.) Lee, whose shrewd and pragmatic style of governing leaves no room for romanticizing the past, once noted that "there was no sanitation and no running water, hot or cold, for many not even electricity," and asked, "And what was there to do? The people could grow tapioca, make children, and drink." He had a point. Anyone who disparages Singapore for being dull and authoritarian has overlooked an entirely different side—one of remarkable accomplishments. Although it began as an impoverished nation with no resources, it has managed to solve the major problems that plague almost every other large urban area in the world today—problems that threaten to balloon into crisis proportions in the United States. Singapore has virtually no poverty, no homelessness, no begging, and little crime. Unemployment is close to nonexistent. The air is clean. Cars are so strictly regulated that traffic flows freely even during rush hours. The prosperity of Singapore, where people lead lives that even many Japanese would envy, is shared widely. The same cab driver who called Singapore dull admitted after a bit of questioning that he grew up in the 1950s in a one-room "shophouse," where a seven-member family both worked and lived. His parents slept on the bed; he slept under it. Today he lives with his wife and two children in a three-bedroom apartment, which they own.

From economics to food, Singapore is a nation of contradictions. Except for Japan, it has the best-educated, most knowledgeable, and most worldly-wise society in Asia, but the government still tries in many ways to regulate its citizens' lives. Although Singapore has no enemies—Communism no longer poses a threat, and the island's relations with its immediate neighbors, Malaysia and Indonesia, are vastly improved—it continues to maintain one of the largest armies in the world proportionate to population and has a ruthlessly efficient and intrusive intelligence agency, the Internal Security Department, or ISD, which is tireless in its pursuit of dissent. Despite the fact that Singapore is a bastion of capitalism, the government owns many of the largest local companies and frequently interferes with economic decisions. The government is so prudish that it bans *Cosmopolitan* as well as *Playboy*, yet the national airline promotes itself with slogans on the order of "Singapore Girl you're a great way to fly." And although Singapore has many "hawker centers," each with an ethnic mélange of food stalls, which offer some of the best street food in the world, young Singaporeans flock to American fast-food restaurants, including no fewer than thirty-four McDonald's.

For any Westerner accustomed to Asian cities choked by pollution, traffic jams, and snarled communications, Singapore is an oasis. The airport is so efficient, the taxis are so numerous, and the roads are so good that a visitor arriving at Changi Airport, on the eastern tip of the island, twelve miles from downtown, can reach his hotel room there thirty minutes after stepping off the plane. That visitor can drink water from the tap; get business cards, eyeglasses, or a tailor-made suit the day after placing an order; and ride a modern subway system whose underground stations as well as its trains are air-conditioned. An international phone call can be direct-dialed as quickly in Singapore as in the United States. Business can be conducted in English, because it is the language that all the schools use. (Only one out of five Singaporeans speaks English at home, though.) While the dreary high-rise buildings convey no atmosphere, Singapore has retained enough greenery to make it a pleasant city for walking. Every block has trees and flowers; the island's entire east coast, facing the South China Sea, is a string of parks and beaches, and only half an hour from downtown are a nature preserve and some semirural areas with farms. No litter mars a walk through Singapore's streets, because a litterbug must pay a fine of up to $620 and undergo counseling. (Cigarette butts count as litter, and many of Singapore's litter baskets—there are forty-five thousand of them—are equipped with ashtrays.) Everything in Singapore is clean; everything in Singapore works.

In a nation known for efficiency, the government is most efficient of all. In other parts of Asia, government services can take an eternity to arrive and then come bound in red tape, the instrument for cutting the tape being a bribe. But in Singapore when someone calls to report a pothole, the Public Works Department fills it within forty-eight hours. The Telecommunication Authority will install a new phone the day after the order is received. Secretaries are so conscientious that a journalist gets unsolicited wakeup calls to make sure he'll be on time for early-morning interviews with their bosses. A bribe, whether a little tip to an employee or a large payoff to a high-ranking minister, represents a ticket to jail. A postman was once arrested for accepting a gift of one Singapore dollar—equal to 62 American cents. A civil servant who receives a present in the mail must send it to a government agency, which puts a price tag on it and then offers to sell it back to the recipient. If the employee doesn't want to buy it, the gift is sold at an auction. Such is the shame attached to corruption that in 1986, when the minister of national development was accused of accepting a bribe to save private land from government acquisition, he committed suicide.

The government of Singapore, ever fearful of snakes in its capitalist Garden of Eden, loves to make rules. The walls of buildings are plastered with rules, telling people what they can't do and how much they have to pay if they dare to try it. The fines represent considerably more than a slap on the wrist, and they're enforced often enough to make most potential miscreants think twice. Eating or drinking on the subway costs the equivalent of US$310, driving without a seat belt $124, smoking in a restaurant $310, and jaywalking, a relative bargain, $30. Few proscribed activities are left to the imagination, as opposed to being posted; for example, in the Botanical Gardens, where "Prohibited" signs threaten to outnumber plant-identification markers, a pictograph warns against shooting at birds with slingshots. Nor do violations always depend for discovery on a passing policeman. Trucks and commercial vans are required to install a yellow roof light that flashes when the vehicle exceeds the speed limit. When a taxi exceeds the maximum speed on freeways of 48 miles an hour, loud chimes go off inside; the chimes are so annoying that the driver is likely to slow down. At some intersections, cameras photograph the license plates of cars that pass through as the light is changing to red; the drivers receive bills for that offense in the mail.

The rules are frequently backed up by publicity campaigns, using advertising slogans, displays at public events, and articles in the leading newspaper, the *Straits Times*, which in all areas enthusiastically fills the role of government lapdog. There have been campaigns to be punctual, to say "please" and "thank you," and to buy frozen pork rather than fresh pork, which, the *Straits Times* said in 1985, "can be dangerous because it can mean living at the mercy of other countries." The government once even urged Singaporeans to "have spontaneous fun." In 1984, Singapore initiated an antispitting campaign, with the distribution of pamphlets, messages on radio and television, mobile exhibitions at food centers and markets, twenty thousand posters on buses and taxis, and, for children, comic strips and a coloring contest. "DON'T SPIT IN PUBLIC—AFTER THE CAMPAIGN, CUL-PRITS WILL BE FINED," a large headline in the *Straits Times* warned, and it also printed dozens of articles, editorials, columns, and letters on the subject. The newspaper didn't confine its warnings to committing the crime in public places. In one article, it quoted a tailor as promising "that he would now spit in drains," and went on, "But experts say that wherever it is done, spitting is unhygienic. It spreads a lot of germs that cause illnesses like tuberculosis, cough and cold, influenza, sore throat, measles, mumps, and chicken pox."

Clean public toilets at shopping malls, food centers, and other public places are among the amenities that make Singapore perhaps the most livable city in Asia. But the campaign that brought them into being, which started in 1988, might be viewed as excessive. A law requiring the flushing of toilets and urinals was enacted, the *Far Eastern Economic Review* reported at the time, "to punish those of its population who have not been properly housetrained." The magazine explained, "Those who ignore the new law do so on peril of a fine of up to S$1,000. And how is this law being enforced? A crack battalion of inspectors from Singapore's Ministry of Environment will be roving public toilets in pursuit of the aberrant nonflushers. This could prove embarrassing for the respectable patrons of such public facilities. How to distinguish the man from the ministry from the common-or-garden Peeping Tom?" When I visited the *Straits Times* library, I requested its file of articles on public toilets and received a folder four inches thick. It included articles day after day, complete with graphic pictures, stemming from calls to "the *Straits Times* Toilets of Shame hotline." In June 1989, the newspaper ran a photograph of a sheepish-looking man staring at the floor as he walked away from a row of shiny-clean urinals. The caption read, "Caught without a flush: Mr. Amar Mohamed leaving the Lucky Plaza toilet without flushing the urinal."

Today, Singapore is a city with almost no poverty. Hong Kong may have grown as rapidly, but in Hong Kong the gap between rich and poor is visible everywhere. By contrast, I never saw anyone in Singapore shabbily dressed, and everyone appeared to have at least a passable place to live. Food is cheap and plentiful. Even low-income Singaporeans have access to high-quality medical care; doctors at public hospitals in the United States might look enviously at the public wards of Singapore General Hospital.

But Singapore was not always so prosperous or so tidy. When Lee Kuan Yew took power, he found himself governing a mosquito-infested swamp dotted with pig and chicken farms, fishing villages, and squatter colonies of tin-roofed shacks. The streets of the central city were lined with shophouses—mostly two-story buildings with ornate façades. A family would operate a business on the ground floor and live on the second floor. Often without plumbing and electricity, and housing as many as ten people to a room, the shophouses may have presented a picturesque sight for tourists, but they were far less agreeable for their occupants. "The Chinese, who constitute the main current of the city, live in utter filth and poverty," *Asia Scene*, a travel magazine, reported in 1960. "Their poverty is phenomenal. One must see with his own eyes to believe it." Compounding the problem of poverty were racial and political tensions, coming both from the Malay minority and from young Chinese infused with the ideals of the Maoist revolution; these tensions frequently spilled out into the streets.

In not much more than a decade, Singaporeans were passing from poverty to affluence, and the nation's economy from a basket case to the powerhouse of southern Asia. The explanation for this transformation, as for nearly everything else that happens in Singapore, rests with Lee Kuan Yew. Lee has put his stamp on Singapore to an extent that few political leaders anywhere in the world have ever matched. Tough and authoritarian although operating under a pretense of democracy, uninterested in personal wealth among a people who devote their lives to financial gain, often rude and contemptuous in a country that runs annual campaigns promoting the virtues of courtesy, Lee embodies as many contradictions as does Singapore itself. "Lee is also the most interesting statesman in Asia," Robert Elegant, a longtime Asia correspondent, has written. "Among those who lead fights for independence, only Lee Kuan Yew afterward ruled wisely. . . . Others failed the transition from revolutionary to ruler: Mao Tse-tung in China, Pandit Jawaharlal Nehru in India, Ho Chi Minh in Viet Nam, and Sukarno in Indonesia. Those great men left disorder—economic, political, and administrative—compounded by corruption."

Singapore has what its economists call a proactive rather than a reactive economy. There are no such occurrences as brownouts or clogged telephone circuits, because everything is well planned. In 1982, although the terminal at Changi Airport showed no sign of approaching capacity, planning began on a second terminal, which opened in late 1990. And although this sprawling new terminal now looks almost empty, planners are already working on Terminal No. 3, which will open early in the next century.

In much the same manner, the sixty-eight-year-old Lee began planning for his succession more than a decade ago. In November 1990, he stepped down as prime minister, the position he had held for three decades, and assumed the post of senior minister, yielding the prime ministership to Goh Chok Tong, who was then forty-nine, and who had been a deputy prime minister. While Lee is still the head of the People's Action Party, the political party that dominates Singapore, and while it's clear that Goh would never make a major move that Lee opposed, the notion of an authoritarian ruler in perfect health and without serious opposition giving up a share of power is hardly commonplace in Asia. "Despite Lee's British training, despite his Queen's English and his highly modern view of economics, as a politician Lee is a traditional Chinese despot," a high-ranking Western diplomat in Singapore explained to me. "I'm saying this in the positive sense: he ranks with the greatest Chinese emperors. But what distinguishes him from Chinese despots and Deng Xiaoping is that he wants to see his legacy survive him. He saw the need, and he saw that stepping down would be in the country's interest." Lee, who seeks control and order above all else, recently offered his own explanation. "Multinational corporations and banks expect things to work properly," he said. "That is only possible with continuity. So my colleagues and I phased ourselves out in a graduated, controlled way to avoid any lurching. . . . I hope the transition will pass imperceptibly. If you can feel a lurch, that's contrary to my intentions."

Singapore is sometimes dubbed Singapore, Inc., because its style of government is so much like that of a corporation, but few corporations have chief executive officers as remote from the center of activity as Lee and Goh. The two men work together at

Istana (*istana* is the Malay word for "palace"), a handsome old colonial building set in the middle of a large park at the foot of the Orchard Road tourist district. Lee occupies the second floor and Goh the third floor, but their press secretaries and their ministers are miles away, in skyscraper government-office buildings. Only their secretaries work with them. This isolation lends Istana an atmosphere that is almost spooky. Where the building's main entrance used to be, there is now only an elevator, opening directly onto a circular driveway. Guards take a visitor up in the elevator to the second floor and then down a long corridor to the waiting room outside Lee's office. There is no activity along that corridor. Doors open into empty rooms, one of them piled high with cardboard cartons. No one walks down the halls or through the waiting room except the guards, young Chinese who look nervous and uncomfortable.

Lee's style of government is a direct reflection of his personality and is shaped little by the sort of protocol that might be expected from a national leader. A blunt man with no interest in small talk, he can cast aside diplomatic niceties and make outrageously provocative statements. Recently, for instance, he said that many Asians did not want Japan to become involved in armed peacekeeping activities because allowing it to do so could be like "giving liqueur chocolates to an alcoholic." He has scant interest in the usual trappings of power: he still lives in a modest house that he bought in the 1950s; he takes Singapore Airlines scheduled flights when he goes on state visits; and he has decreed that there be no pictures of him on the walls of government offices. Lee dislikes putting on a suit and tie. When I interviewed him, he was wearing gray slacks, an open-necked white shirt, and a light-tan jacket zipped up against the air conditioning; at a second interview, three weeks later, he was wearing what appeared to be exactly the same clothes. He has little interest in food, concerts, or movies, and although he reads avidly, his reading is confined to those works of history, political science, and other areas that can give him ideas for improving Singapore. His one diversion is exercise—a quick sequence of jogging, swimming, cycling, and rowing for half an hour each evening. With sparse steel-gray hair, a craggy face deeply lined under his eyes, and an intense gaze that instantly reflects any feeling of annoyance, Lee is a formidable presence.

The quickness and acuity of Lee's mind are impressive to witness. "He can wipe the floor with most of his opponents," as one European diplomat put it. Robert Orr, the former American ambassador to Singapore, told me, "I've never met anyone who thinks further ahead into the future. In conversations and action, he's always likely to be a step or two ahead of other people." That was certainly true when I interviewed Lee, because several times, as I started to ask a long question, he interrupted after only a few words, and he never failed to deduce just what I was going to say. Nor, in almost three hours of discussions, did he ever evade a question; instead, he gave answers so well reasoned that I began to wonder whether he could persuade me that a white wall was actually black. Lee appears to prepare for an interview the way a prizefighter might for a boxing match, by learning all about his opponent. I first had to submit a résumé to his press secretary specifying my education and the articles I had written. Then Lee got hold of one article, twenty thousand words long, and read it so thoroughly that when he discussed it with me he could recite entire paragraphs. The article was on Laos, and, as with everything else he reads, Lee immediately thought about how he could use it for Singapore's benefit. At the beginning of the first interview, he delivered a monologue on ways that Singapore could start trading with Laos, and what difficulties each route would entail. Then his face brightened. "I know," he said. "I'll send my entrepreneurs to Laos and let them find out."

. . . .

In 1950, Lee Kuan Yew returned to Singapore, his birthplace, after four years of study in England, bringing with him a law degree with highest honors from Cambridge. Known then as Harry Lee, he spoke impeccable English but not a word of Mandarin; he could write his name in Chinese characters, but nothing else. His father, an oil-depot superintendent, had wanted Lee "to be the equal of any Englishman." Lee succeeded so brilliantly that George Brown, the British foreign secretary in the mid-sixties, said to him then, "Harry, you're the best bloody Englishman east of Suez."

But Lee immediately cast his lot with the radical Chinese in Singapore, who were agitating for independence from Britain. He shared with them only youth; most had been educated in Mandarin at Chinese schools in Singapore, and many were imbued with the ideals of the Communist revolution that had swept China. "At that time, China was the future," Goh Chok Tong told me. "Almost everyone believed that." Lee became a lawyer for labor unions, working side by side with Communists toward the goal of expelling the British. In 1954, Robert Elegant, who was then living in Singapore, first met Lee; he later wrote about what he had witnessed: "Early in 1954, Harry Lee let it be known that he wanted to be called Kuan Yew. He reverted to his Chinese name to make his anticolonial position unmistakable. He also began to study Mandarin, pasting lists of ideograms to his shaving mirror. He appeared to be abandoning the English-educated elite for the intense world of the Mandarin-speaking militants who were either the willing tools of the outlawed Communist movement or its secret members. . . . In November 1954, when he spoke at the founding meeting of the People's Action Party . . . he wore the cotton shirt and wash trousers that were the uniform of the new radical movement, but he spoke in English." Despite the language barrier, Lee became the secretary-general of the PAP in 1955—the position he still holds, after more than thirty-five years. He said at the time, "I would vote for Communism if I had to choose only between Communism and colonialism."

Ten years later, Lee claimed that he hadn't switched sides when he returned from Britain—that he had actually opposed British rule all along. "Let me say this to show you that I am not an Anglophile," Lee told Seymour Topping, of the *New York Times*, in 1965. "True, I know their culture, their history, their civilization. I have read all about the daffodils, and the bumblebee, and the heigh-ho, merry-ho, and all the rest. It is part of my schooling. They pumped it into me. And I hated what they did, and I joined up with the Communists to get rid of them. But, you know, they had wisdom."

Throughout the 1950s, Lee stood solidly behind his leftist allies. He proposed legalizing the Communist Party and denounced colonialism at every opportunity. "He has warned the English-speaking Chinese that they should either join the revolution or be swept away by it," the *Reporter* magazine noted in May 1959. "At other times he has sent shudders of apprehension down the spines of the British business community with references to the need for nationalizing banking: he applauded the Indonesian takeover of Dutch property and other assets; and he says quite frankly that he intends to turn Singapore's social system upside down." That month, the British granted Singapore, then widely known as the Red City, limited self-rule, allowing Singaporeans to vote for a parliament but retaining control over internal security, foreign affairs, and defense. The PAP, running against an opposition party that was anti-Communist and pro-Western, won forty-three of a total of fifty-one seats, and Lee Kuan Yew became Singapore's first prime minister. The *Straits Times*, which had been one of his severest critics, quickly moved its editorial offices to Kuala Lumpur.

What Lee had achieved was surely one of the most extraordinary political maneuvers in history. He had latched on to a pro-Communist movement, usurped its rhetoric, and seized control of it. He borrowed from the Communists a tactic they had been using so successfully all over the world—the popular-front government that gives way to a Communist regime—and used it against them. "The Kuomintang went into a united front with the Communist Party in China, but the Communists won," I was told by Chan Heng Chee, Singapore's leading political scientist, who was until 1991 its ambassador to the United Nations. "In Europe, when you had the Social Democrats working with the Communists, the Communists won. Singapore is the world's only example of forming a united front with the Communists and defeating them. Lee looked at how they mobilized and learned from them."

I asked Lee whether at the time he said he would rather be a Communist than a colonialist, and advocated nationalization, he was actually flirting with those ideas. "First, we had to get rid of the British," he replied. "To do that, you had to mobilize support from the widest possible group and get as big a majority of the population as you could. If you're not going to shoot the British out, you've got to shake them out, and that means you've got to get the majority with you. First, you've got to get power. Then, having got power, you say, 'What's the problem? Have I said these things? If so, let's forget it.' "

The British understood what Lee was doing; in the 1950s, when the British routinely imprisoned Chinese leftists, he escaped arrest, because they realized that he would eventually be an ally and perhaps the only means of forestalling a leftist take-over of Singapore. But the Central Intelligence Agency was not quite so perceptive as the British. In 1960, fearing that Singapore was falling to the Communists, the CIA tried to put the head of Singapore's Internal Security Department on its payroll. The American who made the offer quickly found himself in jail. Then the United States sent a high-ranking official—to this day, Lee won't reveal his name—to offer Lee $3.3 million to keep the affair quiet. Lee countered that instead he would take $33 million in economic aid for Singapore. He didn't get it. Five years later, when Lee made the story of the bribe public, the State Department denied it. The Americans directed at Lee what from his point of view were probably the two greatest insults possible: first, they treated him as a banana-republic dictator; then they branded him a liar. A furious Lee called reporters into his office and said he would show them incriminating documents and play them incriminating tapes if the State Department didn't admit the truth. The Americans "are not dealing with Ngo Dinh Diem or Syngman Rhee," Lee told the reporters. "You do not buy and sell this Government." The State Department thereupon confirmed the charge.

"If the British officers in the Special Branch had been as unsophisticated as the CIA, I think we would have been forced into the Communist camp," Lee told me. "The CIA didn't really trust the British, because we were running around with the Communists. Obviously, we should have been locked up and disposed of a long time ago. So their conclusion was that the British were inefficient. They wanted to get the jam on us so that they could fix us—believing that we were Communists, I suppose. Why should I take a few million dollars? It's crazy. And then I'm done for."

Lee in fact wasted little time moving against Singapore's leftist Chinese when he came to power. (His government has never shown much interest in distinguishing the non-Communist left from members of the Communist Party. In the early 1960s, many of Lee's political opponents were espousing socialism, not Communism, but Lee has never hesitated to use the word "Communist" to brand political dissidents of all varieties.) He jailed Chinese-language newspaper editors, cracked down on strikes by labor unions, and organized work brigades of unemployed Chinese youths so that he could reach them before the

Communists did. With British help, he engineered a split with the Chinese-speaking radicals he had so forcefully supported in the 1950s. Never one to pay homage to the concept of free-for-all democracy, Lee explained to me with characteristic directness what had happened. "We had taken office with the Communists in our midst," he said. "The British skillfully, not so much by words but by their behavior, led these Communists to believe that if they could win power constitutionally, by getting a majority in the Legislative Assembly, they would be acceptable as the government, provided they allowed the British bases to stay. They misled the young revolutionaries into believing that they could take power, and the revolutionaries came out to whack us. That brought about a split, an open conflict with the Communists, and on the best possible terms for us. And we won, we carried the day. We never gave them a second chance playing at constitutional games."

The key to Lee's strategy was the merger, in 1963, of Singapore into the Malaysian Federation, joining neighboring Malaya and the British colonies of North Borneo, now called Sabah, and Sarawak, which are on the island of Borneo. It was an enormous risk. Lee, although he remained prime minister of Singapore, had to yield ultimate authority over his island to Abdul Rahman, the powerful Malayan leader known as the Tunku, or prince. Rahman had initially rejected Lee's overtures, fearing that the overwhelmingly Chinese population of Singapore would unite with the 39 percent of Malaya that was Chinese to oust the Malays from power. So to join the federation Singapore had to accept the condition of much smaller representation in the Malaysian Parliament than its population should have merited—just fifteen seats, one fewer than those granted to Sabah, which had only about a quarter the number of people. Lee also agreed to make Malay the official language of Singapore. At the time, Rahman told an interviewer that he had accepted Singapore because "I don't want a damn Cuba at my feet." I asked Dr. Lee Siew Choh, who had been a leftist member of Singapore's Parliament in the early 1960s and became one again in 1988, why Lee Kuan Yew had joined the federation on such humiliating terms. "He accepted Malaya without consulting the PAP rank and file," said Dr. Lee, who had spent ten days in jail in 1963 on a charge of coercion against Singapore's government. "Instead of being ruled by London, we became ruled by Kuala Lumpur. Everything we had gained from independence, we lost. On top of that, the terms made Singaporeans second-class citizens. He wanted the federation because it could, if necessary, take action against the opposition and arrest them."

I put the same question to Lee Kuan Yew. "If we were not taken in, there were two perils we faced," he replied. "Economically, we would always be truncated, because we depended on the hinterland of Malaysia for our livelihood. Militarily, it also made no sense to have a small little island. Then there was the other risk, that on our own we could easily have gone Communist. This was because of the appeal Communism had for the majority of the young Chinese-educated, who believed the Communist revolution in China was a great success."

In hindsight, it's not at all clear that Lee needed the Tunku to keep down the left. His own measures of repression were showing signs of working before Singapore joined the federation, and they have succeeded ever since. Some Singaporeans speculate that another element could have been involved in his decision to join with Malaya: the possibility that Lee Kuan Yew might someday preside over the Malaysian Federation himself. "It was nothing but overweening ego and ambition," Francis Seow, Lee's best-known political opponent, who is now in self-imposed exile in the United States, told me. "He was so confident he could repeat in Malaysia what he did in Singapore."

Considering that Lee transformed the flyspeck of Singapore into a world economic power, one wonders what he might have accomplished for Malaysia, with its vast resources of oil, minerals, and timber, and its much larger population. But this was not to be. In 1964, the PAP made its first foray outside Singapore, contesting ten Malayan seats for Parliament and winning one. Lee now says, "By contesting those seats, we alarmed them, because they could see that we could organize and rally not only Chinese but also Indians and Malays in the towns. The urbanized Malays, like those in Singapore, could be reached on the appeal of fair shares for all." This possibility threw nationalist Malay politicians into turmoil, and they attempted to stir up anti-Chinese sentiment in Malaysia. In August 1965, saying that the only alternative was to take "repressive measures" against Singapore, Rahman expelled Singapore from the federation. When Lee spoke to his people about the expulsion, he was in tears. I asked him what emotions he had felt at the time. "A tremendous mixture of conflicting thoughts and emotional pulls," he said. "First, the sheer pity of it all. So much work went into it. Second, the dangers of the future, how to make a living, how to defend ourselves in the long term." Many times in the ensuing decades, the world's press, commenting on Singapore's economic uncertainties and on Lee's heavy-handed measures against his political opponents, ventured predictions that his policies would fail. But so far Lee has known but a single failure—the expulsion of Singapore from the federation.

After leaving Malaysia, Singapore faced desperate economic problems. Even under British rule, it had been a major center for trade. But shipping, warehousing, banking, and insurance could not alone provide enough jobs to bring prosperity. The country needed industry, and here the situation seemed hopeless. Singapore's small domestic market wasn't nearly enough to keep factories busy, and Malaysia had erected high tariffs against goods made in Singapore. "Most factories have cut production drastically," *Time* reported of Singapore in 1966. "They are plagued by strike-prone unions, and face increasingly stiff competition from aggressive and more experienced manufacturers in Hong Kong, Japan and Formosa. Singapore may face insurmountable odds." The problem was compounded two years later, when the British announced that they would withdraw all their troops by 1972, closing down a huge naval base, three airfields, and other facilities. From the British action alone, Singapore would lose about 20 percent of its national income.

Yet by 1969 Singapore was in the midst of an economic boom. "Today, a visitor can hardly move around the island for the piles of red mud from hundreds of construction projects," the *Wall Street Journal* wrote that year. Except for a recession in 1985, the boom has continued unabated, producing economic success of a sort that Singapore's neighbors could only dream about. The statistics are stunning. Year after year, Singapore has achieved economic growth of around 10 percent. Unemployment dropped from 14 percent in 1966 to 6 percent in 1970, 3 percent in 1980, and less than 2 percent today. Workers get fat pay raises—wages rose an average of more than 9 percent in 1990—yet inflation stays low, averaging just 2 or 3 percent in recent years. Per-capita income grew from $500 in 1965 to $12,000 in 1990—a figure surpassed in Asia only by Japan and Brunei. (Japan's higher ranking, however, wouldn't impress a Japanese worker who saw the comparatively spacious apartments that Singaporean workers can afford.) Having attracted more than a billion dollars in new investment in 1990, Singapore sits on foreign-exchange reserves of $27 billion. In the mid-1980s, with skyscraper hotels rising everywhere and most of colorful old Singapore long since reduced to rubble, predictions were heard of a drop in tourism and a hotel-room glut. But in 1990 hotel occupancy stood at 84 percent, a figure that more exotic Asian countries could only envy. After the 1985 recession struck Singapore, the *Wall Street Journal* reported in 1986, "The bonanza years are over." Two years later, the newspaper headlined an article,

"SINGAPORE PLANNERS SEEK WAYS TO CURB NATION'S SURGING, DOUBLE-DIGIT GROWTH."

Singapore's economic miracle owes something to the fact that what might look like free-market capitalism is actually a capitalism carefully controlled and orchestrated by the government. If the people of Singapore have to make sacrifices to keep the economy steaming ahead, the government will impose those sacrifices by fiat. Practically all unionized workers, who make up 22 percent of the work force, belong to the National Trades Union Congress, which in everything but name is an arm of the government; its general secretary, Ong Teng Cheong, is also a deputy prime minister. The last strike in Singapore was in 1986 and came about only after an American-owned company rejected a recommendation of the Ministry of Labor. In 1969, port workers threatened to strike, but Lee Kuan Yew told them that he would consider such a strike to be "high treason," and they backed down. To counter the 1985 recession, the government in effect cut wages, by decreeing a 60 percent reduction in employer contributions to a social security–type fund for workers. "Basically, the union, government, and employers understand that we're all in the same boat," Ong told me. "If the oars clash, the boat won't move. From time to time, we have economic policies painful to some or all workers. We have to pursue the policies, and explain to workers why the decision was necessary."

But many countries have authoritarian governments, and, no matter what their political stripe, their meddling in the economy inevitably leads to disaster. Three factors make Singapore's government different. First, the leaders are incorruptible; their decisions are designed to benefit the country, and not anyone's Swiss bank account. Second, they are unusually competent. Talented young Singaporeans get generous scholarships, including grants for overseas study, if they agree to enter government service. They can rise rapidly through the ranks, reaching top-level positions by their mid-thirties and earning salaries comparable with those paid by private industry. And in time, since the government owns or has a share in so many Singaporean companies, they can slip into comfortable second careers as corporate executives. Finally, Singapore's government is different because its economic planners make pragmatic decisions instead of following rigid textbook rules for running the economy. If a policy works, they continue it; if it doesn't work, they drop it and try something else. This philosophy follows the style set by Lee Kuan Yew. Although to this day Lee hasn't deviated from his perception of a Communist threat to Singapore, he has proved flexible in other areas; for example, the man who supported the speaking of Mandarin in the 1950s to get the radicals on his side, and suppressed Mandarin in the 1960s because it was the language of those Singaporeans who identified with the Chinese revolution, now pushes Mandarin as a sort of vaccine to immunize the Chinese majority against the decadence of Western culture.

What the economic planners devised for Singapore was a way, in effect, of bringing a starving child to robust health by letting someone else pay for the food. To build its economy, Singapore needed entrepreneurs with skills and investment capital. It found the answer in an institution that most other Third World countries whose governments came to power on anticolonial rhetoric shunned: the multinational corporation. The multinationals would use their capital to build factories that could employ hundreds of thousands of Singaporeans. They would bring to Singapore technology and expertise that the locals could learn. And, with their worldwide operations, they would create a global market for made-in-Singapore products. To lure multinationals, Singapore offered far more than the usual tax breaks. The nation built an impressive infrastructure, including transportation and communications second to none in Asia. To develop a skilled work force, schools emphasized technological education. The government made certain that no militant labor unions, no strikes, and no opposition parties threatening nationalization would imperil the country's stability. Above all, instead of imposing red tape, the government acted as a partner in expediting new enterprises. Singapore built shells of factories on speculation, so that arriving companies wouldn't have to spend time planning a new building from the ground up. It created an agency, the Economic Development Board, as a one-stop service to negotiate tax concessions and secure all the necessary approvals from various government agencies. In 1969, Texas Instruments established its first facility in Singapore—a plant to manufacture integrated circuits. The first product came off the assembly line just three months after discussions started.

The ultimate result of all this is that Singapore has built its industrial base with more than 80 percent of the capital coming from foreigners, and the inflow of capital is still continuing. Today, Singapore is the world's second-largest port, after Rotterdam; the banking center of southern Asia; the third-largest oil refiner, after Houston and Rotterdam; the producer of more than half of the world's computer disk drives; and a major center of shipbuilding, telecommunications equipment, electronic components, computer peripherals and software, and pharmaceuticals and medical equipment. Three thousand foreign companies have set up operations in Singapore, including eight hundred from the United States, which is the largest foreign investor. Carlton J. Parker, the managing director of General Automation Singapore, which is a subsidiary of an American computer company, says the system is so fair that he can win bids for government contracts even when his competitor is a firm owned by the Singapore government. "You can explain how your stuff works, what the intelligence is behind it, and you'll win the contract," he says. "If this could happen in places like Indonesia and the Philippines, who knows what their economies would be like? Here I have never had to offer a bribe; in the Philippines, nothing would happen without one. If you ask a question about specifications, it has to be in writing, and a copy goes to everyone bidding, so that we're all on an equal footing. My general impression is that these things go more smoothly here than in the United States."

Singapore government officials refuse to accept the inevitability of economic reverses of any sort. When the British gave up their military facilities, the government converted the naval base into a commercial shipyard, and none of its three thousand employees had to miss a day's work. The Royal Air Force's Changi Air Field was transformed into one of the world's best airports, plus a regional center for aircraft maintenance. As is typical of Singapore, Changi's two terminals are shapeless and lack any hint of aesthetic distinction, but no other airport functions so efficiently. The newly opened Terminal No. 2—named Airtropolis, a word that few Chinese can pronounce—has a sauna, a gymnasium, a nursery, a business center, eleven restaurants, and fifty-one shops, which aren't allowed to charge prices higher than those in the city. In-transit passengers with more than two hours between planes can sign up for a free city tour.

Economic planners averted another potential crisis a decade or more ago, when they saw that Singapore couldn't continue to compete with Hong Kong, Bangkok, and other Asian cities for factories that turn out cheap goods produced by low-cost labor. Singapore decided to change its emphasis to high-technology products—a gamble that, if successful, would dramatically improve the island's standard of living. To drive out low-wage industries like textiles and shoes, the government forced wages up; Singaporeans got an average wage increase of 14 percent in 1982 alone. As a way to lure high-tech enterprises, the government built a "science park," with research facilities for biotechnology, microelectronics, and other growing fields. If a pioneering company had a good idea but no capital, it could locate in Singapore and find a willing investment partner in Singapore's government. The overall strategy brought a flood of high-tech companies to Singapore's door.

Now the government, never one to rest on its laurels where the economy is concerned, is pushing two new plans to spur growth. The first represents a diversification move: taking some of the nation's foreign reserves and investing them in companies overseas—a plan that includes building schools abroad for the children of Singaporeans sent to work for those companies. The second is what is called a growth triangle. Instead of pushing out the remaining low-wage factories and rejecting new ones, Singapore is working jointly with Malaysia and Indonesia to locate such factories in the southern Malaysian state of Johore and in Indonesia's Riau Islands—both adjacent to Singapore—while keeping the manufacturers' corporate headquarters in Singapore itself. The strategy is brilliant: not only does Singapore get new skilled jobs but the country—a Chinese island dwarfed by neighboring Muslim states that posed a real threat in the 1960s—can make the Malaysian and Indonesian economies increasingly dependent on Singapore's existence. "In the Riau Islands, they've set up a joint venture with Indonesians," a Western diplomat explained to me. "This Riau authority is getting a lot of clout to bypass Jakarta's bureaucracy. If Jakarta were running it alone, nothing would happen. Jakarta has had a plan to develop the islands since the mid-1970s, and it had been 95 percent a failure. But now it's taking off. You have Singapore actively assisting Western companies to wade through the bureaucracy and corruption in Malaysia and Indonesia. Creating an economic region with Singapore as the hub insures Singapore's economic growth. And it's also providing political stability because of the growing economic interdependence."

Singapore, the bastion of capitalism, has never hesitated to establish government-owned companies. The government owns or controls some of the biggest banks and insurance companies and also shipyards, hotels, an oil refinery, a steel mill, trading organizations, and many other enterprises. At one point, it owned a driving range for golfers. Not surprisingly, the government's business ventures are highly profitable—even the subway system and the power company—and now that stock in some of the ventures is being sold to the public, in a privatization move, the government is awash in cash. The best known of the government-owned enterprises is Singapore Airlines, which is a paragon of good management. The airline has made a profit every year since its founding, in 1972, and it earned over $500 million in the fiscal year that ended on March 31, 1991—a time when many other airlines had huge losses because the Gulf War reduced travel. Although Singapore is racked by violent thunderstorms most afternoons, Singapore Airlines has never had a crash. It upgrades its fleet so often that it is now replacing all its Boeing 747s with the newest model, the long-range 747-400.

While the government's big investments in private industry might run counter to the tenets of capitalism, Lee Kuan Yew maintains that they have been a vital ingredient in Singapore's economic success. "The only reason the government moved in was that no entrepreneur had the guts and the gumption and the capital to go in on his own," Lee told me. "So we went in and got it going, using government officials who had the drive and the flair. And we are prepared to go into more high-risk areas where Singaporean entrepreneurs are unable to carry that risk, either for lack of daring or for lack of capital."

Singapore acquired the capital to make these investments in an inventive way. The government devised a scheme, or plan—in Singapore, plans are always referred to as schemes—for forced savings on a huge scale. Called the Central Provident Fund, it now takes 34 percent of a worker's salary for a special retirement account; in the past, as much as 40 percent has been withheld. (By manipulating the percentage, the government can inject funds into the economy in periods of recession and cause more to be withheld during boom times, when inflation threatens.) The account pays interest, and the worker can withdraw funds before retirement, but for only two reasons: to buy certain blue-chip stocks, like Singapore Airlines, or to buy a house or an apartment. The fund simultaneously accomplishes three important goals: the government gets a huge pool of investment capital, which at the end of 1990 stood at $23 billion; workers gain a stake in the capitalist system through their stock purchases and help support it at the same time; and Singapore becomes a nation of homeowners—homeowners who want prosperity and political stability to preserve their investment.

Most Singaporeans—87 percent of them—live in the sterile government-built apartment towers, which in some areas stretch so far that there is bus service from one side of an apartment block to the other. From the outside, these apartment blocks could be taken for a New York City housing project: all buildings identical, each without a hint of architectural merit. But the resemblance to New York City ends at their doors, for inside they're immaculate—completely free of vandalism, graffiti, and litter. The explanation lies in the fact that 90 percent of these units—and 80 percent of Singapore's dwellings overall—are owned by the families who live in them, and people aren't going to let the value of their investment drop because the building isn't kept up. The Singapore government builds the towers and then offers the apartments for sale, allowing the buyers to use their Central Provident money for both the down payment and the monthly mortgage payment. A five-room apartment far away from the central city typically sells for around $45,000; a unit closer in costs at least 50 percent more. An owner is free to sell the apartment after five years, and people who bought their apartments in the 1970s can now get somewhere between two and four times the original purchase price. Though the government has no love for those who depend on welfare, it isn't about to see impoverished people sleeping on Singapore's streets, so it rents some of the older, smaller apartments at heavily subsidized prices. Several hundred people—such as families in which the father has been arrested for drug peddling and the mother and children are left penniless—live in government housing free.

Creating a nation of homeowners has done more than keep the housing stock from deteriorating; it has also provided insurance against political or racial revolution, since those who rebel would be acting against their own economic interests. "Underneath everything is the housing policy," Mary Lee, a Singapore journalist, says. "An ordinary office worker can own his own apartment—a situation that would be the envy of anyone in the United States. The government decided that the way to keep the population quiet was to give everyone a stake." The housing situation isn't quite tidy enough, however, to deter the government's rulemakers from stepping in, as they do in almost every other aspect of Singapore life. A single person can buy only a small apartment, and in a less popular area, because "the government thinks if you make it easier for singles they won't get married, and we want to encourage them to have families," I was told by Lim Hng Kiang, then the chief executive officer of the Housing and Development Board. The government also sets size limits for dogs allowed to live in its apartment buildings. And, just in case the pride of homeownership is overwhelmed by an urgent situation, elevators in the apartment blocks are equipped with urine detectors. When the detector senses the ammonia in urine, it locks the elevator doors and activates a hidden camera. An alarm rings at the Housing and Development Board, and the police are dispatched. If the culprit is a child, the parents get a letter of warning. An adult finds himself faced with another of those stiff Singapore fines, and this one can amount to as much as $1,240. On occasion, moreover, the offender will discover his name, or even his picture, in the *Straits Times*. Perhaps fearing that the threat of a fine and unwanted publicity might not be enough, the government also tries to reason with its citizens. When I visited a housing project, I saw a large photographic exhibit on how to take proper care of elevators. One panel was captioned, "Urine causes the lift parts to corrode and makes the elevator smelly."

While Singapore is hardly the entertainment center of Asia, it does offer one pleasant distraction from making money and obeying rules. On days off, families can take an aerial tramway to nearby Sentosa Island, a large and beautiful theme park. Sentosa Island features a wax museum depicting pioneers of Singapore, an old fort from colonial times, nature walks, formal gardens, birds, and displays of coral and butterflies. A monorail circles the island; the stops are numbered, and visitors get a brochure listing the attractions at each stop. The brochure, however, won't inform them about Sentosa Island's one permanent resident, who lives at Stop No. 6, in a guardhouse next to the old fort. Singaporeans seem to have little sense of irony, but tourists who happen upon him and hear his story are astonished to find such a man in a theme park. His name is Chia Thye Poh, and he is currently Singapore's only political prisoner—a man whose life bears a remarkable resemblance to that of Nelson Mandela.

No one guards Chia Thye Poh these days. He is free to receive visitors; his room in the guardhouse, though it is sparsely furnished, has a telephone, and he is confined to Sentosa Island only from 9:00 p.m. to 6:00 a.m. For this degree of freedom, however, Chia Thye Poh has paid a very high price—more than twenty-two years in jail. It's hard to envision Chia as an enemy of anyone, and he certainly doesn't seem a threat to the powerful nation of Singapore. When I visited him, I found a rail-thin man wearing black-rimmed glasses, shower sandals, and white shorts, who was soft-spoken, almost meek, and extraordinarily deferential. He showed a constant concern about my comfort—going to the fort's snack bar to get me a drink, moving my chair so that I would be more directly under the fan. Chia's deeply rooted graciousness and a total absence of ego made his story all the more poignant.

From 1963 to 1966, Chia, a university lecturer in physics, was a member of Parliament from the Barisan Sosialis Party (*barisan* is a Malay word for "front"), a left-leaning group that had split with Lee Kuan Yew's PAP over the issue of Singapore's joining the Malaysian Federation. "We wanted a genuinely democratic Malaysia, including Singapore," Chia said. "We fought for genuine parliamentary democracy, for a rule of law, not rule by one or two ministers. The PAP branded this as toeing the line of the Communist Party of Malaya. After the 1963 elections, three opposition M.P.'s were arrested, and two more in 1966. There were hundreds of other arrests over those years, because many people went out to demonstrate. The government used all means to try to suppress the opposition. In October of 1966, the Barisan M.P.'s resigned because of government harassment. Important issues like Singapore's withdrawal from the federation were never debated in Parliament, since Parliament had become a rubber stamp."

Three weeks after the resignations, Chia was one of the organizers of a rally to protest the Vietnam War, which took place on the eve of a visit to Singapore by President Lyndon Johnson. The rally marked Chia's last day of freedom. He was arrested in the course of the rally, under provisions of the Internal Security Act, which Singapore's government has used against hundreds of political opponents. The act, inherited from the British, allows detention for an unlimited number of two-year periods, without charges and without judicial review. "I was never charged, never brought to trial, never convicted of anything," Chia told me. Only nineteen years later, in 1985, did the government give its first official explanation for his arrest: the minister of home affairs, in an address to Parliament, accused Chia of having infiltrated the Barisan Sosialis to destabilize the government through "Communist united-front activities." Chia told me, "They released no sort of documents. I have never been a member of any Communist Party; I was just performing my duties as an M.P. My activities were all legal, peaceful, and constitutional. I have never advocated violence, and have never been charged with any offense of violence, let alone convicted."

Chia, unlike most other political detainees in Singapore, resisted all attempts to extract a confession. "They tried very hard to break prisoners, to extract confessions from them, to have them confess on television," Chia said. "They made me pay a very high price for not kowtowing to them. In 1966, they put me in a dark cell and said some people had gone insane under such conditions. Sometimes you could hear people kicking the doors as if they had gone insane. I went from one prison to another and was in solitary confinement several times. Sometimes I was deprived of reading material for months at a stretch. They said that there's no end to this, that it will go on year after year if I don't confess, that even if I'm made of steel they have means to break me. I told them that I had nothing to confess, and that if the government had evidence it should try me in open court, where I could see the evidence against me and defend myself. There were daylong interrogations in a freezing-cold room. They pressured my family. But I always thought, No matter how long they keep me this way, someday they will have to release me, because I'm innocent and I have support. It's part of the broad struggle for democracy all over the world. When you are in solitary, there is nothing in the cell. But you can explore, and see faint scribblings from previous prisoners. I still remember one of them. It was a poem in Chinese: 'Ten years behind bars / Never too late / Thousands of ordeals / My spirit steeled.' When you were alone and helpless, and you saw things like that, you were encouraged."

The parallel between Chia Thye Poh and Nelson Mandela, two prisoners of conscience accused of Communist subversion, is striking. Each was in jail for more than twenty years, at least part of the time confined to an island. Each had the opportunity to go free if he would abandon his political goals, and each refused. Chia said that the similarity wasn't lost on his interrogators. "They were telling me that Mandela remained in jail because he had lots of outside support," Chia said. "But they said there's no point in my remaining in jail, because no one remembers me. Mandela at least got a chance to defend himself in court, and now he's a free man. He can travel all over the world. He can take part in politics in South Africa, where the situation is far more tense than in Singapore. But I'm still not free. I don't know why the government should keep me here."

Singapore is clearly different from South Africa: the denial of rights is much more arbitrary and has never been aimed exclusively at the Malay and Indian minorities. Nor is Singapore—as even some former political detainees pointed out when I interviewed them—like Argentina under the generals. "The government knows where to stop," I was told by one of these detainees, who asked not to be identified. "They don't shoot us. They don't maim us. They allow you rehabilitation after you're out." This man said that while he was in jail he was "stripped time and again, blindfolded for three days, kept in an underground windowless room that was very cold." He added, "They had an interrogator who could shout into my ears for twelve hours straight. But on the tenth day, when I was hyperventilating from the cold and the pressure, they rushed me to the hospital."

Yet, short of physical torture and disappearances at night, the human rights record of the Singapore government much more resembles that of a Third World dictatorship than that of an industrial and technological powerhouse whose economy is intertwined with that of the West. Singapore is a prosperous nation with little racial animosity, no external threat, and a government that is genuinely popular, because of the economic growth it has brought. In the eyes of many Westerners, Singapore should have achieved political, cultural, and social freedom as an inevitable companion to the high level of economic development. But Singapore's record lags not only in contrast to the records of Western democracies but also when it is compared with the records of its neighbors, who have their own problems with human rights. Singapore manages to control its citizens more pervasively than does Indonesia, a country that has known bloody repression. It has allowed its press less freedom than has Thailand, even during the period from February 1991 to June 1992, when that nation was under the control of a military junta. The city of Penang, in Malaysia—a nation that has its own Internal Security Act and whose government frequently takes heavy-handed action against political opponents—is filled with public-interest groups that freely criticize the government, but such groups have never been allowed to exist in Singapore.

Several studies of human rights in Singapore have produced substantial evidence that the rule of law has on many occasions fallen victim to the whim of government. In July 1989, the Committee on International Human Rights of the New York City Bar Association visited Singapore to prepare a report financed by the Ford Foundation and the MacArthur Foundation. The report, released in December 1990, amounts to a devastating indictment. "What emerges from this review is a government that has been willing to decimate the rule of law for the benefit of its political interests," the report states. "Lawyers have been cowed to passivity, judges are kept on a short leash, and the law has been manipulated so that gaping holes exist in the system of restraints on government action toward the individual. Singapore is not a country in which individual rights have significant meaning." The United States government, although it is a close ally of Singapore, has also sharply criticized its human rights record. A human rights report issued by the State Department in March 1991 presents an extensive catalogue of abuses. It speaks of "political control of the press, courts, and religion" and points to "credible reports" of mistreatment of detainees and "surveillance of opposition or dissident figures as well as some religious leaders."

Singapore abolished trial by jury in 1969, and judges, according to the State Department report, "have close ties to the Government and its leaders" and "are beholden to the Government for their appointments." In December 1988, a Singapore appellate court ruled against the government, ordering the release of four prisoners detained under the Internal Security Act. The next month, Parliament amended the constitution to eliminate judicial review of Internal Security Act detentions, and the amendment was made retroactive to 1971. In 1990, Parliament passed what is called the Maintenance of Religious Harmony Act, giving the government power to arrest religious workers who it feels are engaging in politics; this act also barred judicial review of their cases. Persons caught breaking into a house or stealing a car, and perpetrators of several other crimes, are subject to lashes with a cane as well as prison; in 1989, the government also decided to cane illegal immigrants. The Bar Association report describes the procedure: "When the rattan hits the bared buttocks, the skin disintegrates, leaving initially a white line and then a flow of blood. The victim must lie on his front for three weeks to a month because the buttocks are so sore."

The feeling of intimidation is increased by laws that are kept on the books but are not enforced, since they could be at any time. During the Vietnam War years, when long hair was connected with drugs and dissent, Singapore police would pull long-haired youths off the streets for involuntary haircuts. Though the regulation against "hair reaching below an ordinary shirt collar" remains, it is now violated by many young Malays. Though homosexuality can be punished by anything up to life imprisonment, one of the largest discotheques becomes male-only every Sunday night, and hundreds of young gay Chinese men gather there to dance and to flirt—but such activities are kept discreet. Though prostitution is illegal, three streets are lined with brothels, and the government requires all prostitutes to get a venereal disease check every two weeks and an HIV test every three months. Many Singaporean men, however, prefer to violate Thailand's prostitution laws.

Opponents of the government have a difficult life in Singapore. The State Department report charges that in the universities "tenure and renewal of appointments can be, and have been, refused to academics whose work deviates from government views." It also points to "substantial evidence that the authorities conduct clandestine searches of the baggage of opposition figures in the airport baggage-handling area." Demonstrations, except for those supporting the government, almost never occur in Singapore. In fact, aside from social gatherings, assemblies of more than five people in public must have police permission. When I interviewed Prime Minister Goh, the government had just announced sharp tuition increases for the universities. I asked him why students wouldn't be allowed to unfurl a banner requesting that the increases be scaled back. "If you allow students to do so, then workers will begin to do so over the slightest grievance," Goh replied. "And if you have several such demonstrations, right away the impression is created that government is not in control of the situation—that the place may became unstable. That will have an impact on foreign investors."

In the area of human rights, the Bar Association committee sees a design resembling that of the former Marxist governments of Eastern Europe. "A basic strategy of the totalitarian governments that were recently toppled in Eastern Europe was to keep society atomized, to keep discontent something that can be whispered among friends but that cannot be transformed into a social movement because people are too fearful to join together as a political force," the report says. "This effort to prevent the formation of a civil society has been the principal strategy of the Singapore government."

When I interviewed a member of the political opposition, he called Singapore "a city of fear." There is much evidence to support this characterization. For instance, in 1990 Russell Heng, who is now a researcher for the Institute of Southeast Asian Studies, wrote a report on Singapore that was called "Give Me Liberty or Give Me Wealth" and was financed by the Rockefeller Foundation. "Two years ago, a Cabinet Minister urged academics and professionals to speak up," he noted in the study. "But when two reporters tried to get the reaction of eighteen of them to the Minister's encouragement, six preferred to keep their views to themselves. Of the remaining twelve, six spoke only on condition of anonymity." Heng also observed that "talking to people for this essay brought some firsthand experience of the irrational fear which exists even among the best-educated Singaporeans," and noted, "One example would be those who rejected phone interviews. Yet others spoke in measured tones and then sent word in a roundabout way to say that they would have said things differently if they were not speaking on the phone."

I asked a high-ranking Singapore official about this climate of fear. The official seemed to have been anointed the house critic of the Singapore government, for he had frequently offered criticisms without repercussion, and in reply to my questions he characterized the attitude of Singaporeans as "Play it safe," and explained, "If you're not sure, don't do it. This syndrome breeds sycophancy. Our friends point out to us that all critics of government are not treated as generously as I am." But later, the official in effect confirmed his own observation by asking that his name not be used.

I saw several examples of this pervasive fear. On two occasions, when I met opponents of the government at hotels for lunch they pointed to people in the lobby and said they were agents of the ISD who were watching us. (I doubted it, figuring that the Singapore government was too competent to allow its security agents to be detected so easily.) Another time, I interviewed an American in the publishing business in Singapore. He later called back, apologizing profusely, to say that he was about to buy an apartment, but first he wanted to know if I was planning to quote him as saying anything critical, because he feared that any such remark would result in his expulsion from the country. And one day, when I beeped my answering machine in Berkeley from my Singapore hotel room, I found a message giving me a phone number in Singapore to call. "Don't identify yourself in any way," the message said. "Just make an appointment to have lunch." I followed the instructions and found myself meeting an establishment journalist. All during lunch, as this journalist described repression in Singapore, he kept glancing nervously over his shoulder, as if he thought he was about to be snatched away. "I never ask questions at press conferences, because if you do they take note of you," he told me. "A number of journalists have lost their jobs." This man held such a negative view of Lee Kuan Yew that he predicted, "There will be a Nuremberg trial in Singapore if Lee loses power—I'm absolutely convinced of it. I see him in no different position from the Shah of Iran or Marcos. Each and every 'Communist' he has detained is not a Communist but an effective political opponent."

The climate of intimidation in Singapore was fueled by a series of events that began in 1987, when the government initiated a crackdown that eventually included actions against Catholic church workers, a prominent attorney who had been solicitor general of Singapore, and a diplomat at the American embassy, who was summarily expelled from the country. These actions seemed to Westerners, at least, to make little sense, because they came at a time when the government appeared to be under no threat whatsoever, from either domestic or foreign opponents; few people could imagine that the political opposition would win more than four or five of the eighty-one seats in Parliament in the September 1988 elections, since it then held only two seats. The crackdown began in May and June of 1987, when the government arrested and detained under the International Security Act twenty-two young social activists, several of them Catholic lay workers. The alleged local ringleader was Vincent Cheng, a former seminarian who had been involved in church-related activities for more than a decade; at the time of his detention, Cheng was helping Filipino women who had been brought to Singapore as maids and then mistreated. The government contended that the twenty-two were part of a "Marxist conspiracy to subvert the existing social and political system in Singapore through Communist united-front tactics to establish a Communist state." The New York City Bar Association committee investigated these arrests, and its report charges that the detainees were subjected to prolonged sleep deprivation and extended exposure to cold, and that at least seven suffered physical abuse in the form of blows and slaps. By the end of 1987, Singapore's television viewers had been treated to their videotaped confessions, which the Bar Association contends were heavily edited, and all but Vincent Cheng had been freed. The terms of their release included a provision that they would not associate with one another in the future. When a British lawyer active in defending Singapore dissidents took some of them to a restaurant, the Bar Association report states, each had to sit at a separate table, and he rotated among them.

In April 1988, nine of the original detainees released a public statement describing their mistreatment in prison and declaring that they had been advocating more democracy and freedom, not a Communist state. Eight of the signers of that statement were rearrested the same day; the ninth was out of the country. The government, which loves to pounce on its victims with the claws of convoluted logic, said that it made these arrests because the former detainees were now claiming innocence, and therefore they hadn't been properly rehabilitated and might still be a danger to the state. This time, the government also put Patrick Seong, one of the lawyers for the detainees, in jail for a month; Seong had been handling his first case outside his usual field, commercial litigation, having agreed to represent several of the defendants because they couldn't find an experienced lawyer willing to take the risk. Seven of the eight who were rearrested quickly agreed to repudiate their public statement, and they signed the equivalent of affidavits reaffirming the truth of their previous confessions. According to the Bar Association's report, the affidavits meant that they would be in criminal jeopardy if they ever tried to issue a contrary statement in the future. But the eighth, a lawyer named Teo Soh Lung, who had founded a legal-aid group for criminal defendants, refused. Instead, she filed a writ of habeas corpus, and for her rebellion she had to stay in jail two more years. Teo and Vincent Cheng were finally released in June 1990.

Cheng, rehabilitated, now works in Singapore as a foot reflexologist; foot massage, many Singaporeans believe, promotes healing and relieves stress. I wanted to interview Cheng but found that there was a Catch-22. A vaguely worded clause in his release agreement indicated that he would have to get permission from the Internal Security Department for any interview. But the mere act of applying to the ISD could mean that he hadn't been sufficiently rehabilitated, since he still wanted to talk about the past. Consequently, he could be sent back to jail.

Instead, I set about trying to see a videotape of Cheng's confession, which had been televised by the Singapore Broadcasting Corporation in 1987. The response I got to this request illustrated the observation about Singapore's climate of fear. An SBC producer informed me that permission would have to come from the prime minister's press secretary; the press secretary, however, said that he would have to take it to the permanent secretary of the Ministry of Information and the Arts, the agency's highest-ranking civil servant. Finally, permission was granted, and one journalist told me privately that he was certain Lee Kuan Yew himself had actually made the decision. Several days later, I sat in a room of the SBC building witnessing an astonishing event. On the tape, four journalists, including a Malay and an Indian, asked Cheng a series of questions about Marxist connections. Although they had pens and notebooks, and the camera switched to them frequently, I never saw any of them taking a note. The sound quality and the picture sequence constantly changed, as if pieces of tape had been spliced, and at one point Cheng's voice wasn't synchronized with his lips. Cheng, thin and frail-looking and soft-spoken, readily confessed to a series of connections with various leftist groups. Some of his answers sounded ludicrously stilted. At one point, he said, "My leftist thinking always left me biased against multinationals. What I didn't understand was whether Singapore can exist without multinationals' contributing to our economy. . . . During my detention, I was given the opportunity to understand Singapore better. I realized I needed to be more positive, to contribute to Singapore." At another point, he noted, "I realize it is very important I take into account the reality of Singapore—Singapore's vulnerability, for example." A friend of Cheng's told me later, "The only way he could protest against this forced interview was to comb his hair in the opposite direction, as a sign it wasn't him."

After seeing the tape, I interviewed a man who, years before Cheng, had also had to make a confession on television about his leftist connections. I mentioned the eerie feeling I'd had in watching Cheng's confession—the feeling that I could just as easily have been in Berlin in 1938, or in Moscow in 1952. The man, who had agreed to the interview on the condition that I not identify him, bridled. "The public confession is very Chinese," he said. "Not to get at the offender but to give a lesson to the audience. It would be a grave insult to Singaporeans if you took the form of these detentions and confessions and simplistically looked at it in your own cultural context. Then it becomes almost Nazi-like behavior; you lump it with North Korea. But when you live here, you realize that Singapore is authoritarian but not by any means totalitarian. The idea is to humiliate people. It's the act of humiliation, not the content of the confession, that is important, to serve as a warning to others."

Cheng and the other social activists were not the only victims of the 1987–88 crackdown. Another was Francis Seow, who ended up in the United States, his career in Singapore shattered. Seow had been a close associate of Lee, serving as solicitor general from 1969 to 1972, and, starting in 1985, as the president of the Law Society, Singapore's equivalent of the American Bar Association. Under Seow's leadership, the Law Society assumed an increasingly independent role, commenting on proposed legislation—a function that the government then outlawed, in 1986. Early in 1988, Seow broke with the government and planned to run for Parliament as an opposition candidate. In May of that year, however, he appeared in court to represent Teo Soh Lung, the one dissident who wouldn't bow to the government, and Patrick Seong, the lawyer for the eight dissidents who himself had been arrested. Hours after his court appearance, Seow was arrested, charged with being in "close contact" with an American embassy diplomat, the political officer E. Mason Hendrickson. Singapore's government expelled Hendrickson from the country, alleging that he had been meeting with antigovernment lawyers "to manipulate and instigate Singaporeans, in order to bring about a particular political outcome." (Seow says that his first meeting with Hendrickson was actually to arrange a cocktail party for visiting American judges.) The government released Seow after seventy-two days, in time for him to run for Parliament but not to organize a broad opposition movement. In the September elections, the PAP took all but one seat, the sole elected opposition member being a lawyer named Chiam See Tong. Seow, however, finished high enough to win a "nonconstituency seat"—a special seat with limited voting rights. (To make sure that Parliament had the window dressing of at least a token opposition, the government had created these special seats for opposition candidates who came closest to winning. They would be doled out as necessary to bring the number of opposition members to three.) The government then delayed the opening of Parliament for five months, saying that its building needed renovation. By the time Parliament finally opened, Seow, who was in the United States for treatment of a heart problem, had been convicted in absentia for tax evasion and fined an amount sufficient to bar him under the law from taking his seat.

"The moment I stepped back into Singapore, I would probably be getting off the plane and into prison," Seow told me from his current home, in Cambridge, Massachusetts. "Lee Kuan Yew is extremely clever. I was definitely a political prisoner; the attention of human rights groups all over the world could be riveted on my case. But if he could shift it onto the criminal plane, tax evasion, he could say that it had nothing to do with human rights. They say I evaded paying my taxes, in that I submitted a false return. That is completely untrue."

The Singapore government, which doesn't worry about bad public relations as a result of its treatment of dissidents, hired private detectives to follow Seow in the United States for seven weeks, beginning in December 1988. The *Straits Times* dutifully reported that Seow "travelled to Bloomington, Indiana, and stayed there over Christmas," and went on, "His stay there was confirmed by purchases of liquor, paid for with his American Express Gold Card. Seow moved on to Seattle on the West Coast of the U.S., five hours by air from Indiana. He was spotted at a house there and photographed sightseeing with 'an unknown Asian lady' in downtown Seattle." While no direct connection was ever proved, the month after Seow's arrest the *Asian Wall*

Street Journal reported that the Banque National de Paris had abruptly canceled a $347,000 line of credit to a Malaysian businesswoman in Singapore whom Seow had been engaged to. Ashleigh Seow, Francis Seow's son and the secretary of one of Singapore's town councils, told me that the woman, a permanent resident of Singapore, was given two weeks to leave the country and never told the reason. "I was there when they served the documents on her," he said.

As for the Hendrickson expulsion, Singapore's government directed a torrent of abuse at the United States in announcing it. Reminiscent of the old *Pravda*, the *Straits Times* reported, on May 11, 1988, the number of demonstrators at a protest rally before the rally had taken place. "More than 4,000 unionists and workers are staging a protest rally today to show their anger at American interference in Singapore's domestic policies," said the paper, which comes out before dawn. On May 31, Goh Chok Tong, who was then deputy prime minister, told Parliament that "the American Constitution—and here I am quoting one Dr. Freeman Dyson—'The American Constitution is designed to be operated by crooks, just as the British constitution is designed to be operated by gentlemen.' " Britain's *Financial Times* wrote of the controversy,

> The fracas between tiny Singapore and the mighty U.S. looks set to go down as one of the more improbable, even bizarre, diplomatic clashes. . . . All this is directed against a country which absorbs a quarter of Singapore's total exports, provides about a third of its foreign investment and whose companies are among the biggest private-sector employers on the island. In addition, it is a country whose defence role in the region Singapore strongly supports.

Did the Singapore government lose all sense of reality in 1987 and 1988, finding itself so embarrassed by bad publicity over the arrest of the twenty-two activists that it kept digging a deeper hole for itself in an effort to get out? I asked Lee Kuan Yew about these events, and about why he appeared in general so contemptuous of the concept of human rights. Lee's answers seem rooted in an era when many countries saw a monolithic Communist conspiracy poised to take over at any sign of weakness, but his words were delivered with such passion and such determination that they also began to resemble something else: to me they sounded for all the world like a father talking about protecting the chastity of his daughter. The only problem, of course, is that in this instance the daughter has by now turned thirty-two.

"We did not arrest them because they were church people," Lee began. "We have a professional organization called the Internal Security Department. Its job is to make sure that the subversion of the Communist Party of Malaya does not swing into the English-educated world. This particular man, Vincent Cheng, tried to use the church as his cover." The activists, Lee said, were trying to create unrest, which was a necessary precursor to the second stage, bombings and assassinations. "It makes no sense otherwise," he continued. "Because, first of all, they were no threat to us, right? None of the twenty-two were any threat to us politically. They were not known public figures. They couldn't have beaten us in any election. You do this, you're bound to have a public reaction which must be adverse, because it comes out of the blue. So why do you want to undertake something with adverse electoral consequences a year before the elections, when these people were no threat to us in the coming elections? Ask yourself that. The Western press spoke as if we were in danger of losing our seats and our majority. But we knew we were in no danger at all, either before or after the action. I told the younger ministers, 'Look, as I see it, this takes about five years before it gets going. You can wait for it to mature and you might find out the ramifications. But you'll run the risk of many more innocent people being drawn in.' "

I also asked Lee about Chia Thye Poh—how a man so modest and considerate could be seen as a threat. As I described Chia's qualities, Lee interrupted, saying, "Chinese Communist style. That is the ideal Communist. You must be humble, you must be very frugal and Spartan, not flashy, not trying to awe or impress people. They impress people by their humility and self-sacrificing manner, a certain exaggerated understatement of themselves, but a steely determination."

While many leaders around the world violate human rights, few won't at least pay lip service to them in interviews with Western correspondents. Paying lip service, however, is not Lee Kuan Yew's style. "I'm not sure human rights are a traditional value, even in Christian societies," he told me. "It's the answer of the West in countering Communism. Democracy countered Communism by sponsoring what has been advanced as the axiomatic truths of free society, which includes freedom of the press and human rights. But are they universal values? Can you prove their universality? If they are in fact of universal relevance, will they not win just by a process of Darwinian evolution?"

Even as Lee Kuan Yew continues to fear a Communist conspiracy, the tattered remains of Asian Communist parties are looking to Singapore as a model of how to maintain tight control over a nation's government and over its people's lives while simultaneously quelling discontent by freeing its economy. Academicians in China have named the movement "neo-authoritarianism"—a system that allows the leaders to keep their party firmly in power yet preside over a booming economy. In his study of Singapore, Russell Heng, the Singaporean researcher, speculates that neo-authoritarianism could emerge as the next ideological challenge to democratic capitalism. The leaders of Vietnam are already speaking openly of their admiration for Singapore, but their ardor might cool when they discover that a major component of Singapore's success is the absence of corruption.

In Singapore, the People's Action Party serves as the basic vehicle for control. Formed in 1954, at a time when Lee Kuan Yew was in alliance with local Communists, the PAP still bears a striking resemblance to Communist parties in its structure. Lee no doubt saw that Communist parties were organized to promote tight discipline and control, two qualities he values, and he has never hesitated to borrow attractive ideas no matter what their source. Accordingly, the PAP's members have no role in choosing the Party leaders or the candidates for Parliament. Instead, Lee screens the members carefully and selects from them several hundred "cadres"—their exact number and their names are secret. The cadres, in turn, elect a twelve-member central Executive Committee. "In the past," the *Far Eastern Economic Review* reported in 1990, "Lee has unapologetically compared the system to that of the Roman Catholic Church, where 'the Pope appoints the cardinals and the cardinals then elect the Pope.' Others have described the cadre-based system as 'Leninist.' Ironically, it was actually imposed on the party by Lee in 1957 against the strenuous objections of the party's left, on the grounds that it would provide an iron curtain to prevent the PAP from being infiltrated by Communists." In remaining secretary-general of the PAP after giving up the prime minis- tership to Goh Chok Tong, Lee still holds the ultimate reins of power. "Goh is perhaps the only head of state in the world who doesn't control his political party," a European diplomat in Singapore noted recently.

Singapore has the trappings of a democracy: its people elect a Parliament, and opposition candidates are free to contest any seat. It is even possible that if the PAP imposed disastrous policies on Singapore—and at the same time chose not to tamper with the electoral system—the opposition could win control. But the opposition has a long way to go. From 1966, when the

Barisan Sosialis delegates walked out, until 1981, when Joshua Benjamin Jeyaretnam won a seat for the Workers' Party, Parliament did not have a single opposition member, and in the 1980s there were never more than two full-voting opposition members. The most recent election took place in August 1991, and although the opposition parties did better than at any time since 1963, the PAP still retained all but four of the eighty-one seats.

Jeyaretnam, who was born in Sri Lanka, is the only opposition figure in Singapore with almost as forceful a presence as Lee himself. Like Lee, he trained for the law in Britain, and his command of the Queen's English is impeccable. When I called on Jeyaretnam in his office, a cramped space he shares with a secretary, and he spoke about what he believes are the injustices in Singapore's society, his powerful voice resounded mightily. Although Jeyaretnam was the lone representative of the opposition in Parliament, the government launched an extraordinary series of actions against him. "Until I got elected in 1981, the PAP was paying lip service to some kind of opposition in Parliament," Jeyaretnam told me. "The moment I got into Parliament, the members were completely stunned, though this was the sixth election in which I had contested a seat. Often, when I asked a question in Parliament, they said I was abusing my privileges. I had to go before the Committee on Privileges four times, accused of making improper allegations against the government. Outside Parliament, the PAP began a systematic campaign to isolate me."

In 1984, Jeyaretnam was accused by the government of misusing Workers' Party funds, and the case went to trial. He was acquitted on three counts and fined a thousand Singapore dollars on a fourth. Under the law, it would have taken a fine of twice that amount to deprive him of his seat in Parliament. Seven months later, the judge who presided over his case was transferred out of the courts and into the Attorney General's office. The government then appealed the case, and in 1986 the appeals court fined Jeyaretnam the necessary $2,000, disbarred him, and sentenced him to a month in jail. Jeyaretnam had the right to appeal his disbarment, although not the conviction itself, to the Privy Council in England, the highest court in the Commonwealth, and he did so. In 1988, the Privy Council delivered a sharply worded verdict restoring Jeyaretnam to the practice of law. The Privy Council Law Lords declared that Jeyaretnam and a codefendant from the Workers' Party "have suffered a grievous injustice," and went on, "They have been fined, imprisoned, and publicly disgraced for offenses of which they were not guilty." The Singapore government then abolished the right of appeal to the Privy Council in such cases. But this still wasn't the end of the story. Lee sued Jeyaretnam for libel and, in 1990, won vast damages, which forced Jeyaretnam to put his house up for sale. "Lee won't let you go," Jeyaretnam told me. "He said several times in Parliament that I had to be destroyed."

While not every opponent gets the attention accorded to Jeyaretnam, his experience does illustrate the perils of being in the political opposition in Singapore. On a subtler level, political opponents face a number of potential obstacles. Even when the government does nothing, opposition candidates can experience substantial setbacks to their careers; for instance, many Singaporeans are unlikely to relish the idea of being represented in court by a lawyer identified with the opposition. "Whether you're a lawyer or an architect or a businessman, your clients want you to get things done," one Singapore professional told me. "A few remarks from the government, and they'll go away. We have a very cautious public, having grown up in these conditions." Opposition candidates have complained about restrictions on their rallies, and about distortion of their views in the government-controlled press. Because trade unions and universities are dominated by the government, they're unlikely to serve as fertile breeding grounds for opposition parties.

In part because of gerrymandering, the percentage of seats in Parliament won by the opposition bears no relation to the percentage of votes it gets. In the August 1991 election, for instance, the opposition parties took almost 40 percent of the vote but won only four of the eighty-one seats. "The PAP has succeeded in preventing this opposition vote from translating into a comparable percentage of seats in Parliament through such techniques as . . . changing the constitutional ground rules at will and combining constituencies and redrawing electoral boundaries for the benefit of the ruling party," the New York City Bar Association report stated. "Following the 1988 general elections, the government imposed percentage limitations on the number of minorities who can live in particular housing complexes. . . . The Singapore government has started to impose quotas on each apartment block and on each neighborhood."

Thus, Singapore is effectively a one-party state, with the ruling party organized on the cadre system. The government has weakened religious institutions, dominated the press, and introduced pervasive censorship. It owns many major businesses and controls the one big labor union. If this has a familiar ring, it is because these conditions—despite the fervent anti-Communism of Lee Kuan Yew—are indistinguishable from those normally identified with a Communist state. Universal employment, good housing for everyone, and the absence of poverty are also part of the Communist rhetoric, the only difference being that in Singapore they have become reality. The analogy can obviously be carried too far—no Communist nation until recent years would have turned to multinational corporations for investment capital, for example. But it raises a fascinating question: Did Communism die because of its inherent deficiencies or because its governments were too corrupt and too incompetent—because there were no Lee Kuan Yews?

Hidden away on the third floor of the Tanglin Shopping Center, in the Orchard Road tourist area, is a little store called D & O

Film & Video. Here, Albert Odell holds court, to talk about movies the way a football fan might talk about the greatest Super Bowls. Odell, once British and now a Singaporean, came from Hong Kong in 1948 to represent film companies that wanted to distribute their movies in Southeast Asia. Today, he runs his video store in conjunction with a silent partner—the government's Board of Film Censors, which has the first crack at all videotapes that enter Singapore legally. "I get a parcel every week, but it's delivered directly to the censors," he told me. "I open it in their presence. The censors have a yardstick to go by: certain words are one hundred percent taboo. They allow 'fuck' but never 'motherfucker.' If 'mother' is involved, it goes. Any frontal bare breast is out, but a side view is O.K. All references to Allah go. In *Young Guns*, a guy might be shot twelve times, and they'll say, 'Reduce it so he's shot only five times.' " Singapore's officials are nothing if not methodical, and they duly type up on a sheet of paper every excision and alteration they require in a film. ("Reduce to minimum the sequence of couple embracing passionately and woman in ecstasy," one alteration reads.) Odell tapes the relevant sheet to the inside of each videocassette box, so the customer can know exactly what is missing. Browsing through the shelves of D & O Film & Video becomes an exercise in R-rated hilarity.

Singapore imposes censorship not only on movies but also on books, magazines, and music. The United States Information Service can't show a film on America before submitting it to the censors. Old Beatles favorites such as "Yellow Submarine" are forbidden, and so are some of the albums by the Rolling Stones, Eric Clapton, and Elton John, often because song lyrics contain references to drugs. All jukeboxes were banned, as a symbol of moral decay, until July 1991, when the government relented and licensed one for the Hotel Asia. Censorship can be the result of whim as well as of policy. I was so curious about the banning of *Cosmopolitan* that I put the question to Lee. "I agree with you," he answered, "*Cosmopolitan* is not likely to degrade or beguile young minds. But I have in my midst ministers younger than I who are fervent Christians, who believe that their daughters should not be reading all this. And one of them was in charge of information and the press, and he decided to ban *Cosmopolitan*." In this communications hub of southern Asia, Cable News Network can be seen only when the Singapore Broadcasting Corporation chooses to broadcast CNN news, because satellite-reception dishes are illegal. "You can get CNN in Saigon, you can get it in Beijing, but you can't get it here," one diplomat complains. When the American embassy applied for a satellite dish, in the mid-1980s, it took the Singapore government two years to grant the application, and then only on the proviso that no Singaporeans—not even employees of the embassy—be allowed to look at programs from it. The embassy is also forbidden to invite Singaporeans to watch American election returns on television.

The government is most careful to keep out anything that might offend Muslims. Because of the tensions between Malay Muslims and the Chinese during the time of the Malaysian Federation, and because Indonesia, a mostly Muslim country, slaughtered tens of thousands of its Chinese minority in 1965, Singapore bends over backward to avoid inciting either its own Malay population or its Muslim neighbors. (In 1965, Lee Kuan Yew said of Indonesia, "They live in a tenement area and they want to come into my little suburban house with its fruit trees.") Until recently, every Malay Singaporean going to college had his full tuition paid by the government, no matter how wealthy his family was; there was no such policy for Chinese or Indians. Several government officials I talked with deplored the fact that Malays don't take as instinctively as Chinese to the pursuit of money, because the result is a Malay underclass in Singapore that, it is feared, could explode at any provocation. "A children's book published in India about the founder of the Sikh religion was banned because he had criticized Islam," a bookseller told me. "We had an art book of Persian miniatures, and one was a picture of Muhammad as a young prince. I had to ink out the face, because Muhammad isn't supposed to be depicted. I got a book on geometric designs in Islamic mosques, and even that had to be submitted to the censors." The government's fear of its Malay minority may be tinged with paranoia. Although Singaporean Malays on average earn less than the Chinese, most still have a substantial stake in the system and have come to be far better off than their counterparts in Malaysia. A young Malay guide from the Singapore Tourist Promotion Board, who showed me the sights of Singapore, told me the story of her family. In the early 1970s, the family of ten lived in a squatters' zinc-roofed, one-room hut, without even a toilet. The roof leaked, she said, and also made the room an oven during the day. Now they reside in a four-bedroom apartment. All her sisters and brothers have good professional jobs, and two of her brothers, who are married, live in five-room apartments.

The workings of censorship can be subtle. The regulations call for all books to be submitted to the censor, but because this procedure can take months for each title, the booksellers generally engage in self-censorship, ordering only books that they know are safe, and not bothering to submit them. "A couple of years ago, some young people started an arts magazine," a man active in the arts community told me. "No bookstore would sell it, and it died." In 1986, a critical biography of Lee Kuan Yew was published in Australia. Called *No Man Is an Island*, it was written by James Minchin, an Anglican priest who had worked in Singapore. The censors didn't ban the book; they rejected it because the cover carried aerial views of Singapore labeled "Courtesy of Ministry of Communications and Information." That, the censors said, implied government endorsement of the book. The 1990 edition of the book dropped the photos, but no bookseller has dared offer it anyway, since a bookseller as well as a book's author and publisher can be subject to a libel suit by Lee. The same holds true for a second critical biography of Lee, written by T. S. Selvan and called *Singapore: The Ultimate Island*, which was published in Australia in 1990. I bought both books in Johore Bahru, the Malaysian city across the causeway from Singapore, where merchants do a booming business in banned books and uncensored videotapes. In my second interview with Lee, I took the books from my briefcase and asked him why Singaporeans couldn't be trusted to read them. It was the only time Lee lost his composure. Of *The Ultimate Island* he said, "And this one I don't even know. . . . It's just rubbish. It's not even a well-written or well-researched book. It's just rubbish. I don't even know of the book." He added, "Anybody can write anything they like about me, but they run the risk of defaming me and ending up paying me damages. That's my counterweapon."

The book industry is a paragon of freedom compared with the country's newspapers. All the newspapers are published by a company called Singapore Press Holdings, and anyone who wants to own more than 3 percent of its stock must seek approval from the minister of communications and the arts; the minister also has veto power over the directors. Government-owned companies and agencies are among the largest stockholders in Singapore Press Holdings, and its current chairman is in addition the chairman of the Port of Singapore Authority, a government agency. Anyone who reads the *Straits Times* might wonder why all this corporate control is necessary, since direct pressure from government officials is never needed. The *Straits Times* operates with a subservience that irritates even some supporters of the government. Day after day, the paper devotes much of its front page to the latest pronouncements of top officials. One day, for instance, a five-column headline over the lead story read "PM: LET'S MAKE THIS THE FINEST NATION," and the article began, "Mr. Goh Chok Tong last night issued an open invitation to all Singaporeans to help build this country into the finest in the world by the end of this century." A Western diplomat who had previously been stationed in Beijing told me, "Reading the *Straits Times* is like reading the *People's Daily*. Basically, the government doesn't like anything it can't control."

Unlike most other countries with a controlled press, Singapore attempts to keep the foreign press in line, too. For several years, beginning in 1985, it fought a running battle with Dow Jones & Co., after taking offense at articles in two of the company's publications, the *Asian Wall Street Journal* and the *Far Eastern Economic Review*. Among other things, Lee twice initiated proceedings against the *Asian Journal* for criminal contempt of court, filed libel actions against each publication, and ordered that the Singapore circulation of each be cut back drastically. When the *Review* responded by ending all circulation in Singapore, the government licensed a local printer to publish pirated copies of the magazine, minus the advertisements, each week, for sale in Singapore. In September 1989, the *Review* wasn't allowed to send a reporter to cover its own libel trial. The next year, Lee, rejecting a request from Secretary of State James Baker, refused to let either publication cover Baker's visit to Singapore. The controversy neared resolution in 1991, however, with each side taking conciliatory steps toward settling the legal battles.

The government has also used circulation restrictions as a weapon against other foreign publications, and in 1990 it enacted harsh regulations applicable to foreign newspapers and magazines that sell copies in Singapore. "The clear intent of the Government was to warn all foreign periodicals that now circulate in Singapore to be wary of their reporting on Singapore lest they cross the vaguely drawn line of 'interfering' in Singapore's 'domestic affairs,' thereby making themselves subject to the restrictions," the State Department human rights report stated.

Never one to hide from his enemies, Lee went to Hong Kong in 1990 and addressed two international press groups; his remarks only strengthened his reputation for combativeness. He blamed television for the deaths in Tiananmen Square, saying it was television coverage of demonstrations in the Philippines and South Korea, rather than a desire for freedom, that had spurred the Chinese students' protest. And he predicted that the Western press now centered in Hong Kong would gratefully flee to Singapore in 1997, when the crown colony reverts to Chinese sovereignty, and work under its rules. Derek Davies, the former editor of the *Far Eastern Economic Review*, wrote that Lee "had the gall to suggest that, come 1997, Singapore would offer the most congenial perch from which Western correspondents could cover Asia. He appeared to be serious. Presumably he believes that, by 1997, the entire 'foreign' press will have been bullied into the pathetic state of the media in Singapore."

Lee clearly takes delight in his battles against his critics. When I asked him how many people he had sued for libel, he replied, "I think about thirteen. Thirteen men in thirty years. Not bad. I haven't lost any of them. I fought only four in court; the others decided to settle. In other words, they withdrew and apologized and paid for my costs and paid a sum of money to charity. A political point was made." Still, the confrontations with the media raise a question: Why should a prosperous country with no government corruption to hide—a nation that seeks to be the communications hub of its region—act so forcefully against the press, against what appears to be its own best interests? The most plausible answer is that Lee Kuan Yew doesn't like what he can't control—and that he sees the independent forces in Singapore today as fueling the potential for destabilization in the future. Censorship in a nation that wants to be a major participant in the world communications revolution might appear to be a contradiction, but Lee has shown in the past that he can successfully counter a well-known adage: he can eat his cake and have it, too.

Nothing seems beyond the scope of the government's manipulation. "They recently had a campaign against obesity," a diplomat told me. "Cherubic kids are prized by Chinese society, but the Singapore government likes them lean and mean." Unlike most other offenses, being overweight is not subject to a fine, but the government did rule that obese recruits will have to undergo five months of basic military training, as opposed to three months for fit recruits. (All males have to serve at least two years in the armed forces.) Overall, however, few campaigns have raised as many hackles as a government effort to get college graduates to marry each other and breed. Government ministers don't shy away from the word "eugenics," despite its negative connotations since the Nazi era. Lee, who initiated the campaign in 1983, once pointed to statistics showing that women with little education have twice as many babies as college graduates, and told the nation in a speech, "If we continue to reproduce ourselves in this lopsided way, we will be unable to maintain present standards. . . . Our economy will falter; administration will suffer, and our society will decline."

Singapore's educational system is intensive, and pupils are subjected to pressure from an early age. One Singaporean banker I interviewed said, "Everyone has private tutors for his children, and it sometimes starts at two or three years old," and he added, "My daughter at age three and a half came home from nursery school and asked, 'Why am I not studying with a private tutor? Everyone else is doing it.' It's hard here to enjoy childhood." By the time a woman graduates from a university, being a housewife holds little appeal for her. But housewives are what many male Singaporean graduates want. Influenced by a Chinese cultural tradition that relegates wives to the home, they shy away from educated women. If present trends continue, the government estimates, two out of five female graduates will still be unmarried at age forty. Foreign men who work in Singapore find a bonanza: the city is filled with attractive, accomplished unmarried women. For the government, however, this situation is a potential crisis.

That's where the Social Development Unit, which is nothing less than an official government matchmaking service, comes in. Only college graduates are eligible; they fill out personal-data forms, and a computer then provides the names of potential partners. "In our culture, there are no singles bars, and it's hard to meet people socially," Ang Wai Hoong, the SDU's director, told me. "Girls read these lovely romantic novels, and our guys are practical-minded technocrats. So when the two get together it's a mismatch." The SDU sponsors lectures on how to date women, along with a variety of other activities, including evening cruises to nowhere that are dubbed "love boats." Then, when the matchmaking succeeds (253 SDU members were matched into matrimony in 1990), the newlyweds are bombarded with a variety of government incentives to have children. The incentives openly rely on the concepts of eugenics. If a working mother has performed at a certain level in tests given to all students in the tenth grade, for instance, she can deduct from her taxes a percentage of her income for each child; the more children she has, the higher the percentage grows. On the other side of the coin, the government instituted a so-called Sterilization Cash Incentive Scheme in 1984 but later abandoned it, along with several other eugenics-inspired schemes. Under this one, low-income families, if neither husband nor wife completed high school, could get $5,000 toward the purchase of an apartment if the wife agreed to be sterilized.

Many female graduates in Singapore, being more interested in a career than in having children, express resentment at being looked upon by their government as high-quality breeding stock. The government's social-engineering schemes have also alienated many Malays and Indians. Now that the Chinese language and Chinese culture are no longer identified with leftist politics, Lee Kuan Yew has been pushing for the adoption of Confucian values, and for the speaking of Mandarin along with English, as a counterweight to what he considers the decadence of the

West—a decadence he sees spreading in Singapore because of its economic ties. (This isn't entirely paranoia. At one of the more popular McDonald's, for example, large groups of Chinese and Malays in their twenties, financed by indulgent parents, sit at outdoor tables all night long, talking and smoking pack after pack of cigarettes. Cigarettes have become a form of protest for rebellious young people, since smoking is the one activity the government tries to stamp out that nevertheless remains legal.) Lee told me that he was encouraging Confucianism "to insure that certain basic core values which held a society together are not lost." Confucianism is also a philosophy that is ideally suited to Singapore, since it teaches absolute obedience to the state and its rulers. But Malays and Indians look upon Confucianism, and upon the periodic campaigns urging the speaking of Mandarin, as dangerous moves that could force them out of the mainstream of Singaporean society. Not all Chinese favor these things, either. "Children are taking their cultural cues from the U.S., but only at a superficial level, like Michael Jackson and Ninja Turtles," a wealthy Chinese industrialist told me. "My children wouldn't speak a word of Mandarin unless someone forced them. We don't want to become like ABCs—American-born Chinese. But will Mandarin be increasingly required for the civil service and business? With the population three-quarters Chinese, the minorities feel justifiably threatened."

When the government uses its authoritarian powers for mainstream causes, like environmental improvement, the results would make any planner in the West envious. Singapore, like many cities around the world, has been threatened with slow strangulation by the increased use of cars. But unlike the other cities, the government of Singapore can dictate stringent restrictions on car ownership and get away with it. Because of government taxes, the same models of cars cost two or three times as much as in the United States. (The cost drops substantially if you agree to use the car only at night and on weekends.) There is a quota on the number of new cars allowed, and the government holds a monthly auction of rights to buy these cars. The annual road tax ranges from a few hundred dollars to well over a thousand, depending on the size of the car. The owner pays extra for the right to drive into the central business district during rush hours, and soon sensors will be embedded in the roads so that the owner can be billed for other rush-hour driving, such as driving on freeways. Combined with excellent public transportation, the result is clean air and few traffic jams.

Even in the earliest days of Singapore's development, Lee insisted on environmental controls for industry. When I asked him what he considered the biggest mistakes he had made as prime minister, he didn't mention the collapse of the Malaysian Federation first. Instead, he told me about "a beautiful patch of green right in the middle of our harbor called Keppel, which had a golf course," and he went on, "But we were so desperate to get our industrialization going that I was persuaded by my colleague the minister for finance to allow a Japanese company to set up an oil refinery there. It was a fire hazard and a blight on the landscape. And now they've sold out, because they lost money."

High government officials in Singapore not only get salaries commensurate with those of corporation executives but also occupy offices luxurious enough to resemble the finest corporate suites. Even by that standard, the office of the minister of trade and industry is something special: it is huge, with tasteful high-tech decor, and is situated on the top floor of the Treasury Building, with a commanding view of the harbor. Its occupant is Lee Hsien Loong, who is often known as B. G. Lee, because he held the rank of brigadier general when he left the army, at age thirty-one. Besides being the minister of trade and industry,

B. G. Lee, at forty, is deputy prime minister and the heir apparent to Goh Chok Tong. He is also the son of Lee Kuan Yew.

B. G. Lee dismisses the relationship as unimportant. "After a while, they're not interested in who your father is but in what you're doing," he told me. Lee Kuan Yew hasn't got off so easily: his critics frequently question why the son of the prime minister rose so rapidly in what is supposed to be a meritocracy. After meeting B. G. Lee, however, it becomes impossible to attribute his status merely to nepotism. A graduate of Cambridge and Harvard, fluent in Mandarin and Bahasa Malaysia—the language of Malaysia—and formidable in his native English, he is a powerful intellect and a master of words; every off-the-cuff remark he makes is phrased as if a speechwriter had taken days to polish it. Unlike his father, he wears a suit and is smooth in manner, betraying none of his emotions in his face. During my interview, he laughed heartily after every answer. Although in Asia laughter is often a sign of being ill at ease, he appeared so supremely confident that I began to wonder whether he was instead laughing with pleasure at the brilliance of his response.

Like his father, Lee Hsien Loong takes a hard line toward the governing of Singapore. He sees no need for a relaxation of censorship. "If we took a poll of the population, there would not be a dramatic change in censorship standards," he said. "Do we want to have Washington, D.C.,'s Thirteenth Street in Singapore? Most Singaporeans would say no." (Few Singaporeans are as worldly as their deputy prime minister, so in reality a reference to Washington's center of sleaze would draw only a blank stare.) Nor does he feel that the foreign press should report on Singapore as it sees fit. "We start with the proposition that Singaporeans have to be masters of their own households, and foreigners are guests," he said. "Does it hurt us? Banks grow at the rate of 15 percent a year, multinationals come in. I don't think it hurts our reputation to have taken on Dow Jones and not to have been bested by them." On the question of demonstrations—even relatively innocuous ones, such as those by students protesting tuition increases—Lee was firm. "It would be a sad thing if we had to solve our problems this way," he said. "I don't think a demonstration in this part of the world would be like a campout on the Mall in Washington. Our answer is this: We fully concede we're not like America."

Also like his father, Lee can be tough. When he came to Washington in 1989 to speak to the Asia Society, a business group, he used the occasion to attack America's human rights policy, saying that the United States should continue to defend Southeast Asia but should keep out of its internal affairs. He said that it "puzzles us that U.S. human rights groups and government officials should so confidently prescribe for us, as a panacea for progress and stability, U.S.-style press freedoms and 'human rights.' Can the Singapore government really be so benighted and wrongheaded as not to see what is so patently in Singapore's interests? . . . Speaking English does not make us an Anglo-Saxon people, much less make us Americans. . . . We are not a Western society, and have never sought to become one." When I remarked to Lee that it must have taken courage to make such a speech in Washington, he replied, "The audience wasn't hostile. Businesspeople don't mind having liberals shot at."

The contrast between B. G. Lee and Goh Chok Tong is dramatic. Goh's father died when he was ten, and the family survived on his mother's earnings as a schoolteacher. He grew up speaking the Fukien dialect at home, and although he got a master's degree in economics at Williams College, his English is no better than adequate, and on occasion it is difficult for a Westerner to follow, because it has a Singaporean lilt. A friend's father "was amazed that I should choose to make a living as a politician," Goh once said, adding, "Fortunately, this is Singapore, and our people place greater value on substance and results than on the gift of gab." Goh—who, like Lee Kuan Yew, often dresses informally—is tall and thin, sits ramrod straight, and was visibly nervous during my interview. Especially in contrast to the self-assurance of the two Lees, Goh's awkwardness makes him seem refreshingly human, and Singaporeans appear to be fond of him. But Goh, too, can be tough. He played a major role in the arrest of the church workers and in the battle with Dow Jones, and in 1990 he told a public gathering, "If people behave in a manner that will threaten the wider interests of Singapore, they will feel the firm smack of the government."

Few people would envy Goh his position. On one side is Lee Kuan Yew, who heads the PAP, takes an active role in running the government, and, in 1988, told Singaporeans, "Even from my sickbed, even if you are going to lower me into the grave, and I feel that something is going wrong, I'll get up." On the other side is Lee Hsien Loong, who openly aspires to Goh's position. "If I can do the job, I want to be prime minister someday," he told me. I asked Goh how he survived, sandwiched between two such forceful personalities, one of whom threatens to come back from the grave if necessary. "Well, I think that's because I'm relaxed," he replied. "I'm not wearing Lee Kuan Yew's shoes. I'm wearing my own shoes, which are much smaller than his. I think that B. G. Lee is in many ways like his father. But he knows that to govern Singapore you want a team that can work for Singapore. So he's very supportive as No. 2." Goh calls Lee Hsien Loong "an obvious successor." (The succession became less certain in November 1992, when Lee Hsien Loong began chemotherapy treatments for malignant lymphoma, which is cancer of the infection-fighting lymphatic system.)

Goh became prime minister in November 1990, offering the prospect of a changed Singapore. With the release of Vincent Cheng and Teo Soh Lung a few months before, Singapore was down to its last political prisoner, Chia Thye Poh, and he is now a part-time prisoner at that. Goh has filled his speeches with references to making Singapore a more enjoyable, less restrictive place to live and has pledged that the government will move toward a less paternalistic role. He has told Parliament that "the society which we want to bring about will be more refined, more compassionate, kinder and gentler, to borrow President Bush's words," and added that "there will be greater freedom for Singaporeans to make their own choices and to express themselves." Then, in August 1991, he called a snap parliamentary election for the final day of the month—two years earlier than was required by law. Goh said that he was making the election a test of his plans for liberalization, and that if he didn't get sufficient support "we can all go back to authoritarian government." For once, Singapore's opposition, so often cowed and ineffective, came up with a brilliant strategy. Its architect was Chiam See Tong, the only full-voting opposition member of Parliament and the leader of the Singapore Democratic Party, which, along with the Workers' Party, forms the bulk of the opposition; the two parties hold similar views and stand to the left of the PAP. Chiam won his first election to Parliament in 1984; he told me that Lee Kuan Yew had campaigned against him then by pointing out that Chiam's opponent had got better test scores in high school. Chiam, a lawyer who is extremely meek and mild in manner, persuaded the Workers' Party to allow PAP candidates to remain unopposed for forty-one of Parliament's seats, and so guarantee that, no matter what the size of the opposition vote, the PAP would remain in power. Chiam sensed the mood of the electorate perfectly. Clearly, there was widespread dissatisfaction with the government's authoritarian, paternalistic policies, but many more voters would be tempted to express that dissatisfaction if they could be absolutely certain that they wouldn't be throwing the PAP out of office, and thereby imperiling the economic prosperity they hold so dear. The result was that the PAP lost ground, its share of the vote dropping to 61 percent from 63 percent in 1988. The drop translated into only four seats, but it was still the opposition's biggest victory since 1963. And it put Lee and Goh in a real bind: Goh had wanted the vote to be a referendum on his plans for liberalization, but Chiam had turned it into the opposite. Many of those who voted against the PAP were asking for more liberalization, not less.

What will happen now is far from clear. Goh said after the election that "life cannot go on as before," but he gave no hint of what he meant. Some students of the Singapore political scene speculated that Lee Kuan Yew would push Goh aside in favor of Lee Hsien Loong, who might quickly turn a kinder, gentler Singapore into a tougher, more brutal Singapore. Singaporean journalists I spoke with noted that the business community was trying to persuade Lee Kuan Yew that it didn't want a crackdown against the opposition—possibly the one move that could bring about the instability that Lee so fears.

If the hard-liners win out, can Singapore continue to survive as an anachronism—an economic power aligned with the West but resisting the democracy and freedom sweeping through the world? The tendency would be to answer no. The only problem with such an assessment is that when it comes to Singapore, the doomsayers have yet to score a point. Lee Kuan Yew has proved them wrong on every possible occasion over the past twenty-five years.

The problem is the same for the other scenario, that of liberalization. Goh has done little more in his first year of office than to ease somewhat the censorship of movies. Jeyaretnam, the Workers' Party head, remarked that "nothing has changed in this administration except that men can now go see films in which women show their bodies." Goh's promises of greater freedom have been expressed only in generalities, and when I interviewed him I tried to press him on the particulars. I asked if he could name any issues on which he and Lee Kuan Yew disagreed. "Issues, no," he replied. "But maybe the style, the way of doing things." We discussed the rules and the fines for breaking them that are posted all over Singapore. "My own goal is for us to move into a position one day where we don't need to have all those fines put up," Goh said. "The rules would be there, but they would not be intruding into your consciousness every day. That means a newer generation must be put through schools, to be socially educated that this is the norm of behavior. I think it would require twenty or twenty-five years before we can move to that situation."

LAOS
The Forgotten Country

FOR ANYONE accustomed to American roads, the drive east on Route 9 across the 120-mile width of southern Laos is a bone-jarring experience. As Route 9 leaves the port city of Savannakhet, on the Mekong River, the asphalt ends, and the views are obscured by clouds of dust kicked up by passing trucks. After a few miles, the pavement starts again, but for many stretches the surface undulates like a washboard, and there are countless potholes. Yet this narrow, two-lane road, which would be considered laughably inadequate anywhere in the United States, is for Laos a veritable superhighway. Far more typical of the country than Route 9 is Route 13, on which one drives from Vientiane, the capital, to Luang Prabang, the old royal capital, 140 miles to the north. Much of Route 13 is little more than a dirt path snaking through mountains, a road so bad that there is no bus service between the two cities, although they're the most important cities in Laos. But Route 13 hardly represents the worst of the country's transportation problems. When David Merchant and Lois Foehringer, an American couple working on aid projects in Laos for the Mennonite Central Committee, the relief and development arm of the Mennonite Church, visit Phong Saly Province—the northernmost province of Laos, on the China border—they have to travel for three and a half days by boat and then are met by provincial authorities and given a jolting ride up the side of a mountain in a four-wheel-drive truck. The truck itself arrived by boat, having been cut into two pieces for the voyage. For eight months or so of each year, Phong Saly Province is accessible only by helicopter, because the water level is too low for boat traffic.

There were no such problems on Route 9. It had been built during a ten-year period, starting in 1978, as an aid project sponsored largely by the government of Vietnam, with Hungary, Czechoslovakia, and the Soviet Union contributing bridges, and internees in a Laotian "re-education camp" supplying some of the labor. As I bounced along the first ninety-odd miles in a four-door Japanese truck in the company of the driver and four government officials, I was able to view an Asian landscape unmarked by the centuries—a procession of rice fields and primitive villages, the houses of wood, bamboo, and thatch standing on stilts to keep them above the floods of the rainy season. We climbed into the foothills of the Annamite Mountains, which straddle the Laos-Vietnam border, and the scenery slowly changed from paddy fields rimmed by dikes to rocky, overgrown terrain. And then my Laotian interpreter began to point out bomb craters, often twenty or thirty feet in diameter, along the side of the road. Some of the poorer villages, lacking bulldozers, were built on a sea of craters; to get from one house to the next, you had to walk along the rims. At Xepon, a village of five thousand that serves as a district capital, one crater, a few yards from the road and almost at the front door of a house, contained a large rusted-metal object—a bomb that had never exploded.

Just a few minutes' ride past Xepon lies the village of Ban Dong, twenty-one miles from the Vietnamese border. Ban Dong is built on the flotsam of war. Parts of airplanes and casings of bombs serve as support beams for houses, as boats on a nearby river, and even as bowls for food. One homeowner has transformed a bomb crater into a decorative pond, the banks lined with a neatly stacked display of artillery-shell casings. A circle of cluster-bomb canisters makes a border around a big shade tree. Two cluster-bomb canisters attached to the ends of a wooden pole have become a barbell for weight-lifting exercises. And children play on a pile of war debris stacked in the center of the village; the metal, which represents the area's only "cash crop," will soon be shipped by truck to Savannakhet and sold to Thailand as scrap. At Ban Dong, we parked our truck and walked along a narrow, rutted dirt road that intersected with Route 9. No sign identified the road; there was nothing to indicate that it wasn't just another of the dozens of tracks that crisscross the Annamite Mountains. But this particular track happened to be one of the best-known roads in the world: it was the main route of the Ho Chi Minh Trail.

The Ho Chi Minh Trail, and especially this key junction near Xepon, had been central to America's nine-year secret war in Laos, orchestrated by the Central Intelligence Agency and directed from the American embassy compound in Vientiane. Although the CIA managed to recruit a mercenary army of thirty thousand Hmong, an ethnic group that lives in the mountainous regions of Laos, and although several hundred American fliers lost their lives in Laos, news of the operation had been successfully hidden from the American people for most of the time between 1964 and 1973. Many of the details didn't emerge until 1987, when Christopher Robbins, a British journalist, published a book on the secret war called *The Ravens*, which was based on interviews with many of the American pilots who fought in it; they used "Ravens" as their code name for the war. "There was another war even nastier than the one in Vietnam, and so secret that the location of the country in which it was being fought was classified," Robbins wrote. "The cognoscenti simply referred to it as 'the Other Theatre.' The men who chose to fight in it were handpicked volunteers, and anyone accepted for a tour seemed to disappear as if from the face of the earth. The pilots in the

Other Theatre were military men, but flew into battle in civilian clothes—denim cutoffs, T-shirts, cowboy hats, and dark glasses."

The American effort was two-pronged: the first aim was to disrupt the flow of men and matériel coming down the Ho Chi Minh Trail from North Vietnam to South Vietnam; the second was to cut the route across the Plain of Jars, in the north, which the Pathet Lao, the Laotian Communist forces, might take from their strongholds along the Vietnam border if they decided to march on Vientiane. The war was fought largely with bombs—an unprecedented rain of bombs. By 1973, when the bombing stopped, the United States had dropped 2,093,100 tons of bombs on Laos; the tonnage was a third higher than that of the American bombs that devastated Nazi Germany in the Second World War, and three times the tonnage dropped during the Korean War. The total number of sorties during that period was 580,944—an average of 177 a day, or one planeload of bombs every eight minutes around the clock for nine years. The cost of the bombing was $7.2 billion, or more than $2 million a day. (That daily figure is almost exactly the amount that Laos—a nation where the average life expectancy is forty-five, and the government is so poor that many of its teachers have had to go without salaries—received in all of 1988 from other countries, United Nations programs, and private relief groups to finance seventy-seven health and education projects.) Yet the bombing failed to achieve either of its objectives. Year after year, the Ho Chi Minh Trail was improved, to the point where it had an oil pipeline and underground repair shops, and could accommodate the largest available tanks and trucks. By 1971, North Vietnam had used it to move 630,000 troops into the south and to keep up a steady stream of supplies to equip and feed them. And the bombing certainly did nothing to stop the Pathet Lao forces from building up their strength; peasants being bombed out of their homes made easy recruiting targets, and in 1975 Pathet

Lao troops entered Vientiane victoriously without firing a shot. On December 2 of that year, meeting in the gymnasium of a former American school in Vientiane, the Pathet Lao abolished the monarchy and established the Lao People's Democratic Republic, thereby taking over a nation whose economy lay in ruins.

Few American visitors have had an opportunity to travel along the Ho Chi Minh Trail and observe the devastation that still remains from the bombing. But any unease I felt at the prospect of doing so quickly evaporated thanks to the reception I was accorded. Those who lived through the bombing, and even those who were maimed by it, treated me with unfailing courtesy and cheerfulness. On our way up Route 9, my interpreter, who was an employee of the Foreign Ministry, had suggested that since we would arrive in Xepon too late for dinner we should stop to buy food, so at a roadside stand we picked up barbecued chicken and a bag of frogs grilled to a crisp, both extricated from a swarm of flies. But when we arrived in Xepon, where we were to stay at the district leader's house, we discovered that he had arranged a special dinner for us at the local restaurant. The dinner included at least a dozen courses, but he apologized profusely, saying that he hadn't had enough notice to plan anything elaborate. In my honor, the meal concluded with a delicacy that occasionally finds its way into Laos from neighboring Thailand—a platter of Spam.

The district leader, a jovial man of forty named Lahoun Maphangvong, described his life under the rain of bombs. "Nothing stood on the earth," he told me, through my interpreter. "Every building was destroyed. We all went into the mountains and lived in caves, or else stayed in the jungle. My family and I lived in the jungle about eighteen miles from Xepon for eight years, from 1964 to 1972. We dug a pit to sleep in, and covered it with logs and thatch. We grew our own rice, and the North Vietnamese troops gave us essentials, like salt. The heaviest bombings were in 1965 and 1966. During that time, much of the land was destroyed by defoliants sprayed by the airplanes. When the spraying took place, it looked as if everything had been burned by a fire; every leaf fell off every tree. The defoliants got into the drinking water and the vegetables, and some people died from that. There was much vomiting and there were skin diseases, and many people couldn't eat." The use of defoliants remained a secret far longer than the bombing itself. Only in 1982 did the United States Air Force confirm charges by antiwar groups that it had dumped two hundred thousand gallons of herbicides on Laos in 1965 and 1966.

I asked Lahoun (in Lao, people are addressed by their first name, not their family name, even when an honorific is used) a question about what had been for me one of the greatest puzzles of the Vietnam War: Why did the bombing of the Ho Chi Minh Trail—a bombing whose tonnage per square mile was the greatest in history—fail to disrupt North Vietnamese supply lines? I told him about an interview I had had in Bangkok with Robert Karniol, the Asia-Pacific editor of *Jane's Defence Weekly* and an experienced analyst of military tactics. Karniol had said that bombs were simply not effective weapons against a guerrilla movement in the jungle. "Essentially, all that happens is that you make a few holes in the ground, and they are later filled up," he had said. "You destroy a few trucks, and they are replaced. You kill some people, and they are replaced also. You can make things uncomfortable, but airplanes can't stop people. You have to physically possess the territory."

Lahoun nodded in agreement, and told me what he had witnessed when the bombs fell: "During times when the bombing was too intense for trucks, the soldiers took the supplies and balanced them on poles. Then they put the poles on bicycles, and walked alongside the bicycles on small paths under the cover of jungle. The airplanes couldn't see them there. The North Vietnamese lost a lot of troops, but the supplies never stopped coming."

Lahoun went on to say that the suffering didn't end with the cessation of the bombing. The United States had carpeted the Ho Chi Minh Trail, the Plain of Jars, and other areas of Laos with cluster-bomb units, or CBUs. A "mother bomb"—a canister that looked like a giant pea pod—would be timed to open at a predetermined altitude after it was dropped, scattering tennis-ball-size bomblets over an area of about five thousand square yards. Each bomblet—called an antipersonnel bomblet by the military and a *bombi* by the Laotians—contained about two hundred and fifty steel pellets. Some of the bomblets were rigged to detonate on hitting the ground, spraying all the people and animals in the area with pellets. Others would sink into the ground and detonate only when something hit them. Thousands upon thousands of these bomblets are still buried today, and they are frequently set off by an unsuspecting farmer swinging a hoe. "When you set off a *bombi*, an explosive device blows the pellets out, and they can scatter six or eight feet around," I was told by Jacqui Chagnon, who worked in Laos for the American Friends Service Committee, and from whom I learned about the *bombis*. "So if children are playing by the side of their parents, they are often killed or injured as well. On the Plain of Jars recently we were clearing land about the size of two football fields with a metal detector, to build a teacher-training school. We found eighteen *bombis*, two medium-sized unexploded bombs, and one large bomb buried nose down so that we couldn't defuse it. We had to bury the whole bomb. In Xieng Khouang Province, on the Plain of Jars, anywhere from five to ten people are killed or injured by *bombis* every month." The injured, if they're near enough to the provincial capital, can seek medical care at the province's one hospital, which was built by Mongolia. It has no general-anesthesiology facilities, no sophisticated techniques to stop bleeding, no way to deal with shock.

Early the next morning in Xepon, Lahoun was standing outside his house talking with a neighbor—a woman who had only one leg. I asked her if she would tell me her story, and she readily agreed, speaking cheerfully and with complete ease, although she had been told that I was an American. In 1968, when she was nineteen, she said, she had stepped on a *bombi* on her way through the jungle to work in a rice field. Local villagers took her to a makeshift hospital that had been dug into the ground in the jungle, and a North Vietnamese doctor amputated her shattered leg. The leg was replaced by a prosthesis that the villagers made for her from a bombsight tube recovered from a downed American airplane.

"Just a week ago, three teenage boys in a nearby village hit a *bombi* while they were digging a garden," Lahoun said. "One of them, who was fifteen years old, died after two days, because a pellet had penetrated his brain. The two others survived, but they'll have to have operations to remove pellets from their bodies."

After breakfast, the government officials and I set out in our truck for a tour of the area. Not only had the wreckage of planes and bombs been fashioned into many essentials of life—swords into plowshares—but the sale of scrap metal had provided the money to rebuild the villages that the bombing had destroyed. In one instance, however, potential scrap metal had been left untouched. The wreckage of two South Vietnamese tanks still stood near Ban Dong, as a monument to a battle, code-named Lamson 719, that took place in 1971—one of the most disastrous undertakings of the Vietnam War. After six years of futile bombing, Lamson represented a change in tactics, an effort to cut the supply lines by seizing the strategically important portion of the Ho Chi Minh Trail around Xepon. The battle plan had been devised by the Americans, but the South Vietnamese, aided by American air cover, did the actual fighting. According to Christopher Robbins, the invasion was planned at the Pentagon, and the planners used a map showing no topographical features, and so were unaware that the South Vietnamese would have to cross high mountain ridges, which ran north and south, while the North Vietnamese could pour reinforcements in through a series of valleys. With bad weather limiting air support, the invasion turned into a rout: of the 17,000-man South Vietnamese invasion force, 5,000 were killed or wounded, and 176 Americans died. All that remains of the battle today is the two wrecked tanks. Laughing children who had been following us ran to clamber over them.

That afternoon, we stopped back in Xepon to say goodbye to Lahoun and thank him for putting us up at his house; he had refused to accept any money, explaining that he had been doing his duty as a district official. This time, Lahoun, who had smiled almost constantly, even when he was talking about the horrors of the war, was unusually solemn. He had apparently spent the day making calculations and entering figures in a notebook, and he clearly wanted to present them to me in as formal a manner as possible, to impress me with their gravity. He sat at the head of a table, motioned to me and my interpreter to be seated, and cleared his throat and began. "The district of Xepon extends along Route 9 for seventy-five miles, to the Vietnam border," he said. "We had been a liberated area since 1960, and that was one reason we were one of the most heavily bombed regions. In our district, there are two hundred villages. The bombing destroyed 6,557 houses—every house in the district. Five thousand buildings that were used to store rice were also destroyed. In the nine years of war, fifteen hundred people died in Xepon, out of a population of forty-five thousand. Eighteen hundred cows and water buffalo were killed out of about six thousand. In four villages, the majority of the people died. Since 1975, at least three persons a year in the district have been killed by a *bombi*."

"The Laotians have the ability to live with contradictions in a way that Westerners can't," an American who lives in Vientiane told me. And everywhere in Laos contradictions, paradoxes, ironies abound. They can be seen in little things. At one of the bustling outdoor markets, a Laotian teenager walks down the street wearing a gray T-shirt stenciled "U.S. AIR FORCE." In Vientiane, every day at dawn and dusk, loudspeakers blare out the broadcasts of the municipal radio station, but now instead of urging people to fulfill their day's production quota the announcers read commercials for soft drinks, soap, textiles, and beer. At Lao Radio and Television, the deputy director—from such a Francophone family that he has both a French and a Lao name and didn't learn to read and write Lao until he took lessons from a monk while he was studying at the Sorbonne—escorted me on a tour of the premises, speaking elegant British-accented English. As we entered the English-language broadcasting studio, a shrill-voiced female announcer was denouncing "the lackeys of American imperialism."

In all of Laos, however, the most striking contradiction lies in the boomtown atmosphere of Vientiane; the city seems almost phantasmagorical in view of the desperate poverty that grips this nation, which was ravaged first by the Vietnam War and then by Stalinist economic strictures imposed by the Pathet Lao. By every objective yardstick, the Laotian economy barely functions. Per-capita income is $156 a year. There are so few exports that the sale of overflight rights to commercial airlines is one of the major sources of hard currency. More than eight hundred American companies have revenues each year larger than Laos's entire gross national product: it was $546 million in 1988. The latest count shows 6,451 telephones in the entire country, and many of them don't work; when I tried to phone a high Laotian government official from Bangkok, I first had to call a Thai businessman in Vientiane, and he agreed to send someone to get that official for my second call, half an hour later. Until 1990, Laos was connected with the world, except for Thailand and the Soviet Union, by a single phone line: only one incoming or outgoing international call could take place at any one time. (Now, thanks to an Australian aid project, calls are routed through an Australian satellite.) The infant-mortality rate is 109 for each 1,000 live births—three times that of Thailand and more than ten times that of the United States. Illiteracy is so widespread that candidates at one teachers' training school complete grades one through five so that they can then teach grades one through three. In this country, which is the size of Oregon and has a population of just four million, more than three-quarters of the people live in rural areas, subsisting on what they can grow and what they can hunt in the jungles. One American aid worker had traveled widely around Laos, and in a mimeographed newsletter he described life in a typical village:

> The diet is a monotonous parade of rice, soup broth, and fermented fish. School is a little bamboo hut with grades one through three; the nearest junior high school is at least a day's walk away. The village doctor uses herbs and roots to cure sickness. The nearest clinic is 20 miles away, but remember you have to walk. Sickness and death are frequent companions of the young and elderly. Life is a struggle, with most of one's labor consumed in monotonous tasks like carrying water, pounding husks off the rice, and hoeing the soil.

Such poverty can also be seen in Luang Prabang, an ancient city of Buddhist temples and pagodas that stands in a northern valley carved from the mountains by the Mekong River, and whose physical isolation has served as an effective barrier to any economic changes. Although Luang Prabang is the religious center of Laos and the site of the former Royal Palace—which the Pathet Lao maintain for visits by tourists, even though they deposed the king—it has only one channel of transportation besides the tortuous road from Vientiane, on which the 140-mile trip may take as long as four days. That channel is a single flight each day from Vientiane, on a rusted Antonov-24 owned by Lao Aviation, the state airline. A round trip costs a Laotian $16, which is a month's salary for many workers, and even someone who is able to come up with the $16 has trouble getting a seat because foreigners, who pay $65, have priority. Northern Laos is the poorest part of the country, and Luang Prabang—with a population of sixty thousand, which makes it the third-largest city, just behind Savannakhet—has remained relatively unchanged for decades. Water buffalo lie asleep on the streets; Buddhist monks hold out their bowls for donations of food; Hmong women, dressed in black clothing blazing with bright-colored embroidery, walk in from mountain villages to sell jewelry and embroidered fabrics. During the driest period, when for a few months water levels are low and there is little hydroelectricity, lanterns provide the only illumination for most of the city. The airport consists of a landing strip and a tiny two-room building; departing passengers can wait at home until they hear the plane arriving from Vientiane.

If Laos as a whole speaks of backwardness and poverty, Vientiane delivers an entirely different message. Still called Vieng Chan by Laotians (Vientiane is a French-imposed version of the name), it looks like a city that has awakened from a long sleep and gone excitedly to work. Vientiane is a capital of no special beauty, since most of its buildings are decrepit and badly in need of paint. Its broadest avenue, Lane Xang, is the disastrous result of an attempt to create a boulevard in the Parisian style. (Lane Xang, which means Land of a Million Elephants, is the name of the ancient Lao kingdom.) The avenue runs about a mile, from the Presidential Palace, on the Mekong River, to a huge monument on a traffic circle that is meant to resemble L'Etoile, in Paris. The monument, whose construction started in the 1960s, with American cement intended for a runway at the airport, looks like a squat, ill-proportioned version of the Arc de Triomphe topped by an astonishing wedding-cake structure resembling an Oriental palace with Byzantine spires and Gothic gargoyles. When you climb to the top of it, the buildings of Vientiane, all of which are small and unimposing, seem to disappear beneath the tropical foliage. Croaking frogs in ditches alongside Lane Xang Avenue outnumber pedestrians, and the traffic circle, which could accommodate hundreds of vehicles, gets only a trickle of cars, mostly Russian and Japanese. Still, they represent an automotive boom compared with the vehicles that existed here a few years ago. Most people in Vientiane get about on bicycles.

Although Vientiane may not have fulfilled the vision of French colonialists who dreamed of a European-style capital, it does have considerable charm. In the evening, the sun is a fiery red ball as it disappears into the Mekong, and then the twinkling lights of Thailand appear in the distance. Every morning, sidewalk food stalls offer basketfuls of freshly baked baguettes, which are one of the few French influences remaining; the Laotians eat the baguettes with fish sauce sprinkled on them. Many of Vientiane's neighborhoods resemble self-contained villages, with rutted dirt roads and traditional bamboo-and-thatch houses on stilts. A Western visitor who leaves the commercial and government areas and walks through these neighborhoods is mobbed by curious children, and adults extend greetings with shy smiles. Visitors to Vientiane before 1975 saw a wide-open city, where brothels and drugs were as readily available as they were in Bangkok, but today Vientiane displays a puritanical innocence, which seems much more in the Laotian character. Laotians are delighted to respond when a Westerner approaches them to start a conversation, but no one will come up to you outside your hotel to lure you with the prospect of taxis, guides, cut-rate merchandise, or hinted-at pleasures; such aggressiveness, common in almost every other Third World country, is alien to the Laotian temperament. I never saw a beggar in Laos, and no child ever asked me for candy or money. "They're the ultimately tolerant people—they never get upset," a World Bank official in Vientiane said. "If you give them something, they say 'Thank you.' If you give them nothing, they also say 'Thank you.'"

What was once a torpid colonial capital had been further sedated by a Communist government that made individual initiative a potentially dangerous activity. As late as 1988, residents say, most of the stores in the central commercial district were shuttered and unoccupied. But suddenly Vientiane sprang alive, and now almost all the stores are active. The biggest market, which covers acres of ground not far from the Presidential Palace, is overflowing with the latest Japanese electronic goods, Thai clothes, and Thai foods; it is called the Morning Market, but that has become a misnomer, for it's now jammed throughout the day. A few years ago, there was no such thing as a Laotian restaurant in Vientiane. Now Laotian food is served at dozens of places, and new ones are opening almost every week. The drab buildings housing hotels, restaurants, and shops are today incongruously brightened by strings of blinking Christmas-tree lights, and the Lane Xang Hotel, the best in town, also features on its façade a flashing neon hammer and sickle. And in a country whose dour, serious-minded government stamped out any remnant of night life when it came to power fifteen years ago, at least a dozen discotheques are now blasting their music past midnight, for although a curfew remains on the books it is universally ignored.

The new restaurants, the discotheques, the stereos in the market, and the other aspects of a revitalized Vientiane owe their existence to a manifestation of *perestroika* that is extraordinary even in the current world of upheaval in the Communist bloc. The economic reforms of other Communist nations have been preceded by new leadership, bringing new ideas, but the Laotian version of *perestroika* did not result from any change in leadership: most of the elderly, hard-line Pathet Lao who still govern

Laos have worked together since the Second World War, when they headed an arm of Ho Chi Minh's Indo-Chinese Communist Party. Nor were the reforms spurred by street demonstrations: Westerners who live in Vientiane say they haven't heard of a single protest—not a peep of dissent from any source. Yet the Pathet Lao leadership, without abandoning its Marxist rhetoric, and without allowing the smallest degree of political opposition, has instituted an economic restructuring as broad as anything to be found in Eastern Europe today. Although Laos was firmly under the sway of the former Soviet Union and, particularly, Vietnam, these reforms preceded the advent of Mikhail Gorbachev by many years—they started in 1979, when the state backed off from its policy of collective farms—and have run well ahead of hesitant efforts by the Vietnamese to change their own economy. Known as *chin ta nakan mai,* or "new thinking," the Laotian reforms can also be described as "*perestroika* without *glasnost,*" or the carrying out of economic reforms without accompanying political changes—precisely the formula that failed so disastrously for the leaders of China. The secretive Pathet Lao have cast off the Stalinist economic doctrines and broken dramatically with the past.

Laos's economic reforms would impress the most unrepentant capitalist. In agriculture, farmers can now own their land, and, provided only that they pay taxes on their earnings, they can dispose of their crops in any way they want, at free-market prices; if a state agency needs to buy rice or any other crop, it has to compete with private traders on the open market. As for the state-owned agricultural cooperatives that still exist, they must either show a profit or go out of business. The same applies to state-owned businesses and factories, and they now make their own decisions on production, investments, and pricing. Banking has been liberalized, and the first commercial bank, 70 percent owned by Thai investors, opened its doors in 1989. A new investment code, enacted in July 1988, authorizes both joint ventures and wholly owned foreign-investment projects. Foreign investors can repatriate their profits and, under the code, are protected against nationalization. This liberalized investment code lured a significant, if unlikely, participant when the Hunt Oil Company—owned by a Texan whose family is known in part for its militant anti-Communism—signed a contract to explore for oil in southeastern Laos. "Privatization" is a word frequently heard; the government has leased its cigarette factory to a Thai investor, and a sheet-metal plant to a Thai-Laotian joint venture. Khammone Phonekeo, the vice-minister of industry, told me that even Lao Aviation might become private. "We're still open," he said. "We don't know which things to keep."

It's not necessary to pore over investment codes and other regulations to recognize the dimensions of the reforms. A visitor to Vientiane experiences one result of the "new thinking" the moment he tries to change money. There is no black market, because the Laotian kip now floats free against the American dollar and the Thai baht, and all three currencies are readily accepted. (Visitors who use kip face one disadvantage, however: the largest kip banknote is worth only about seventy American cents, and most moneychangers try to palm off notes smaller than that. My first day in Laos, I changed a hundred-dollar bill without specifying the denomination of banknotes I would get in return, and I ended up with a plastic bag containing at least five pounds of currency.) In Laos, the setting of the exchange rate involves what is surely one of the world's most literal enactments of a "free market": early each day, an employee of Laos's central bank walks through the Morning Market to see how many kip the shopkeepers are offering per dollar, and what he finds determines what the nation's official exchange rate will be.

The fruits of these economic reforms can be observed all over Vientiane. To buy gasoline a few years ago, for instance, it was necessary to wait in a long line at a state-owned station and present a ration coupon; but now there are several private gas stations, and a big Shell station in the center of town—one that would look at home in the United States—stays open until midnight. The gas stations are getting new business because, though Vientiane has yet to witness its first traffic jam, cars and other motor vehicles are being sold in increasing numbers. For example, the owner of a wool factory who sells his cloth to Thailand told me that he has provided his extended family with two Toyotas, a Volkswagen, and two motorbikes. All over Vientiane, teenage boys in blue jeans, with hair over their shirt collars, zoom around on motorcycles or motorbikes, causing havoc on streets where drivers are normally so polite that they stop with a smile for the most brazen pedestrian. Just a few years ago, the hair length of those teenagers could have landed them in a re-education camp.

The government's new policy includes putting out the welcome mat for anyone who wants to participate in the economic rebirth—even those Laotians who were interned in re-education camps in 1975, or who fled the country. A few years ago, Souban Sritthirath, the deputy foreign minister who is in charge of relations with the West, made a trip to the United States to tell Laotian-Americans precisely that. "I said to them that if they want to contribute to the development of Laos they should move back to start a business," Souban told me. "We'll give them all their property back if they stay six months and abandon their new citizenship." The American embassy in Vientiane has reported that hundreds of Laotians who are now American citizens have returned for visits without incident, but so far only one has moved back to start a business. I met a returnee from France one night while I was eating at a place called Somchan's Pob & Restaurant. Seeing a Western face, the Pob's owner, Douane Siharth, sat down to tell me his story. "I lived in Paris for seven years, and before that I lived in the United States and Australia, but I'm a Laotian, and I missed my country," he said. "So three years ago I returned, and now I have this restaurant, an export business, and a computer center. I also started a night club called Feeling Well—I had to argue with the government for three months to get that name approved. I started Somchan's, which is named after my wife, because foreigners who came to Vientiane would ask for Laotian food, and there were no Laotian restaurants. I set this up for foreigners." The menu at Somchan's attracts foreign visitors with such specialties as "grilled small intestine," "underdone grilled," and "very spicy delicious bowel salad."

Few of the stories of newfound prosperity are more dramatic than that of Domon Bilavarn. A colonel in the Royal Lao Army, whose family owned the Vieng Vilay Hotel, in Vientiane, he had gone to the United States in 1960 for a training stint with the American armed forces. When the Pathet Lao took over, they confiscated the hotel and sent him to a re-education camp, where he was assigned to bridge and road construction and was cut off from any contact with his family. In 1988, his camp was closed down. The government gave Domon back the Vieng Vilay, and the Laotian tourism agency actually invested money in it in return for a share of the ownership. With a second partner, a Thai hotel owner, Domon had enough capital to begin major renovations. When I interviewed him, crews of workers had already gutted the hotel, a brick structure in the central commercial district. "We're going to make this a first-class hotel—forty-two rooms," he told me. "There has been no problem with the government about anything. Whatever I need to import, it's O.K. Now I have my hotel and my home back, and my life in Laos is very good." Domon, the forced laborer turned capitalist, would admit to only one difficulty: the spate of building was creating a shortage of skilled workers. "It's a real problem," he complained. "There are no people with construction experience."

The history of Laos offers some insight into why the Pathet Lao leaders were willing to cast aside traditional Communist economic doctrines. For centuries, tiny, landlocked Laos has been a pawn in the hands of far more powerful countries, which coveted it for its strategic location, bordering China on the north, Vietnam on the east, Thailand and Burma on the west, and Cambodia on the south. As a result, Laos, which itself has never launched a war, has known hardly a moment of peace over the years. Although it has historically been a battleground between the Siamese and the Vietnamese kingdoms, it was also conquered by France in the 1880s and by Japan in the Second World War, and then underwent the final, climactic struggle with the forces of the United States and Thailand on one side and the Vietnamese and their subservient allies the Pathet Lao on the other. Modern-day Laos is a French creation, not a Laotian one; the French colonialists, who brought in Vietnamese to run the country, set the borders of Laos in consultation with neighboring powers, allowing the Laotians themselves no say. The result is a nation of at least sixty-eight ethnic groups, many of them traditionally at odds with the lowland Lao, who live on the Mekong plains and make up about half the population. The Hmong, one of the sixty-seven other groups, were ready recruits for the CIA's secret army; young men who had never seen a car or an electric light were plucked from primitive villages and put into jet fighters and helicopter gunships. When the Pathet Lao took over, Vang Pao, the leader of the Hmong, fled to Thailand—with his six wives and twenty-nine children, according to an extensive report on him in the Fresno *Bee* in July 1989. Tens of thousands of other Hmong also left, and today there are more than a hundred thousand in the United States—many of them living near Fresno, in California's Central Valley.

Although Laos became the forgotten country of Indochina in

1975, it played a central role in the region starting in the 1950s, with the increasing aggressiveness of the Vietnamese Communists—the Vietminh—and their Laotian counterparts, the Pathet Lao. In 1953, when the Vietminh established a stronghold in northeastern Laos, the French decided to protect the approaches to Luang Prabang by occupying Dien Bien Phu, a strategic Vietnamese outpost on the Laotian border. That decision cost the French the Indochina War. In 1960, President Dwight Eisenhower called Laos the key to Southeast Asia. It was Laos, not South Vietnam, that played the role of the crucial domino: if the Vietminh took over Laos, the reasoning went, they could launch an invasion of their historic enemy Thailand. The Vietminh left nothing to chance in their relationship with the Pathet Lao, since the Laotians, the most tractable of the civilizations of Southeast Asia, possessed a legendary ability to be somewhere else when the bullets were flying. The American press frequently mocked the performance of the Royal Lao Army during the Vietnam War. One American military officer was quoted at the time as calling it "without a doubt the worst army I have ever seen—it makes the South Vietnamese army look like storm troopers." Nor was the Lao air force about to waste the potential of its American-supplied planes by confining their activity to bombing runs; more typically, the Laotians used the aircraft to ferry passengers for money or to smuggle opium. They would bomb miles away from the target if they even suspected the presence of antiaircraft guns, Robbins noted in *The Ravens*. Sometimes they wouldn't show up at all, if they thought the day would be unlucky. And, according to Robbins, "The Lao preferred to use the most expensive ordnance, ordering CBU-25 canister bombs as often as possible. . . . The Lao pilots brought the empty canisters back to sell the aluminum, having already snipped off the umbilical cords to sell the wire."

The Pathet Lao were different, because of their subordination to the Vietminh. Joseph J. Zasloff, a professor of political science at the University of Pittsburgh, who is one of the few American specialists on Laos, told me that "in Vietnamese eyes the Pathet Lao weren't all that impressive." He went on, "When I wrote a book on the Pathet Lao, I interviewed a Vietnamese adviser to them, and he sounded like an American military officer describing the South Vietnamese. The Vietminh were crucial to the development of the Pathet Lao. They recruited the leaders, they trained them, they had advisers there, and during the Vietnam War they had their own troops fighting in Laos." Of the three top Pathet Lao leaders, two had Vietnamese wives. The third, Kaysone Phomvihane, who has headed the Laotian Communist Party since its formation in 1955, is himself half Vietnamese. The son of a Vietnamese civil servant in Savannakhet, he attended a *lycée* and law school in Hanoi. In 1975, he became the prime minister of the newly formed Lao People's Democratic Republic. He ruled Laos until his death at age 72 in November 1992, and was succeeded by another longtime Pathet Lao hardliner, Finance Minister Nouhak Phoumsavan, 78.

The secretive Kaysone, who lived in a cave in Sam Neua Province near the Vietnamese border during the years of the American bombing, was a figure largely unknown to the rest of the world. In the 1960s, the American press, which in those days covered Laos thoroughly, hardly acknowledged Kaysone. Instead, the press depicted an epic struggle between two half brothers. On one side—sometimes backed by the Americans and at other times the object of CIA plots—was Prince Souvanna Phouma, the neutralist, always willing to seek a compromise. His political adversary—even though they remained personally fond of each other—was Prince Souphanouvong, the so-called Red Prince. French-educated, cultured, and autocratic, these two members of the Lao royal family went their separate ways politically in 1949, when Souphanouvong cast his lot with the Vietminh. He had become radicalized by his contacts with French Communists during a year he worked on the docks at Le Havre, and in 1945, when he was a thirty-three-year-old highway engineer in Vietnam, he first met Ho Chi Minh. "My father lived entirely from his salary as an engineer," the Prince's son, Khamsai Souphanouvong, who is a high Laotian official, told me. "He had no land, no house. No one thought who was the prince, who was the worker—they were all Communists." Souphanouvong was named prime minister of the resistance government in 1950; with the Pathet Lao takeover, he became the president of Laos. He gave up that job in 1987, because of a stroke.

While Souphanouvong maintained ideological "purity," Souvanna Phouma presided as prime minister over a series of coalition governments that spanned twenty-four years, from 1951 to 1975; he tried desperately—in the face of plots, counterplots, and coups, some of them aided by the CIA—to steer Laos on a neutral course that would satisfy all sides. An elegant man who spoke fluent French and was a lover of French wines and big cigars, Souvanna willingly suffered many indignities in his effort to save his country. Leonard Unger, who was the American ambassador to Laos in the early 1960s, recently told me of one such instance. In 1963, when Unger was in Saigon meeting with Secretary of State Dean Rusk, he received a middle-of-the-night phone call from his deputy telling him that an attempted coup against Souvanna was in progress, led by a right-wing general. Unger returned to Vientiane immediately. "I found out Souvanna was at home, but he was essentially a prisoner, because his whole compound was ringed by the dissidents," he said. "I had to get to him and tell him all was not lost, that the United States was supporting him. So I drove down a driveway parallel to his compound, walked to the fence, and leaned over. He came out on his balcony, and he could hear what I said if I shouted. Reporters were all around listening, I was shouting, and he was on the balcony shouting back. The French ambassador was there, and he immediately dubbed it *la diplomatie à la 'Roméo et Juliette.'* " Souvanna was a genuine patriot hopelessly squeezed on one side by the rigidly anti-Communist Americans and the rightist factions in the Lao army and, on the other side, by the militant Pathet Lao and Vietminh, who would agree to compromises and then brazenly disregard them in their effort to gain control of Laos. "Neutrality was not a fashionable idea at that time," Souvanna's son Prince Panya Souvanna Phouma told me in an interview that took place in Bangkok, where he works as a business consultant. "The problem was that nobody cared about Laos. We are at the crossroads of several frontiers, and everyone thought that Laos could be of use. The Americans acted as if they were blind. There was no relation between the problems of Laos and the reaction of the Americans."

While political machinations embroiled Vientiane, and American bombing devastated the countryside, the Pathet Lao leaders waited patiently in the caves of Sam Neua Province until an opportune time to move. In the summer of 1975, sensing that the Pathet Lao would soon gain control of the whole of Laos, the British ambassador, Alan Davidson, flew to Sam Neua to witness an entire shadow government functioning in a network of caves. "I was the first non-Communist to be received there," he told me, in a telephone interview from London. "I hoped very much to see Kaysone and some of the other leaders we hadn't met, but that was not to happen. They had a sort of hotel cave, and then we visited a hospital cave and a theatre cave, where I was compelled to dance with a Pathet Lao danseuse. Souphanouvong's cave was very elegantly furnished, with a carpet, a bookcase, and the sort of sofa and armchair regarded as chic in that part of the world. The hotel cave, however, was distinctly Spartan, with a naked light bulb and only cold water from an outdoor tap. There was a 10:00 p.m. curfew, and at 9:56 the Pathet Lao foreign minister told us we had four minutes to brush our teeth before the light went out. It was a little bit crazy and surreal."

By 1975, Laos was a ravaged country. For many years, education, medical care, roads, and communications had been largely ignored while Vientiane subsisted on an inflated wartime economy, and that economy collapsed with the end of the Vietnam conflict. Entire provinces lay in ruins from the American bombing. After years of venality, corruption, and political infighting manipulated by foreign powers, Laotians of many political stripes welcomed the Pathet Lao takeover. This bloodless coup demonstrated for the first time that the Pathet Lao, despite their close ties to Vietnam, were capable of imposing uniquely Laotian solutions—in this case, a government incorporating the tolerance and the lack of aggressiveness that distinguish the Laotians from their neighbors. What happened was extraordinary: After overthrowing the government of Souvanna Phouma and abolishing the royal family, the Pathet Lao didn't execute the prince and his followers, expel them from the country, or even throw them in jail. Instead, they immediately named Souvanna and the king, Savang Vatthana, advisers. And the United States, the country that had bombed Communist-held areas of Laos for nine years, was invited to maintain its embassy in Vientiane. This flexibility of the Pathet Lao would be demonstrated again when the time came to change the course of the economy.

By most accounts, Souvanna's position was not just an empty title, either. In 1977, the *New York Times* reported that "the 76-year-old former prime minister still lives quietly in his old residence, occasionally attending diplomatic dinners," and went on, "He has decided to stay despite pressure from his family to join them in exile in France. Treated with deference by the government, he has been named a special adviser and attends the monthly cabinet meetings and other important functions." When he died, in 1984, he was given an elaborate state funeral, attended by Kaysone himself, who rarely appeared in public. The king was not so fortunate. In 1977, the government, fearing that insurgents from Thailand would attempt to organize a coup built around him, since he was still revered by many Laotians, sent the royal family into internal exile in Sam Neua Province. Under the harsh conditions of the mountainous jungles of the northeast, the king and the queen died. No one knows the details of their deaths, which the government officially acknowledged only in 1990. When I toured the Royal Palace in Luang Prabang, a palace guide, who willingly told me all sorts of stories about the king's life, only laughed nervously when I asked about his death. To this day, no details have emerged on the fate of the crown prince, Vongsavang.

The Pathet Lao's willingness to impose a homegrown solution didn't extend to two other major problems: what to do with the army officers and bureaucrats of the old regime, and how to handle an economy that had been destroyed by war. In both areas, the Pathet Lao opted for the precedents set by previous Communist liberation movements. As a result, they inflicted grievous harm on the country, causing many of the economic problems that Laos is struggling to overcome today.

Souphanouvong, the new president, with his French education and his internationalist outlook, could have steered Laos on a more centrist course, which might have brought Western aid. But from the beginning it was clear that Kaysone, the new prime minister—he appeared at a reception on December 5, 1975, and that was the first time he had been seen in public since 1958—was to be in charge, with Souphanouvong occupying a figurehead role. To Davidson, the former British ambassador, the role assigned Souphanouvong seemed logical, since this urbane, Westernized man was so different from the other Vietminh and Pathet Lao leaders, whose outlook had been shaped by years of a harsh existence in the mountains and jungles. "You couldn't really have a Communist country dominated by the princes and the ruling class educated in Paris," Davidson said.

Kaysone and the other Pathet Lao leaders made two grave errors almost immediately. First, they rounded up somewhere between thirty thousand and forty thousand people and put them in re-education camps; the internees included many civil servants and officers of the Royal Lao Army. This action, combined with a mass exodus of the Laotian elite across the Mekong River to Thailand, stripped Laos of those who were capable of restoring the economy and running the agencies of government. In the United States, I spoke with a man who had been sent to one of these camps; because he is applying for political asylum, he asked that his name not be used. This man, who speaks elegant French, was a colonel in the Royal Lao Army from 1960 to 1975. "The Pathet Lao invited the hundred highest-ranking officers to their regional headquarters to watch a film about their goals and to hold a meeting," he told me. "They sent out official invitation cards. But when we got there the Pathet Lao troops surrounded us. They said that they were taking us to the north for a visit to discuss what is happening to the country—that a big group of people would be waiting to welcome us with flowers. They flew us to Sam Neua Province, to a camp on the Vietnamese border. It wasn't fenced in, but it was a mountainous area with a river on one side, and guards blocked the only path to escape. They took our military uniforms and gave us civilian clothes, and we got a new set of clothes once a year. We cut branches to construct shelters, and used banana leaves as beds. There was no medicine; a lot of people died from malaria. Each morning, they rang a bell at five and assigned jobs for the day— to cook rice, cut wood, work in the fields. When the sun went down, we ate dinner, then sat in a circle to talk about the deficiencies of the old government and to engage in self-criticism. There was no physical torture, but a lot of psychological devices, mindless rules just to control you. They let us write letters home, but then they read them to see what we were thinking, and never sent them. I was in the camp for twelve years, until 1987. I was sent to dig a canal, to build a school, and I was hitched to a plow to do the work of a water buffalo."

Faced with the prospect of a re-education camp, hundreds of

thousands of Laotians chose to flee the country. Since 1975, 343,000 Laotians—roughly a tenth of the population—have registered as refugees in Thailand. The new government was being run not by highly skilled people but by thousands of cadres from areas that the Pathet Lao had controlled. "The Pathet Lao, when they came out of their caves, knew how to conduct guerrilla wars, but they didn't have the slightest idea of how to run a nation," a Western aid official in Vientiane told me. Just as in the French-colonial days, personnel brought in from Vietnam helped to run the Laotian government—only, this time, of course, they were Vietnamese from the opposite end of the ideological spectrum. In addition, more than forty thousand Vietnamese troops were stationed in Laos. The Pathet Lao took over a country bereft of money and resources. The previous government had depended on foreign aid, mostly from the United States, for 80 percent of its budget; now this aid was cut off, and those fleeing the country were taking with them everything that could be turned into a liquid asset. Facing severe shortages and rampant inflation in a nation with a per-capita income that was then less than ninety dollars a year, the Pathet Lao set about imposing a Stalinist system: they collectivized farms, nationalized the tiny industrial base, and centralized control of prices and all other facets of the economy. The government made it clear that it was regulating every aspect of life. Long-haired youths were told to get a haircut; women were required to wear the traditional long native skirt; everyone was expected to engage in communal rice and vegetable growing on evenings and weekends, and children had to be taught in Laotian instead of French. "Laws are being enforced now," the *New York Times* reported in 1976. "No one locks his car doors anymore. There are even traffic rules, and people are beginning to obey them. If a violator is caught, the vehicle is confiscated."

How did Vientiane, under the same Pathet Lao leadership, switch to unrestrained free enterprise, zooming motorbikes, and jammed discotheques? As anyone finds who asks any question involving Laos, getting a straight answer from government officials is not easy. Even an interview is hard to come by, since in Laos, although it is facing shortages of many commodities, a stifling bureaucracy is in abundant supply. Strict protocol controls every government transaction; when I went to the Ho Chi Minh Trail, for example, I ended up being accompanied not only by my government interpreter and a driver but also by officials of both the administrative and the information sections of Savannakhet Province, and a security guard besides. (In typical Laotian fashion, the security guard was armed with nothing more deadly than a camera. Even in Vientiane, there is almost no evidence of a police or a military presence.) My first interview came only after a week-long process of writing letters and submitting questions, which were sent off to the relevant ministries and seemed to be mainly disregarded, in the hope that the problem would disappear before anyone had to do anything about it. My interpreter, who handled these negotiations, would shake his head sadly every morning and say about the minister under discussion, "He is a very busy man." At one point, he drew up an impressive appointment chart, showing the time at which each official was to be interviewed. However, none of the ministries had yet responded to the interview requests; the appointment chart represented the interpreter's fantasies about what would happen. I discovered that journalists aren't the only ones to encounter bureaucratic difficulties in seeing government officials. A Soviet diplomat in Vientiane told me, "The Soviet ambassador has to wait a few days or a week to get an appointment even with a first deputy minister, not just Kaysone. They're all very busy. What they're doing, no one knows, but they're very busy. No one wants to take responsibility. 'Well, of course, we'll think it over—yes.' "

A government official's monthly pay is barely enough for a couple of tanks of gasoline. My interpreter, who had sufficient status to have worked for the Laotian government in New York, India, and Australia, was supporting a wife and two children on twenty dollars a month. A first deputy minister makes about forty dollars, hardly more than a desk clerk in one of the newly privatized hotels, but he does get a government-supplied house and car. Khamsai Souphanouvong, who is the second-ranking official in the Ministry of Economics, Planning, and Finance, told me, "Workers in a factory now get a higher salary than mine, and I am responsible for finance all over the country. I buy things from the market and cook them myself, and go to restaurants only for official business. But during our period of fighting in the jungle no one got a salary. Some years, we didn't even have salt. We had to sacrifice ourselves for our country." Some government officials supplement their income by holding a second job—often during government hours—or by growing vegetables in their back yards and raising chickens and pigs. A Western diplomat told me he once saw a high Laotian official selling quail eggs in the market before going on to his office. For those whose idealism may have faded, extra income from corruption may be readily available in the newly open economy. In Bangkok, I met a Thai businessman whose company sells to Vietnam and Cambodia but refuses to do business in Laos. "I gave a Laotian official a bribe of ten thousand baht"—four hundred dollars—"and he kept the money but never came through with the deal," he complained. "For Vietnam and Cambodia, we have to pay people in the government, too, but at least they deliver for us."

The low salaries are matched by dismal working conditions. Government buildings are dank and filthy, because there are no maintenance staffs; employees are supposed to clean their own offices on Saturday mornings. Few dignitaries have receptionists or secretaries, and even my Foreign Ministry interpreter had trouble finding the offices of people I was supposed to interview. When we did corral the proper official, the interview sometimes turned into a lecture, which I wasn't permitted to interrupt. Kham Ouane Boupha, vice-minister of agriculture and forests, took forty-two minutes to answer my first question. A stern-looking man wearing wire-rimmed glasses, who brought his own interpreter and ignored mine, he watched me closely during the translation. If I looked up even for a moment, he pointed to my notepad and made a writing motion with his thumb and forefinger. These interviews, since I was asking many questions about the revitalized economy, included lots of statistics, and the statistics confirmed a warning I had had from Western diplomats—not to trust any figures I heard, since statistics in Laos were notoriously unreliable. One high economic official told me that foreign investment in Laos had totaled $100 million so far; a second official, of similar rank, put it at $70 million; and a Western embassy that had just completed a study of the Laotian economy claimed that the most accurate figure was $5 million. In Savannakhet, a bustling city that sprawls for several miles, a local official insisted that the population was just twenty thousand; Westerners in Vientiane said that it was actually seventy thousand.

Yet the interviews did help to explain how the Laotian version of *perestroika* came about. In different ways, several of the government officials' explanations had a common theme: Over the centuries, as the Laotians fell victim to one foreign power after another, they survived by turning inward—by developing a strong sense of national identity intertwined with their Buddhist beliefs. What evolved was a Laotian way of doing things. But two Pathet Lao moves—the Stalinist economy and the re-education camps—were taken wholesale from the Vietnamese, and it eventually became clear that neither was working. So the Pathet Lao leaders, behind their image as a rigid dictatorship, had to exercise great flexibility. What happened was best explained to me by Somphavan Inthavong, a key economic planner, who is one of the most articulate of the Laotian leaders. "To survive, we must have a very Asian philosophy," he said. "We must be like the trees that curve with the strong winds. We changed when history bent us to the point where if we didn't change we would break. We had made many errors in the first ten years of the new regime, because we had little experience and wanted to copy the big countries. But we do better when we go our own way. To copy means to refuse to see that you are in a different stage of development. We are a country the size of West Germany with just seven percent of its population. We can potentially grow crops on four million hectares of land, but now only four hundred thousand are under cultivation. Last year, our rice production exactly met our needs, but we couldn't distribute it evenly. Where are the roads? It's cheaper to buy rice from Thailand than to bring it up from the south of Laos. So our change has been motivated mostly by our internal needs. But it should not be denied that, in addition to the internal reasons, Laos has been shaped by economic and political influences from the outside world. Every day in Laos, you can tune in Thai television and watch CNN in color." To emphasize the degree of the government's flexibility today, Somphavan said, "The man who came to see me just before you was one of the leaders of the rightists in the old regime, a vice–prime minister. All countries must change. We have a different way, a Laotian way, of doing things."

As is true of every major decision in Laos, the central figure in bringing about the economic changes was Kaysone. "He's very busy, because he's the only man who makes the decisions on all vital questions," the Soviet diplomat in Vientiane told me. (While many of the diplomats in Vientiane readily agreed to interviews, all asked that their names not be used.) "That's not very good, and that's why Laos lags behind in many ways. Kaysone can't get people to do things. This is one of the main problems here: the old generation is still in power." Kaysone, a distinguished-looking man with a round, fleshy face and graying hair receding at the temples, lived in the same clandestine manner he developed in the caves of Sam Neua. Until he visited Japan and France in 1989, he had never traveled outside the Soviet bloc except for two visits to Thailand. He almost never granted interviews, and my repeated requests to see him were rebuffed with the usual explanation: "He is a very busy man." Although Kaysone had never been to the United States, his house was a little slice of Americana. Along with many other Pathet Lao leaders, he lived in Kilometre 6, an American-style suburb on the edge of Vientiane, complete with ranch-type houses built by the United States during the Vietnam War. (The kilometer counting starts at the Presidential Palace, on the Mekong River.) Kilometre 6 can be reached by a half-mile-long road from the main highway. Since I saw no guards around, I asked my cab driver to let me off on the highway, telling him I would walk in as far as I could get. Although he had previously been fearless in taking me around Vientiane, this time he refused even to slow down, saying that he would be arrested if he did.

By several accounts, Kaysone possessed a keen mind. "I've met him many, many times," the Soviet diplomat said. "He's a very clever man. One of his advantages is that he likes to learn from everybody. He acknowledges his mistakes, and he knows what should be done to build his country." Kaysone seemed capable of expounding on all sorts of subjects. When in 1990 he addressed a conference of Laotian bankers, he spoke for the entire day, with only a break for lunch. He described in detail the backward state of the country's economy and noted that when there was capital available it was usually either wasted or used for immediate needs, not for long-term projects. "Shortages exist in rice, foodstuffs, fertilizer, farm tools, and other staple items," he told the bankers. "But the market is inundated with whiskey, beer, cigarettes, and other types of expensive goods imported from foreign countries."

The nearest he came to discussing the economic reforms

publicly was in a February 1989 interview with Grant Evans, an Australian sociologist who is an expert on Laos. Evans asked him, "Why did you have the old policy?"

"Well, they had done it that way in other socialist countries, and I thought I understood how it should be done," Kaysone replied. "So we tried it out here. It worked in some situations but not in others. Then [in 1979] we had to slow down, and then change direction." He noted that "the real change began in 1985," and said, "It was then that we really began to tackle the problems of prices, values, and money. We began experiments with a more flexible pricing policy. . . . If we are not good at controlling the macroeconomic relations between goods and money, we'll have the same problems as China."

To an outsider's eye, the economic reforms might look like unbridled capitalism. But Laotian officials patiently explained— one of them while sitting beneath a map of Laos that had a picture of Engels taped to it—that sound socialist principles were lurking underneath. The teachings of Lenin, they said, give the free market a vital role in the transition to socialism— you have to pass through a capitalist stage on the way to true socialism, and Laos had never done this.

"Is it the goal of Laos to be a socialist state?" I asked Boun Omme Southichak, one of the officials who oversee foreign investments.

"Sure, but we need some time," he replied. "We have to go step by step. We don't know how far away socialism is; it depends." The unwillingness of the government to abandon its ideological baggage makes for schizophrenic scenes these days in Vientiane. The biggest bookstore sells nothing but publications from Communist countries, but a couple of blocks away you can buy a television and watch four channels from Thailand. (The Thai and Laotian languages are so similar that people who speak one can easily understand the other.) While Laos's television station still serves as a propaganda mouthpiece for the government, its salesmen are pounding the streets trying to persuade businessmen to buy commercial time. Students still have to pass an exam in Marxism to graduate from a university, and one student told me that—at the same time that the government was leasing state-owned factories to capitalists—his Marxism teacher was lecturing on how factories under capitalism exploited their workers.

I asked the student whether he had pointed out the contradiction.

"You don't ask questions," he replied. "You just take down what the teacher says."

It seems axiomatic that changing the economic system of an impoverished country in a way that frees some of the people to get wealthy while the vast majority remain very poor must create resentment—particularly if the economic freedom is not accompanied by fundamental political reforms. I assumed, therefore, that it would be easy to find Laotians critical of their government, at least in private conversation. But I found none at all. One Western ambassador told me he had never met a dissident, and explained, "The young Laotian would say, 'We have freedom to travel, we have discos, we have economic reform.' I don't see any sign at all of political pressure for change; I can't imagine where it would come from." Another diplomat noted, "The Voice of America broadcasts an hour a night, and it's very well listened to. They get Thai television and radio. So the seeds have been planted. But there's no indication that anything is sprouting."

"Laos is a different country, Oriental in thinking," said a Russian diplomat. "People are very passive politically here. Their thinking is that if they have rice that's good, but they don't necessarily want to have more rice. Inevitably, there will be dissent, but probably not for several years more."

I spoke to a couple of Laotian journalists and discovered that they, too, adhered firmly to the government line. The press isn't needed to expose any shortcomings of government, a Vientiane reporter told me. "The government has meetings every day, and they talk about all these problems," he said. "Laos won't be like Eastern Europe, because people follow Buddhism, which tells you to stay together in peace."

Finally, I took to stopping people on the streets who looked like students of college age, and inviting them to practice English with me. That invitation is certain to get a response, because among the young people of Laos, English has replaced French as the second language. One day, I was lucky and encountered a group of about twenty students who were eager to talk. But when I turned the conversation to politics my audience shrank to one. A dissident by no stretch of the imagination, this student was at least willing to answer my questions frankly. "All the students know what has happened in Eastern Europe," he said. "We found out about it by watching CNN on Thai television. We all know what happened in China, too, but what could we do? Here everyone is too busy running around making money. This is not like Eastern Europe, where there are so many demonstrators. In Laos, if there had been any sort of demonstration the police would have outnumbered the critics."

The absence of dissent can't be explained solely by the presence of neighborhood block wardens, who keep an eye on comings and goings, for in the past few years the trappings of a police state have been substantially reduced. A few years ago, Westerners living in Vientiane couldn't invite a Laotian to their house without first clearing the invitation in writing with the Ministry of Foreign Affairs. Today, that procedure has been eased, and Westerners and Laotians can be seen dancing together in discotheques. (In the early days of the discos, the government decreed that dancers had to stay two feet apart, but that regulation is no longer enforced.) Anyone, even a former internee in a re-education camp, can get a passport; for that matter, you can now visit Thailand for a day without a passport. A passport costs fifty-five cents and takes a couple of months to receive, but the process can be speeded up if you pay extra. All former Laotian citizens can come back to visit, whatever their politics. In 1975, for instance, Prince Panya Souvanna Phouma discovered that he was about to be put in a re-education camp, presumably because he was working at the Ministry of Finance. (Souvanna Phouma's three other children, who weren't government officials, had no such problem.) Panya escaped across the Mekong to Thailand, and in 1990 he returned for the first time. "I was received very nicely," he told me. All over Laos, I met visitors who fled in 1975 and had returned to check on things. By most estimates, the number of former Laotian citizens returning now exceeds the number of those fleeing across the Mekong.

The Laotian government claims that it has closed all the re-education camps. That claim is impossible to verify, but it is known that the population of political prisoners has dropped dramatically from the 1975 figure, which was more than ten thousand. The State Department says, in its 1989 Human Rights Report, that it knows definitely of only thirty-four people who have been incarcerated since 1975, and that the total number of political detainees in the country is somewhere between that figure and "over one thousand." The report concludes, "Many former camp prisoners apparently have been able to obtain work. Some of them now have responsible, professional positions both with the government of Laos and with international organizations present in Vientiane."

Although the better treatment of political opponents hasn't led to toleration of any sort of opposition party, there has been some loosening of restraints. Until four years ago, the Laotian Communist Party made all government appointments—the minister of health, for example, would have no say in who his deputies were to be—but this control is now less strict. Moreover, in parliamentary elections in 1989—the first since the Pathet Lao took over—121 candidates were allowed to run for 79 seats, and 14 of the winners weren't Party members. The Parliament, called the Supreme People's Assembly, is being given some real power, for the first time, and it is now drafting the regime's first constitution. (Since 1975, Laos has been without a constitution and without a code of civil law, and their absence is considered one impediment to attracting foreign investment.) Western diplomats in Vientiane, however, don't view the parliamentary elections as a precursor of major political changes. "The elections were something of a farce, since all candidates were approved by the state in advance," one ambassador said. "The political system has not changed at all; Laos is a tightly run one-party socialist state, and is likely to remain that way." Government officials are quick to dampen any speculation that political change might be coming. Souban, the deputy foreign minister, told me, "It's not like Eastern Europe here, because we have a just economic policy and we've liberalized our thinking. Because our economic policy is correct, there are no demonstrations. There couldn't be demonstrations in the future. . . . The non-Party members in Parliament share the policies of the Party. All the people in Laos agree with the government."

Many Laotians do indeed seem genuinely to admire their government. The opening up of the economy, after so many years of total deprivation, has led to something approaching a state of euphoria. Everyone in Vientiane seems proud of the abundance of material goods now available, even if most residents can't afford to do more than window-shop for them. But there is a second, and more important, explanation for the absence of dissent, and that lies in the availability of the Mekong River as a safety valve. Dissidents can simply cross the river to Thailand. There are no patrol boats on either side to stop anyone wanting to leave Laos, and those Laotians who cross can melt easily into the population of northeast Thailand, which consists largely of Thais whose ethnic origin is lowland Lao. Many Laotians are able to join relatives or friends; my interpreter, for instance, told me that all three of his brothers live in Thailand. This is the crucial difference that has allowed economic reform to succeed in Laos unaccompanied by political changes, while the same attempt failed so dramatically in China. Almost no one in Beijing could even dream of escaping to the West, but in Vientiane it's as easy as taking a boat across the river. Those Laotians who haven't done so are here because, for one reason or another, they have chosen to stay.

The Mekong has lately proved to be a two-way street, for a few of those who fled have been returning, with arms, to harass the Laotian government. The insurgents include Hmong and lowland Lao from refugee camps in Thailand, and also assorted bandits and opium smugglers. Each winter during the dry season, they move into Laotian villages from across the border and ambush trucks, particularly on Route 13, massacring the passengers, including women and children. In 1989, the attacks were especially brutal; in late December, newcomers burned down an uncooperative Hmong village and ambushed a six-truck convoy on Route 13, killing twenty-eight civilians. It's likely that the attackers include at least a few Laotians who have become American citizens; the Hmong leader, Vang Pao, who is a naturalized American, is widely believed to be one of those involved. The possibility that Americans might once again be fighting in Laos does not please the United States government, which views the fighters as little more than drug smugglers. The State Department says that the United States is not supporting them directly or indirectly.

Even those knowledgeable about the insurgents differ in their estimates of the number of rebels, which range from two hundred to thirteen thousand. Although the insurgency poses no threat to the stability of the Laotian government, the Pathet

Lao fear that the sniper attacks could imperil the badly needed foreign-aid projects now in progress in the countryside. That happened in the summer of 1981, when a World Bank consultant studying a possible road-building project died in a bazooka attack north of Savannakhet. The perpetrators were never discovered, but the World Bank dropped all consideration of road projects for the next five years. The attacks on Route 13 are probably one reason that in the fall of 1989, after opening Laos for several months to anyone who applied for entry, the government stopped issuing visas to individual tourists. Some of the less prosperous new tourists, it turned out, were putting themselves in danger by trying to hitchhike to Luang Prabang instead of taking the plane.

In January 1990, the government may have struck back vigorously at the insurgents. According to an article in the Bangkok *Post*, insurgent leaders accused the government of bombing ten villages where their forces had established a foothold; they claimed that 183 people were killed and 5,000 left homeless. The article noted, "Thai-Lao border intelligence sources said the reports could be genuine." The article raised the question of whether the Laotians were fighting against a guerrilla movement with the same tactics that the Americans had used during the Vietnam War—in effect, destroying villages in order to save them. No foreign embassy in Vientiane has direct evidence of any bombing of villages, although diplomats say they are certain that some sort of bombing—perhaps of rebel camps—did take place. When I put the question to Souban, he dismissed it with a wave of his hand. "They don't threaten our security at all," he said. "Do you think we need MIG-21s to bomb five or six people in the mountains?"

The insurgents, who call themselves the United Laotian National Liberation Front, declared in late 1989 that they had established a provisional revolutionary government, operating on Laotian soil. A probable explanation for all this activity is that the rebels fear they are about to lose their traditional sanctuary in Thailand, because Thailand is finding participation in Laos's newly open economy a far more profitable enterprise than covert support of an anti-Communist insurgency. The turnaround in relations between the two historic enemies (Thai "volunteers" had fought in the CIA's secret army, and American planes bombing Laos had taken off from Thai territory) has been dramatic. From December 1987 to February 1988, Thailand and Laos fought a bloody border war over disputed territory, which cost a hundred Lao and five hundred Thai lives. In February 1989, just a year after that conflict ended, Kaysone was in Thailand grandly declaiming to his hosts, "Mountains may collapse and rivers may run dry, but let the Laotian-Thai friendship last forever." The newfound relationship makes considerable sense, since the two cultures are so similar and since, by Laotian standards, Thailand is an enormously wealthy superpower and a potential source of desperately needed investment capital. "Once the barriers are down, there's a natural affinity with Thailand," Joseph Zasloff, the University of Pittsburgh Laos specialist, said. "And there's also a new mood in Thailand, characterized by the prime minister's slogan 'From battlefield to marketplace.' "

Indeed, Thai investors—and also Thai government officials and high-ranking army officers, who, characteristically, don't let their official duties interfere with the opportunity to make personal profits—have been courting Laos assiduously, and Thai companies have provided a large share of the new investment in Laos. The well-stocked markets of Vientiane that give the city such an aura of prosperity are selling mainly Thai consumer goods, from food and medicine to television sets. "The Laotian economy is becoming dependent on Thailand," a Western ambassador told me. "I think the government is more comfortable being an economic province of Thailand than being so closely tied to Vietnam. The Laotians have nothing at all in common with the Vietnamese except political ideology. Now Australia has agreed to build a bridge across the Mekong, and it will be finished in 1994. That will make it much easier for the Thais to rape and devastate Laos." That ambassador isn't the only one to use harsh words in describing the relationship; the Laotians themselves sometimes seem to be having second thoughts about it. On July 4, 1989, the state-owned Radio Vientiane broadcast a speech accusing Thailand of using economic power to dominate Laos, because armed force had not succeeded. "Having failed to destroy our country through military might, the enemy has now employed a new strategy, attacking us through the so-called attempt to turn the Indochinese battlefield into a marketplace," the speaker said. The Laotian government quickly attempted to calm the ensuing uproar with the lame explanation that the speech—in a country where all the media are rigidly controlled—didn't reflect official views.

The trade problem is particularly acute in respect to timber. In early 1989, Thailand banned logging in its few remaining forests, and it has since been covetously eyeing the timber resources of its neighbors. This puts its policies in sharp conflict with those of Laos, which has shown a sensitivity to environmental concerns which is unusual in the Third World. For several years now, as one example, some of the ethnic minorities in mountainous areas who have been destroying the forests through slash-and-burn agriculture have been offered material inducements by the government to relocate in the lowlands. "In most countries, it starts at the bottom," Richard Salter, a Canadian forestry consultant working in Laos, said of environmental awareness. "People get concerned and go after the politicians. But here the interest is at the very top. When Thailand banned logging, the Thais were literally over here the next day. They said, 'We'll pay anything,' and they were refused. The government seems willing to lose short-term economic benefits for long-term environmental considerations. That's very unusual."

Although Laos has banned the export of unprocessed logs

since early in 1989, disregarding the Thai appetite for timber is not as easy as putting a regulation on the books. For the Laotian army, for corrupt provincial officials, and for many peasants, timber represents hard cash in an extremely poor country. Some observers think that logging continues at the same level as before—only, now, illegally, so that the central government is deprived of the revenues. In the course of my drive to the Ho Chi Minh Trail, and on a day trip north from Vientiane, I saw logs all along the road. Those who know Laos well say that the problem is most acute in Xaignabouli Province—the one province of Laos that is on the west side of the Mekong River and so has no water boundary with Thailand. Xaignabouli is controlled largely by the Laotian military, and, according to some accounts, huge areas are being clear-cut, with both Laotian and Thai military officers pocketing the proceeds. I asked Somphavan Inthavong, the influential economic planner, about this, and he was more candid than other government officials, who simply deny that the problem exists. "There are good Thais and bad Thais," he said. "We cannot just by a decree make those who are bad go away. Guards alone in the forest can't do the job, so we have to rely on the villages. We're giving villagers the title to surrounding forests, telling them they can use the timber for their own purposes, like housing and charcoal. That way, they will protect it."

At the same time that Thailand has strengthened its ties with Laos, Vietnam appears to have willingly backed off from its position of strong influence over the Pathet Lao government. For many years, the Vietnamese kept between forty thousand and fifty thousand troops stationed in Laos. Soviet and American diplomats agree that all these troops are now gone, with most of the withdrawals having taken place in 1987 and 1988. It's possible that some military advisers still remain, but diplomats think that, if so, the advisers are now more involved with construction projects than with directing the Laotian military. Why the change? One reason is the easing of tensions in Southeast Asia, including the improved relations between Vietnam and its two traditional enemies, China and Thailand. The reduced threat from both makes Laos less strategically important to Vietnam. A second explanation lies in Vietnam's own economic problems, which make it less feasible to support thousands of troops in Laos. "They're good fighters, and they waged war for many years," a Soviet diplomat explains. "But now they're tired of it. They need many things; they have a lot of problems."

Thailand isn't the only country to look more favorably on Laos today. Relations with China are reported to have improved as a result of Kaysone's visit to Beijing, in late 1989. Laotian officials seem confident that, overall, foreign aid will rise in the future, with grants from the West more than compensating for any cutbacks from Eastern Europe. This is a key concern, because, by anyone's accounting in this land of muddled statistics, foreign aid is what keeps Laos functioning. Khamsai Souphanouvong says that in 1989 Laos received a total of $200 million in grants and loans from foreign countries and international agencies, and that almost three-quarters of the aid came from the Communist bloc. He puts Laos's 1989 government expenditures at $300 million.

The positive glow from economic reforms and improved relations with its neighbors can't mask the enormous problems that Laos still faces. While the VCRs in the markets of Vientiane and the privately owned Mercedes sedans waiting at the Savannakhet airport to pick up arriving passengers demonstrate that Laos is starting to develop an entrepreneurial class, they are not signs of a prosperity with deep roots. Overwhelming poverty still grips the countryside, with many villages lacking doctors and schools, and depending on subsistence farming, because there are no roads to get crops to market. The government has only the most meager resources available to provide medical care and education, and to repair the nation's shattered infrastructure.

Vientiane's Mahosot Hospital, the largest in Laos, provides a dramatic example. Built in 1972 by the Americans, in a campuslike setting, it fell into complete disrepair under the Pathet Lao. "There was not a single toilet that flushed, no hot water, not a working drain," an official from the United Nations told me. "The operating room has no windows, and its air conditioning hadn't worked for ten years. In 1990, we contributed something less than $200,000, and that paid to disinfect everything, paint the walls, fix the toilets, clear the drains, and take care of other problems. But after we got the drains working we discovered that they didn't go anywhere; all the sewage simply drained underneath the buildings. There's no program to dispose of medical wastes; they're just tossed away with everything else. And the government has no money to pay a maintenance staff to keep things running; there's not even money to replace light bulbs. So everything could go back to what it was. But we had to do something."

Most of the patients at Mahosot Hospital are being treated for malaria. I spoke to a French doctor studying malaria in Laos, and he told me that it is by far the leading cause of death for infants and children, and that it afflicts one out of four Laotians. The doctor said he had determined that a significant program of malaria control in Laos—local spraying, distribution of mosquito nets impregnated with an insecticide, and treatment of the disease—would cost only $800,000 a year. "But there's no money to finance operating expenses here," he said. "Just no money. There's no money to buy equipment, pay people, buy gasoline— there's simply no money."

Dr. Vannareth Rajpho, the vice-minister of health, told me that doctors earned less than thirty dollars a month, and that some, in poor provinces, had to go as long as six months without pay. "We're spending in Laos one dollar per person a year for medical care," he said.

There are so few skilled administrators in Laos that the country isn't able to use efficiently what little foreign medical aid it now receives. "Today, they've built clinics in many villages, but the question is: Do they function?" a Western aid worker asks. "Medicines arrive from UNICEF and are locked up until they expire, because no one knows what to do with them. Russian medicines aren't used, either, because no one can read the labels saying what they are." At many ministries, long rows of offices lie vacant most of the day, because many of their occupants are out working at second jobs. Somphavan Inthavong told me that Laos had recently had a Soviet offer of a cement plant. "We would have had to build new roads, and to maintain it, so we refused it," he said. "Where would the technicians have come from? If you don't have a big stomach, you can't eat a big amount of food. Of the foreign aid we now receive, we can use only sixty percent efficiently. The absorptive capacity is the key."

The Laotian economy faces some fundamental problems, hidden by the veneer of prosperity resulting from the economic reforms. Agriculture still dominates the economy, and 95 percent of the farm production is rice. Years of little rain, such as 1987 and 1988, can therefore wipe out all other progress. The manufacturing sector is so small—just 4 percent of the gross national product—that it barely exists; one of the few manufactured exports from Laos is toothpicks. The government's budget deficit stands at 60 percent of expenditures, and the deficit has to be financed through foreign aid. The absence of skilled managers means that some of the joint-venture investments are amateurish at best. Late in 1988, a Thai company that engaged in scrap-metal trading established a joint-venture airline called Lao-Pacific. The agreement called for the Thais to contribute the capital and the Laotians the expertise. The "expertise" came from the curator of the national library in Vientiane, who left her job to become the chief Lao partner in the venture. Lao-Pacific has already folded.

There is considerable pessimism in Vientiane among Western

residents who know Laos well. One of the country's major difficulties, they say, is its low level of visibility. "What will the
Laotians do when they lose Russian and Eastern European aid
because those countries are facing their own economic problems?" one Western diplomat asks. "Who is going to fill their
dance card? And what will happen when peace is reached in
Cambodia? Everyone will feel guilty about the Cambodians, and
Laos will be lost in the shuffle. It's a country of four million
people sitting between Thailand and Vietnam, each with more
than fifty-five million people—how does Laos compete with
them on its own?"

Ironically, one of the optimists is a man who had to flee Laos
in 1975—Prince Panya Souvanna Phouma, the former prime
minister's son, who now lives in Bangkok. Educated at the Harvard Business School, and fluent in Lao, Thai, French, and
English, Panya came back from his trip to Laos deeply impressed, and he isn't sure that the relative prosperity of Thailand
is more enviable. "There is peace now in Laos," he told me in
Bangkok. "Go to the countryside, see the people. Roads are
being built, people are being taken care of. Do you want them
to be workers in hotels? Do you want them to cut down their
forests? Is it economic progress when the hill tribes in Thailand
become beggars in Bangkok? Fifteen years is a short moment in
time; give them more time. When you're a landlocked country,
and everyone is ogling you because you have a small population
and lots of territory, it's a wonder Laos is a nation today. I say,
'Stay closed, solve your problems slowly.' The Laotian people
should be careful, and keep what they have untouched."

The embassy of the United States occupies a sprawling compound of low-slung white buildings in the center of Vientiane,
an easy walk from the Morning Market, the Mekong River, and
the central commercial district. From those buildings Americans

once ran a secret war and directed many of the activities of a subservient Laotian government. Today, the buildings hold just eight Americans—three diplomatic officials and a support staff of five. They're relatively young, knowledgeable about Laos— the second- and third-ranking officials speak fluent Lao—and free of the antagonism stemming from the Vietnam War that still colors American relations with Vietnam and Cambodia. They travel widely in the country, sometimes risking days of isolation in primitive conditions while waiting for the weather to clear enough for the old Russian-built helicopters of Lao Aviation to pick them up. For the past dozen or so years, the State Department and the government of Laos have been engaged in a delicate diplomatic dance—a couple of steps together for aid projects and then a couple of steps apart for a round of rebukes—but these days the two are closer than they've ever been. American disapproval of the Pathet Lao, once expressed by the onslaught of bombs, is now confined to diplomatic wrist-slapping. The rank of the head of the American embassy in Vientiane, for instance, was itself a form of wrist-slapping; until 1992, he was a chargé d'affaires, not an ambassador. Laos shared this stigma with only two other countries, Ethiopia and Grenada.

There is an American embassy in Vientiane today only because of the peaceful nature of the Pathet Lao takeover. The violent Communist conquests of South Vietnam and Cambodia sent the Americans packing, but the Pathet Lao indicated from the outset that an American presence would be acceptable. Laos, like Cambodia, has a government that was initially dominated by Vietnam and supported by tens of thousands of Vietnamese troops, but in the case of Laos the peaceful transition in 1975 provided some continuity, and today the United States manages to deal with the Laotian government in a near-normal fashion while refusing to recognize the government of Cambodia because of its Vietnamese ties. Washington has lately had little to complain about, because it has made two major demands on

Laos—cooperation in dampening the opium trade and permission to search for the remains of Americans missing in action—and the Laotians have made significant attempts to meet them.

Laos is the world's third-biggest opium producer, although it lags well behind the first two—Burma and Afghanistan. As with every other Third World drug producer, defining the problem proves a lot easier than solving it. Opium cultivation has been traditional for a hundred and fifty years among the ethnic minorities in the mountains of northern Laos—ethnic minorities that have generally been estranged from and out of touch with the central government. The government has not been eager to deal with these minorities, but recently it did approve the start of a crop-substitution program. In an agreement signed in 1989, the United States pledged $8.7 million over a six-year period for the program, in the remote northeast, only about seventy miles from the former Pathet Lao caves of Sam Neua. (Whether all this money will actually be appropriated, however, is open to question.) According to the agriculture and forests official Kham Ouane, livestock, soybeans, and several other crops can actually prove more profitable than the opium poppy, provided that roads are built to get the products to market. The United States is financing the roads. In return, Laos has agreed to make a "maximum effort" to stop the opium trafficking, although it's uncertain how a country with its paucity of resources can halt the flow of drugs. In 1990, Laos was removed from the "decertification list"—a list that blocks American aid to countries that refuse to cooperate in curbing narcotics. The only countries decertified are those that get little or no American aid anyway, but the presence of Laos on the list had been a major sore point in Laotian-American relations—especially since the United States had accused Laotian civilian and military officials of participating in the drug trade. Discussing the renewed certification of Laos in testimony to Congress, a State Department official said,

"High-level involvement of both military and civilian officials in the Lao government . . . continues to plague constructive cooperation with the U.S. It is difficult to balance corruption and ongoing trafficking activities on the one hand with the beginnings of cooperation on the other."

I discussed this statement with a well-informed Western ambassador in Vientiane.

"I don't believe that narcotics trafficking is organized on a national basis by the government," he said. "If it were, it would be the only organized thing in this country. But there's no doubt about a certain amount of involvement by individuals, particularly in the army."

The question of Americans missing in action in Laos—the number is now 533—has also been thorny. While there is no hope that any of the Americans will be found alive, the United States insists on conducting excavations for their remains, so that the bones can be transported back to the United States for proper burial. The concept of elaborate, costly searches in Laos for American remains has been a bitter pill for the Laotian government, since thousands of Laotians were killed in the bombings and more die from *bombis* every year, and there has been no offer of American compensation. But the Laotian government recognized that the searches were being proposed as a prerequisite for better relations with Washington, and the two sides began to work together in 1985. The United States pays for the excavations, which are conducted by American-Laotian teams. There have been eleven digs so far, and they have yielded the remains of thirty-two Americans. (Inexplicably, the Laotians, while agreeing to these excavations, have turned down American offers of metal detectors and other means of finding and detonating the remaining *bombis*. Perhaps the Laotians feel that such aid would be humiliating to accept, but the government isn't saying.) Souban, the deputy foreign minister, says, "The spirit of cooperation between the Laotians and the Americans in the excavation teams has been very good and very much appreciated. We want to create an atmosphere of trust and understanding. We want the people of the two countries to forget the hard times of war. We hope that by eradicating the past the United States government can change its thinking."

A major goal of the Laotian concessions on drugs and on the searches has been to encourage American aid—aid that could help repair the damage caused by the American bombing. But so far the amount of aid—charted to the last dollar by the United States embassy in Vientiane, which is eager to seize on any proof of better relations—has been so tiny that the total figure would finance the building of no more than three miles of highway in the United States. In five separate years, the United States donated emergency rice shipments, worth a total of $10,590,000. Over four years, it sent $135,000 in medical supplies, the last contribution being duly recorded as $4,000 worth in 1987. The crop-substitution program has brought $700,000 so far. All these figures add up to $11,425,000 in American aid over a fifteen-year period—approximately the average amount spent for five days of the nine years of bombing.

Should the United States feel obligated to offer some sort of compensation for the damage done by the bombing? American government officials who reject the idea argue that the bombs were directed against North Vietnamese supply routes, not against Laotians, and that any additional damage was unintentional and unavoidable. But their argument loses its force when the Plain of Jars is considered. This rolling meadowland, ringed by mountains, 110 miles northeast of Vientiane, was itself the object of hundreds of thousands of tons of bombs. The Plain of Jars was nowhere near the North Vietnamese supply routes, but on it were the roads that the Pathet Lao and the North Vietnamese would have had to take if they had attempted to march on Vientiane and Luang Prabang. In addition, there were reports that the Plain of Jars was used as a dumping ground for the bombs of American planes that were turned back from bombing runs over North Vietnam because of bad weather. "The Plain of Jars is simply littered with craters," a Western diplomat who has been there many times says. "It's hard to believe there were so many targets." The jars themselves—more than a hundred ancient stone urns, whose origins are unknown—came out relatively unscathed; only a few were shattered by the bomb blasts. The inhabitants of the plain fared significantly worse, and by 1969 most of the 130,000 residents of Xieng Khouang Province had fled. The Laotians say that 8,038 civilians in the province were killed by the bombing, 11,345 children were orphaned, and 353 villages were razed.

Many of the Western diplomats and Western aid workers who live in Laos feel that the United States has a debt to pay. One official of an international organization who visits Laos frequently puts it this way: "Along the Ho Chi Minh Trail, the Americans systematically bombed and bombed until everything was gone. The American people should understand that they owe the Laotians something. Laos is comparable to some of the worst countries in the Sahel in terms of health care. That's an atrocity; it's just not Asia. If you cross the river to Nong Khai, in Thailand, life expectancy goes up fifteen years. I'm German, and we paid war debts to Poland and to Israel. The United States has an equal obligation."

If the United States ever recognizes such an obligation, it already has a precedent for carrying it out—a precedent that demonstrates how the world's richest country can work hand in hand with one of the poorest countries. It's a precedent that eliminates the waste, corruption, and bureaucratic inertia so often associated with foreign aid, replacing them with enthusiasm and egalitarianism. This is the search for the remains of the missing Americans—the excavations carried out with Laotian participation by an American interservice military group, called the Joint Casualty Resolution Center, in conjunction with the

United States Army Central Identification Laboratory in Hawaii, or CILHI. To be sure, the operations are in no way meant to be foreign aid, and the Laotians involved in the excavations benefit only incidentally. Nevertheless, the effort gives an illuminating picture of what American aid to Laos could accomplish if reconstruction projects were modeled on it.

I had heard from the American embassy in Vientiane that an excavation was going on near Xepon, where I was headed. While the embassy officials couldn't give me its exact site, they agreed to radio the excavators that I was coming. It turned out that when my Laotian companions and I reached the Xepon area we didn't have to ask directions. Just a few miles down the Ho Chi Minh Trail from Route 9 we saw the blades of a Lao military helicopter. Turning onto a path to drive toward it, we came upon a surreal sight: a United States military camp, complete with green army tents and three black Jeep Cherokees. There were no American soldiers around, but dozens of Laotian villagers had walked for miles to witness what was clearly the entertainment spectacle of the year. A Laotian teenager offered to take us on an hour-long hike, through the jungle and up the side of a mountain, to where the Americans were working. Part of the hike was along the rims of bomb craters, and at one point we passed a rusted bomb casing with the words "DISPENSER AND BOMB—122 LBS." neatly stenciled on its side. I was relieved to be following a local villager, who was familiar with the jungle, not only because of the bomb craters and possible bombs but because the Americans told me that this jungle, like that of nearby Vietnam, is the home of the so-called one-step snake. It gets that name because after it bites you the afflicted limb must supposedly be hacked off before you take more than one step, or else you'll die. (When I returned to the United States, I inquired about this "one-step snake," which I had first read about during the Vietnam War. John Behler, the head of the Department of Herpetology at the Bronx Zoo, said that it was a myth, that there's no snake in Laos or Vietnam whose bite would be fatal in less than fifteen minutes.)

The trail took us into a clearing, where an American army sergeant sitting at a wooden table was serving as sentry. He registered not a flicker of surprise at seeing a sweat-soaked American and five Laotians burst out of the jungle. He simply looked up and asked "May I help you?" in a tone that made it plain that, whoever we were and wherever we came from, we could go right back if we didn't have official clearance. Fortunately, the Americans here had received the embassy's radio message, so I was taken on a tour by Major Hugh Klipp, the head of the recovery team. We walked around what turned out to be a professional archeological dig, complete with an anthropologist who works for CILHI. The area, where photo-reconnaissance and interviews with villagers had indicated that a plane might have crashed, was roped off into sections, and workers were digging up soil, putting it in buckets, and sifting it through screens in a search for bone fragments. "What we're doing is an obligation to brother soldiers," Major Klipp told me. "They earned the right to come back to their families. The Laotians consider this somewhat curious, but to us it's really important that we bring back our dead. I can't say it's 'Spare no expense,' but there has never been a request where I've been told no. I have the army, marines, a navy doctor, an air force technician—each service is committed. Airplanes are provided from all over the Pacific. It's a total government commitment. You never hear anyone say 'We can't.' It's always 'What can we do to make this happen?' "

Particularly striking was the cooperation at the site between Americans and Laotians, all of them casually dressed in T-shirts. Each American soldier digging a shovelful of soil was paired with a Laotian, hired from a nearby village to do the same thing. When the soil was sifted through a screen, an American held one end of it and a Laotian the other. Major Klipp himself had a Laotian equivalent at the site. Every American wore a name tag with his first name spelled out phonetically in Lao, and the Laotians wore English name tags. One bilingual American officer and one bilingual Laotian officer did the translating. Even though the Americans and the Laotians had been together only six days, one sensed a genuine affection and camaraderie, expressed through constant bantering. "We're not associated with the Vietnam War by the villagers," Major Klipp said. "The Laotians couldn't be more gracious—not only that, but these guys are good workers. When the Laotians work with us, they see men, women, blacks, whites—how diverse the American people are."

Major Klipp suggested that I go back to camp and interview the navy doctor, Jennifer Ruh. As part of the agreement setting up the excavations, the United States allowed the doctor at the site to examine local villagers and dispense whatever medicine was available. The news traveled by word of mouth, and, in an area with no other medical care, Dr. Ruh had found herself inundated. "I've seen seven hundred Laotians in six days," she told me. "They come from five or six different villages. There are a lot of upper-respiratory infections and skin diseases, and a lot of cases of worms. Our medical supplies ran out so quickly that yesterday I had to take the helicopter to Savannakhet and get more medicine for them. They're just delighted to see a doctor. It's the main spectacle around here. Sometimes fifty people watch all day." When I left Dr. Ruh's tent, at noon, there was a long line of people waiting patiently for her impromptu clinic to reopen, at two. Some of them carried live chickens, which they planned to give her as an expression of gratitude. But this heaven-sent privilege of medical care was not to last long. Two days after my visit, the excavation was shut down. It was a failure, for no remains were found. The camp was dismantled and packed up, and life on the Ho Chi Minh Trail returned to normal.

CAMBODIA
The Khmer Rouge Have Returned

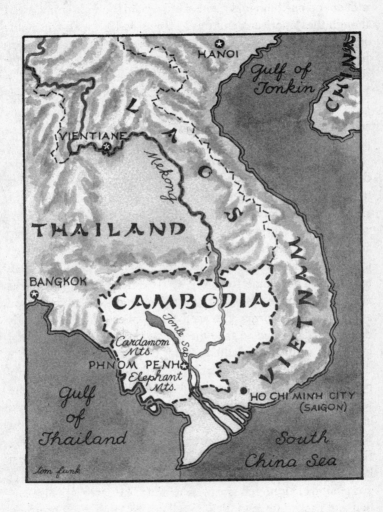

PHNOM PENH is a boomtown. Evacuated by the Khmer Rouge during their reign of terror over Cambodia from 1975 to 1979, then choked until 1992 by an economic boycott that the major Western powers imposed on Cambodia to put pressure on its Vietnamese-installed government, this once-elegant French-colonial capital has sprung back to life with an astonishing resilience. The arrival hall of the airport terminal reflects the new theme of commercialism with a huge sign saying "Welcome to Cambodia—Heineken Beer." The ride into the city gives glimpses of workmen everywhere, restoring office buildings and sprucing up old villas as quarters for the Western relief organizations that are flooding into the country. The trucks of these groups, with identifying initials and insignias painted on the doors, are all over town—a veritable alphabet soup of aid, ranging from ACR (Australian Catholic Relief) to YWAM (Youth with a Mission), and including an umbrella organization, CCC (Cooperation Committee for Cambodia), that has been set up just to keep track of them all and to prevent duplication of aid projects. The thousands of United Nations troops and civilians now pouring into Cambodia to administer the peace agreement signed in Paris in October 1991—an agreement under which the Cambodian government allowed back into Phnom Penh the three rebel factions that had sought for more than a decade to overthrow it—are finding that they can buy a cornucopia of goods that have managed to appear despite the years of poverty, deprivation, and boycott. "You can get almost anything here," one UN official told me. "We send someone out for light bulbs, and he'll come back with four different kinds, from four different countries. We've even bought an electric typewriter with English letters." The newly arrived Westerners are fueling a boom in restaurants, and Cambodian entrepreneurs are scampering to take maximum advantage of it; on Achar Mean-Boulevard, the main street, the Bayon Restaurant has hung up signs to lure customers with the news that cobra is in season. In this city, whose population, now nine hundred thousand, is still less than half of what it was before the Khmer Rouge took over, planning for the future used to be limited to figuring out how to stay alive. Now a poster on a bulletin board at the CCC urges runners to sign up for the Phnom Penh–Mekong Marathon.

Perhaps the most jarring sight in Phnom Penh is the abundance of new Mercedes-Benzes and BMWs, the vehicles preferred by people who, through smuggling and other illegal activities, have managed to pluck a fortune from a city that was only recently in shambles. These cars compete for the roads with far less substantial cars, motorbikes, and cyclos—three-wheeled pedicabs in which the passenger sits in a basket-shaped front seat and the driver pedals from behind—and this competition sometimes leads to disaster. The rules of traffic in Phnom Penh are governed more by the easygoing ways of Cambodians than by any set of laws, and it's considered perfectly acceptable to drive on the left side of the road, facing oncoming traffic, if you're going to turn after a block or two. Vehicles generally enter an intersection from all directions simultaneously without stopping, moving very slowly and then jockeying for position. The Mercedes-Benzes and BMWs, however, rudely interrupt this delicate ballet, roaring through with their horns blaring and sending the other vehicles scattering. At night, many of the expensive cars can be seen parked outside the former Samaki ("Solidarity") Hotel, which has a new coat of paint and its original name back, which is Le Royal. Le Royal now has a blasting disco, so loud that it can be heard blocks away. You enter the disco through a special gate, where a guard sits at a desk and politely asks customers for their guns; he arranges them neatly in a drawer with coat-check tags on them. Inside the disco, swarms of Vietnamese prostitutes descend on unaccompanied men. With lighter skins and more experience than Cambodian women, they dominate the market, and apparently find Phnom Penh more profitable than Saigon.

Not only Westerners but also the Khmer Rouge are remarking on Phnom Penh's prosperity. Son Sen, the Khmer Rouge leader who specialized in overseeing the torture of those about to be put to death, and who is back in Phnom Penh because the peace agreement gives the Khmer Rouge a share of power, wrote, "While in the car, I noted that there were people everywhere. Everybody looks well." Son Sen and his cohorts, who once condemned Phnom Penh and most of its inhabitants to death, must surely have been surprised to see this city showing signs of becoming the most beautiful capital in Asia, with its broad, tree-lined boulevards, its handsome French colonial villas and Buddhist pagodas, and the pleasing Cambodian architecture of the Royal Palace compound, which fronts on the Tonle Sap River at its confluence with the Mekong. Investors haven't missed the news of Phnom Penh's resurrection, either. When I visited the city in December 1991, Japanese, European, and even a few American businessmen were jammed into the handful of passable hotels, which had taken advantage of the influx by doubling—or, in some cases, quadrupling—their rates. One day, I met three American investors who had just arrived with visions of building hotel complexes on land they would pick up for bargain prices. I saw them again a couple of days later, looking crestfallen. Although real estate transactions in Cambodia are the riskiest of ventures, given the instability of the country and the destruction by the Khmer Rouge of all property-ownership records, the Americans discovered that rampant speculation had nevertheless driven the price of land and buildings up to a level about equal with that in the United States. Four days before Christmas, when government troops opened fire on student protesters, these three American investors and most others headed for the nearest exit—a twice-a-day Bangkok Airways propeller plane to Thailand.

The ostentatious wealth of the nouveau riche in Phnom Penh seems phantasmagoric, for Cambodia is one of the world's poorest, most war-ravaged nations. Life remains unchanged in the city's back alleys, where people live in hovels with no water and no electricity. And even these residents are better off than those in the countryside, where farmers try to scratch out a living with no fertilizer, no equipment, and a network of roads and bridges that lies in ruin. In Cambodia, government ministers earn ten or fifteen dollars a month, and lesser employees and soldiers go for months without a paycheck; tens of thousands of amputees, victims of several million land mines planted during the decades of conflict, survive on what little they can gain from begging; and the sick suffer and die because the few primitive hospitals are reserved for soldiers and for the wealthy. Cambodia has a desperate shortage of teachers, doctors, and every other sort of professional, for the Khmer Rouge meticulously sought out and slaughtered everybody with an education. In 1975, the country had 485 doctors; only 43 survived to see the end of the Khmer Rouge era.

The expensive cars on the streets of Phnom Penh, appearing amid all the privation, represent the spoils of peace—the fruits of the venality, corruption, and manipulation that began sweeping through the city almost from the moment that the peace agreement seemed a possibility. By late 1991, the corruption had reached such a level that students who were repelled by it took to the streets for several days to demonstrate. Demonstrations in Cambodia have been dangerous under any regime, and these were no different, as the government responded by ordering its troops to shoot into the crowds and by announcing new repressive measures. "My greatest fear is that the world will start pouring more money in here, and that the corruption will increase to the point where the country will collapse," a government official who is shocked by the conditions in Phnom Penh told me. The scene there today recalls vividly the unbridled greed of another era—the early 1970s, when Cambodia became a victim of the destabilization caused by the Vietnam War, and the rightist government of General Lon Nol plundered the country. In 1969, the United States had launched a secret bombing campaign on Vietnamese targets in eastern Cambodia. A year later, with American support, Lon Nol overthrew Prince Norodom Sihanouk, who had ruled Cambodia since 1941, first as king and then as head of the government. Sihanouk responded by joining with his former enemy, the Khmer Rouge—whose name he himself had coined, to designate the indigenous Communist guerrillas of Cambodia. Headed by Saloth Sar, who used the *nom de guerre* Pol Pot, the Khmer Rouge forces in early 1970 numbered just five thousand, but they grew rapidly because of opposition to American bombing and by posing as the protectors of and providers for the poor, the true nationalists fighting against the foreign-backed government that was looting Cambodia. In 1975, the Khmer Rouge, supported not only by peasants but also by many educated Cambodians, who saw no other alternative to the corruption that was tearing their country apart, marched victoriously into Phnom Penh.

Whatever the resemblance between conditions in Cambodia today and those of the early seventies, one big difference exists: this time the Khmer Rouge don't have to fight their way into Phnom Penh to establish a presence there. In addition to Son Sen, another of their highest-ranking leaders and some aides and bodyguards are in the capital as part of the peace process. These delegates are being protected by the troops of their arch-enemy, the Vietnam-backed Cambodian government, which since 1984 has been headed by Prime Minister Hun Sen. A second layer of protection is offered by United Nations peacekeeping forces, which started arriving in Cambodia in early 1992. That the troops of Hun Sen's army are guarding the walled compound that formerly housed the French governor-general and now serves as the Khmer Rouge residence and headquarters is no small irony, for Hun Sen was among a group of Khmer Rouge officials in eastern Cambodia who broke with Pol Pot and escaped to Vietnam in 1977. Their change of allegiance could have been as much an attempt to save their necks as it was revulsion against Khmer Rouge genocide, for Pol Pot had turned against Vietnam, his former ally, in a paranoid fury and, suspicious even of Cambodians, had begun purging the ranks of Khmer Rouge officials based near the Vietnamese border. He didn't stop there: on several occasions in 1977, his troops staged raids into Vietnam itself, massacring thousands of Vietnamese civilians and driving hundreds of thousands from their homes. In December 1978, after Pol Pot refused to negotiate or to accept international supervision of the border area, Vietnam invaded Cambodia, and in January 1979 it captured Phnom Penh. Vietnam then installed the government that still rules Cambodia; Hun Sen, who was only twenty-seven years old, was named foreign minister. The Khmer Rouge fled to the Thai border, and Prince Sihanouk, who had spent the years of Khmer Rouge rule imprisoned in the Royal Palace, fled to Beijing.

Now Sihanouk, too, is back in Phnom Penh, also maneuvering for power, but in a very different setting—one created by the peace accord, which emerged from a nineteen-nation conference held in Paris in October 1991, under the auspices of the United

Nations. To satisfy all the participants, the peace agreement set up three different governmental units, which are operating side by side. One is the Hun Sen government: it is still administering the country, but it is doing so under UN supervision, to make certain that it doesn't interfere with a free election process. Second is the UN itself, carrying out the biggest peacekeeping operation in its history. The UN has in place 15,900 soldiers, 3,600 police, and 2,400 civilians, all under the banner of UNTAC, the United Nations Transitional Authority in Cambodia. For this country of fewer than 9 million people, UNTAC is undertaking a $2 billion effort to repatriate 330,000 refugees on the Thai border; disarm the more than 400,000 soldiers and militiamen and demobilize 70 percent of them; and organize free elections—no easy task in a nation that has never known free expression, a free press, or a secret ballot. The third governmental unit, a new body called the Supreme National Council and headed by Prince Sihanouk, has taken over the "sovereignty" of Cambodia from the Hun Sen government. The SNC has twelve members—six from the Hun Sen government and six from the opposition, which means two each from the Khmer Rouge, the Sihanoukists, and the Khmer People's National Liberation Front (KPNLF). The last two factions—the former supporting Prince Sihanouk, the latter headed by Son Sann, an ardent anti-Communist who in 1967 was briefly prime minister in the Sihanouk government—have small armies of their own on the Thai border. The SNC as a whole has only a small staff and no administrative functions, and so possesses no real power, but its existence allows Western nations to lift their economic sanctions and send diplomats to Phnom Penh; the diplomats can be accredited to the SNC, making it unnecessary to recognize the Vietnam-backed Hun Sen government. In tangible terms, the Khmer Rouge get only a sixth of the seats in a powerless body. But the intangible benefits are enormous, since the Khmer

Rouge gain a new legitimacy. The peace agreement provides them with protection, freedom to move within Cambodia, and freedom to promote their cause on radio and television.

If the peace process works according to plan, the Khmer Rouge will contest for power this time not on the battlefield but in the election booth. That fact still doesn't diminish the shocking starkness of what has happened: the Khmer Rouge, among the worst mass murderers of the twentieth century, have returned. It is as if the Nazi leaders, instead of being punished at Nuremberg, had been invited back by the Allies to participate in the governing of postwar Germany. It is a situation that clearly delights the Khmer Rouge. In November 1991, a Khmer Rouge radio broadcast called on Cambodians to "forget the past." Son Sen, who holds one of the two Khmer Rouge seats on the SNC, told a reporter from Agence France-Presse, "I am very happy to be here because we are so warmly welcomed by our compatriots. They call me Uncle."

Son Sen's boast of a warm reception turned out to be somewhat premature. On the morning of November 27, 1991, the day after his interview, Khieu Samphan, the second Khmer Rouge representative, flew to Phnom Penh. As his motorcade from the airport passed Phnom Penh University, it was mobbed by peaceful student demonstrators waving banners. That afternoon, hundreds of people gathered outside the Khmer Rouge compound. A group of young men hurled stones, tore down the gate, and ran from room to room throwing furniture, carpets, clothes, and papers out the windows, and other protesters tossed it all onto a bonfire. In a second-floor bedroom, the men ransacking the house found Samphan cowering in a closet and proceeded to beat him. Foreign press photographers sent around the world two unforgettable pictures: Khieu Samphan, a frightened, white-haired man of sixty, with blood streaming down his face, first wearing a pair of underpants on his head to stem the bleeding, then wearing a helmet. Samphan and Son Sen ended up in an armored personnel carrier of the Cambodian army and were taken to the airport and put on a plane to Bangkok. They returned to Phnom Penh a few weeks later, this time carefully guarded by troops of the Hun Sen government.

Many publications wrote about the incident as a case of an enraged population that couldn't bear to see its former torturers return. For example, a Washington *Post* editorial commented on the attack, "Forgetting the past means forgetting the people who were murdered. That is precisely what the Cambodian people are unable and, to their credit, unwilling to do." The Hun Sen government attempted to reinforce this impression. "We cannot forget, but we still must abide by the peace agreement," an official of the Foreign Ministry told me. "But for the simple people it is different. We were told that people from the countryside came to Phnom Penh and waited three or four days for Khieu Samphan to arrive. One widow said she would keep trying to kill Khieu Samphan as long as he stayed in Cambodia. The Khmer Rouge had killed her husband, and then had come back and killed her children in front of her." This explanation for the citizens' outrage seems logical, for the Khmer Rouge had made no attempt to project a new image—to present younger and gentler faces. Instead, they had sent to Phnom Penh as their representatives two of their most barbarous leaders from the 1970s. (Pol Pot, who remains in charge, prefers to work from behind the scenes, in Thailand.) When the Khmer Rouge ruled Cambodia, Son Sen, who still holds the title of defense minister of Pol Pot's Democratic Kampuchea Party, personally directed the operations at Tuol Sleng, a former high school in Phnom Penh that was the Khmer Rouge torture center, where those suspected of disloyalty were taken on their way to the killing fields. Tuol Sleng has been preserved as a museum, to remind visitors of the Khmer Rouge atrocities; it displays hundreds of photographs of the victims, as well as bloodstained clothing and torture instruments. Khieu Samphan's past was equally grim. Samphan, who has held the title of president of Democratic Kampuchea since 1976, is a French-educated economist, whose doctoral thesis at the Sorbonne, on economic development, provided the intellectual framework for the Khmer Rouge's decision to evacuate the inhabitants of Cambodia's cities to the countryside; that decision is often attributed to Samphan himself. His duties in the late seventies also included acting as host at macabre "last suppers" for Khmer Rouge officials who were about to be purged and executed. Samphan would invite the officials to dinner and attempt to allay any suspicions they might have, so that they wouldn't try to escape.

While Cambodians had every justification for rising up in anger and attacking the Khmer Rouge compound, the fact is that nothing in Cambodia happens spontaneously. The decades of repression have bred caution for every situation. The return of Prince Sihanouk to Cambodia, on November 14, 1991, after thirteen years of exile, was without doubt an occasion for celebration; Sihanouk is still revered by some Cambodians as a god-king, and he symbolizes a happier, peaceful past. The government planned elaborate welcoming ceremonies at the airport, ending with a motorcade in which Sihanouk would ride triumphantly in the back of a 1963 Chevrolet Impala convertible, which had been lent by a Thai newspaper, because Sihanouk wished to be seen in such a vehicle as a remembrance of his days of glory. Yet even for this historic, nonthreatening event the government felt compelled to order its employees to attend the ceremony, and schools issued similar orders to their students. Nor was there any spontaneous reaction when the first advance contingent of UN troops arrived in Phnom Penh. "In Namibia, when we came in we were cheered on the streets by the people," a UN official told me. "Here there has been no reaction. They've learned: Don't trust anybody, don't ask questions."

I went to the campus of Phnom Penh University, hoping to meet a student willing to talk about what had happened on the day of the attack on the Khmer Rouge compound. A student who spoke excellent English—I will call him Sok—came up to me almost immediately. Sok felt that the Hun Sen government had attempted to sabotage the peace process, and he was so outraged that he was anxious to tell the entire story to a Westerner; I was able to confirm enough details of his story to be convinced of its credibility. Though Sok was severely critical of Hun Sen, he could hardly be called a supporter of the Khmer Rouge. In 1975, his family had been sent from Phnom Penh to Kompong Cham Province, northeast of the capital, to work on a farm. In 1977, at the age of eight, Sok was taken from his parents and two sisters as part of the Khmer Rouge policy of breaking up families. They sent him to a farm to work with other boys. "One day, the Khmer Rouge supervisor of the boys asked me if I wanted to see my mother and father," Sok told me. "I said I would like that very much. But then some of the boys warned me that I shouldn't go with him, that I would be killed. So I ran away into the forest. I went to the house of friends of my parents, and they told me my parents had been killed the night before. I found out that the Khmer Rouge had murdered my two sisters also. My father was a math teacher, and my mother taught literature; maybe that was why they were killed, but I don't know. I lived alone in the forest for two years, sleeping at night in a hole in the ground. I drank water from the river, and sometimes I met people who gave me some rice and bananas." After the Vietnamese invaded Cambodia, a soldier befriended Sok, and he lived with Vietnamese troops for a year. Then he stayed at a UNICEF orphanage for a time and, later, at a refugee camp on the Thai border. When fighting on the border became too intense, Sok crossed back into Cambodia. All this time he had been trying to learn English, and in 1988 he went to Phnom Penh, passed an English exam, and enrolled in a course of study that would train him to be an English interpreter. Sok was a fervent human rights advocate, and he wanted me to use his real name, so that he would become a test case to see if the Hun Sen government would in fact allow freedom of speech, as the peace accord required. I told him that I couldn't do it—that he had already suffered enough for several lifetimes.

Sok recounted how the student demonstrations began. The day before Khieu Samphan's arrival, he said, the head of Phnom Penh University canceled classes and called all the students to a meeting. "We were given signs to carry that had slogans like 'Down with the Khmer Rouge' and 'The Khmer Rouge cannot take power in Cambodia again,' " he said. "All the slogans were written at the Ministry of the Interior. No one wanted to demonstrate—we didn't want to throw the peace away. But we were forced to do it. That afternoon, we went out for the first demonstration. Those who were studying English had been told not to go, because we could talk to foreigners, but I went anyway. We walked around the city for an hour holding the signs. That night, we listened to the Voice of America, which said Cambodian students had demonstrated against the Khmer Rouge, and we laughed. The next day, classes were canceled again, and we were told to go out to the highway and wait for Khieu Samphan to come from the airport. There was a procession of cars, and we didn't know which one Samphan was in, but the police pointed him out to us. He was waving at the students and smiling. I looked at his face and saw he was not worried; I think he knew this was the government's plan. That afternoon, a friend came to my house and said we should go to the Khmer Rouge headquarters and see what was happening. There were demonstrators of university age, but they weren't students. I could tell from their accent when they spoke Khmer that some were Vietnamese. These Vietnamese broke down the front gate. I saw a policeman motioning to them to go into the house. As the demonstrators shoved forward, the police moved back."

A few days later, I saw a videotape of the demonstration that had been taken by SPK, the Cambodian press agency. The tape clearly backed up Sok's account of complicity by the police and soldiers guarding the house. Hundreds of people had indeed gathered outside the compound, but almost all of them appeared to be passive onlookers. Only twenty or thirty young men were involved in the actual vandalism. They were far outnumbered by the police and the soldiers, who a couple of times could be seen laughing and smoking cigarettes. At one point, when the front gate was half down, a policeman gave a boost to a demonstrator to help him climb over the gate. Hun Sen later explained that his only alternative would have been to order the police to shoot into the crowd. But the videotape made that explanation seem duplicitous, since the police could easily have hauled away the couple of dozen demonstrators, and since they had no trouble rescuing Khieu Samphan when they decided to.

The incident was astonishing. Overnight, the Hun Sen government had made the hated Khmer Rouge seem almost deserving of sympathy, with Khieu Samphan looking like a kindly old man mercilessly pummeled by thugs. Moreover, if the Khmer Rouge had been so inclined, the ransacking of the compound alone could have sabotaged the peace process, which depended on the participation of all the factions. If that had been the government's intent, however, the Khmer Rouge—who have been vocal supporters of the peace accord all along, and have repeatedly requested that the UN troops arrive as quickly as possible—were having none of it. Khieu Samphan and Son Sen had ordered their ten North Korean–trained bodyguards not to use their pistols, and even during the attack, Samphan on a couple of occasions managed a weak smile for the cameras.

Why would the Hun Sen government, barely a month after signing the Paris peace accord, instigate a public-relations fiasco that threatened to undo the peace? Any plausible answer has to take into account the fact that, while the UN peace process is neat and logical, neatness and logic do not apply to the tradition of government in most of Southeast Asia. Cambodia has long been a country of intrigue and machination, and such activities continue alongside the Western-inspired peace process. They are found in the Royal Palace, among Sihanouk, his Eurasian wife, Princess Monique, his sons, and the royal advisers. They are found in the Cambodian government, where Hun Sen, who is relatively liberal, is doing constant battle with a faction of hard-liners who disavow the tag of "Communist" solely as a concession to the times. These hard-liners, who favor the peace process only to the extent that it enhances their opportunities for corruption, control the Interior Ministry, which Sok said had prepared the signs for the demonstrators—and the Interior Ministry does not go to Hun Sen for permission to act.

That Hun Sen has been able to gain some real power in a government of hard-liners who have sought to use him as a figurehead is a tribute to his skill. For a decade, starting in 1967, when he was sixteen, he devoted himself to the Khmer Rouge cause, first as a courier and eventually as deputy commander of a regiment based near the Vietnamese border. Along the way, he was wounded five times, losing his left eye to shrapnel in April 1975, on the day before the Khmer Rouge captured Phnom Penh. While there's no direct evidence that Hun Sen himself participated in Khmer Rouge atrocities, it's hard to believe that a military commander in Pol Pot's army would ever resist orders, and many Cambodians I spoke with still resent him for his Khmer Rouge past. In 1977, Hun Sen and other Eastern Zone officials fled to Vietnam; they provided the core of the leadership for the Cambodian government that the Vietnamese installed in 1979. First as foreign minister and then as prime minister, Hun Sen was used to present a more compassionate, liberal face of Cambodia to the outside world, while in many instances the Stalinist hard-liners in the government dictated policy. Although he instituted numerous repressive measures over the years, at least some of them were clearly required for his political survival. Through his travels and diplomatic contacts, Hun Sen has become far more polished: handsome and appearing even younger than his forty-one years, he favors French double-breasted suits, but on informal occasions he looks as if he had stepped out of the pages of an L. L. Bean catalogue.

Hun Sen's nemesis in the government is also a former Khmer Rouge official. He is Chea Sim, who, at sixty-one is the chairman of the National Assembly and the head of the Cambodian People's Party, which in 1991 dropped the hammer and sickle and the name "Communist" but in other ways remained unchanged. Chea Sim, who blames "external reactionary forces" for the student unrest over rampant corruption in Phnom Penh, clearly recognizes the need for the more benign Hun Sen to be the Cambodian government's front man during the peace process, but who is actually running the country at any given moment is a matter of guesswork. For instance, when Chea Sim started accompanying Sihanouk on trips outside Phnom Penh in early 1992, speculation arose that he was the person in charge. He is thought to control the Interior Ministry, the secret police, and the National Assembly, while Hun Sen has the loyalty of the intellectuals in the government and strong support in the Defense and Foreign ministries; the army appears to be split. The attack on the Khmer Rouge compound could well have been a rearguard action by the hard-liners—if not to thwart the peace process, then perhaps to warn Hun Sen of the potential strength of the Chea Sim faction.

Like Hun Sen and Chea Sim, Prince Sihanouk is tainted by

Khmer Rouge associations in his past. However, Sihanouk is a different sort of person. He was never bound by ideology but, rather, motivated by a desire somehow to insure Cambodia's survival during the decades of unceasing interference by outside powers. Sihanouk's overwhelming ego, his high-pitched giggle, and his love of the finer things in life, such as a daily snack of foie gras and caviar washed down with champagne, have frequently made him an object of ridicule in the American press. His constant political shifts have earned him the description "mercurial"; it is used so often that it has practically become part of his name. But many of the Western diplomats in Phnom Penh express considerable respect for Sihanouk. Charles H. Twining, a longtime Indochina expert who is the United States Special Representative to the SNC, told me, "I see Sihanouk over his whole history as a man who has maneuvered and twisted and turned with one object: to keep Cambodia independent." More than anyone else, Sihanouk is given credit for persuading the four Cambodian political factions to join in the peace agreement, despite the years of rancor.

With his courtly manners and elegant French, Sihanouk cuts a princely figure. Sheltered by China and North Korea in the 1980s, he lived in lavish palaces in Beijing and Pyongyang. China allotted him an annual stipend of $300,000, which he still receives, and one of his advisers told me that China spent as much each year maintaining his palace as it did on the upkeep of the Forbidden City. When Sihanouk returned to Phnom Penh from Beijing in November 1991, he brought with him three chefs, two banquet waiters, and a doctor to check his food for poison, all of them Chinese. Kim Il Sung, the North Korean dictator, whom Sihanouk describes as his best friend, celebrated the occasion by sending as a gift twenty-six bodyguards. Dressed in Mao suits and looking fierce, they present a stark contrast to the Cambodian soldiers stationed at the entrances to the Royal Palace, who frequently laugh and banter. Sihanouk has behaved graciously in his public encounters since his return to Phnom Penh. After a diplomatic reception at the Hotel Cambodiana, the one modern hotel in Phnom Penh, I saw him walk through the lobby, pausing to greet every hotel employee and hugging some of them. Now seventy, Sihanouk has distinguished silver hair, yet, inexplicably, his official portrait, appearing all over Phnom Penh and as a thirty-foot-high poster above the main entrance to the Royal Palace, shows a man thirty years younger, with heart-shaped lips colored ruby red.

The only figure in Cambodia who commands widespread respect, Sihanouk returned to Phnom Penh as the glue that would hold the peace process together. "Basically, the whole thing depends on Sihanouk," a UN official told me. "He's extremely important in this whole drama. If the agreement breaks down, we're out. There's no question about it." The Hun Sen government cooperated by announcing, almost immediately after his arrival, that it would recognize him as head of state—the position he held before Lon Nol ousted him in 1970. The government also quickly rewrote a bit of history to explain away Sihanouk's dalliance with the Khmer Rouge over a twenty-year span. "In fact, he was a prisoner of the Khmer Rouge after 1971," an official of the Foreign Ministry replied when I asked about Sihanouk's background. "Right before the 1979 liberation, he was kidnapped by the Khmer Rouge and the Chinese from the Royal Palace. From 1979 until the time he came back to Phnom Penh, he was a hostage of the Chinese." For his part, Sihanouk, who had once called Hun Sen a "one-eyed lackey" of Vietnam, took to describing him as his adopted son. Then, just nine days after his return, Sihanouk revealed some startling news. He said that his political party, the Sihanoukists, headed by his son Prince Norodom Ranariddh, would join with the Cambodian People's Party—the party of Hun Sen and Chea Sim—to form a coalition to govern Cambodia. Like the attack on the Khmer Rouge compound that would come four days later, this act threatened to sabotage the peace process, since the agreement called for Sihanouk, as the head of the SNC, to be neutral. But again the Khmer Rouge failed to rise to the bait. A few days later, Sihanouk, perhaps realizing his error, backed off, but the two parties are still expected to present a joint slate of candidates in the 1993 elections.

During my visit to Cambodia, I had lunch at the Hotel Cambodiana with Julio Jeldres, who has described himself as Sihanouk's special assistant; some Cambodia-watchers consider him Sihanouk's chief of staff. It is difficult to talk to Jeldres and not think of him as a character from a novel come to life. A bearded Chilean who calls Australia his home, he speaks in hushed, conspiratorial tones and draws an immediate stare from any diplomat who enters the hotel dining room. How did a Chilean-Australian come to advise a Cambodian prince? Jeldres says that he wrote a letter to the Cambodian government in 1967 asking for information about the country, and that Sihanouk answered it personally. This started a correspondence that lasted until 1981, when Sihanouk invited Jeldres to come visit him in North Korea. Jeldres had been with Sihanouk ever since. When I saw Jeldres, he was so disillusioned, he was about to quit and leave for Australia. (He returned in September 1992, to head an institute promoting democracy.) At our lunch, Jeldres was clearly angry and in a mood to speak bluntly. His complaint was that Sihanouk, instead of leading the peace process, had become its victim, confining himself to ceremonial functions while a corrupt Phnom Penh government was destroying Cambodia. "The immensity of the problems hasn't hit him yet," Jeldres said. "We wanted him to move quickly—he could maintain his neutrality and still take action. But now everything goes back to the Hun Sen administration. Sihanouk says we have to be practical and defer to the government. I have been slipping away and seeing the back streets of Phnom Penh at night, and it couldn't be worse: the squatters, no electricity, no water, no toilets. But the prince's motorcade always takes the same route, and he doesn't see any of this. I don't think there is a single idealistic government minister, one who refuses money. Sihanouk can do a lot of things for this country, because people love and respect him, but he is losing that respect."

A great surprise in speaking with Cambodians is to learn of the depth of their resentment against the Hun Sen government—the government that liberated them from the genocide of the Khmer Rouge era. It is as if the taste of freedom had stimulated their appetites, and now they wanted a feast. Half measures were no longer enough. Sok, the student who told me about the demonstrations against the Khmer Rouge, put it this way: "The situation has gone from worse to bad." For example, he said, although the Hun Sen government claims to have abandoned Communism completely, students at Phnom Penh University must still take a compulsory course in the philosophy of Marx, Lenin, and Ho Chi Minh. But now there are two differences. "This year, it's only once a week for three hours," Sok said. "Last year it was two days a week, and before that three days. I have the same teacher as last year, but he's changed his ideas. This year, he says that Ho Chi Minh and Lenin were not such good people. Now I can criticize them in my exams."

I asked Sok if he could gather together some students to discuss politics, and a couple of days later I met a group of seven on the university campus—a pleasant place, with buildings scattered in a parklike setting. The students were afraid to talk where they could be overheard, so we walked to the house of one of them and sat in his bedroom with the door shut. Sok and another student who spoke good English translated. As the conversation progressed and all seven started to loosen up, they became almost giddy at realizing that they were having an uninhibited discussion with an outsider. But none of them felt that the UN was about to usher into Cambodia an era of free speech and human rights. "If someone is caught and taken away by the Phnom Penh government, we don't know where he's gone," one student explained. "Suppose we find his body one month later. Then we know what happened, and we can go to the UN. But what good does that do, since he's already dead?" The students were outraged by the corruption. "Hun Sen is the prime minister," one said. "His elder brother is a provincial governor, and another brother is in charge of communications for the government. If I'm not a friend of Hun Sen, when I finish my studies I will have to become a cyclo driver." Nor did they have kind words for Sihanouk. "The old people like him, but the young people don't," another student said. "We are educated, and we understand what he did to Cambodia. In 1970, he went to China and supported Communism for Cambodia." While they agreed that "everyone hates the Khmer Rouge," they accepted at face value the Khmer Rouge's claim of trying to protect Cambodia from outside domination, and particularly from Vietnam. This is a key point that the Khmer Rouge are using in their attempt to take over Cambodia once again. Only for the KPNLF's Son Sann were there no harsh words, but that was because none of the students knew much about him.

A week after this discussion, and a few days after I left Cambodia, something unprecedented happened in Phnom Penh: a truly spontaneous demonstration. Where the inspiration for the demonstration came from is easy to deduce, since Cambodian television, which is controlled by the Hun Sen regime, had repeatedly broadcast the videotape of the attack on the Khmer Rouge compound, along with the government's claim that the attack was spontaneous. Apparently, no one had thought of what the consequences of this propaganda move might be, and now Hun Sen had to deal with the real thing. The demonstration was a protest against corruption—a subject that, because it interferes with their lives at the moment, inflames Cambodians with a passion that exceeds the memory of the Khmer Rouge atrocities. The rumor had spread through Phnom Penh that the minister of communications, transport, and posts, Ros Chhun, had commandeered a house and evicted six families who had been living in it, so that he could refurbish it and sell it, presumably to newly arrived diplomats, UN agencies, or aid groups, who pay huge sums for housing. Hundreds of people surrounded the house, broke the windows, hauled the furniture out, and built a bonfire. The demonstration ended peacefully after police played a recorded announcement by Hun Sen that he had fired Chhun, who is a close associate of Chea Sim—and, according to one report, his brother-in-law—and three of Chhun's deputies. "I understand that you are angry about corruption," Hun Sen said. "The government will resolve this problem."

A new demonstration the next day had a less happy ending. This one, by medical students, quickly escalated, with demonstrators throwing rocks and the police firing into the air. According to Western reporters on the scene, by evening the army was patrolling Achar Mean Boulevard and shooting into crowds of demonstrators. One journalist reported overhearing the vice-minister of the interior instructing the soldiers several times on a two-way radio to "do what is necessary to protect yourselves," and adding, "Do you understand me?" The toll was at least eight dead. The government closed the schools for two weeks, instituted a 10:00 p.m. curfew, and passed a law banning all demonstrations without prior government permission. Hun Sen told reporters the curbs were necessary because investigations into the violence had pointed to "armed elements," which his foreign minister suspected were Khmer Rouge supporters. But not everyone was buying that story. I talked on the phone with Khieu Kanharith, a former newspaper editor and a leading Cambodian dissident. He expressed some strong views, even though he had recently become an adviser to Hun Sen. "Hun Sen lost a lot of his credibility because of the demonstrations," Kanharith said. "He didn't know how to handle the situation. He should have tried to find an ombudsman to talk to the students. To use violence against the demonstrators was a big mistake. They weren't asking to topple the government; they were only asking for social justice."

By coincidence, I had taken a tour of the medical school ten days before the demonstration, and had found conditions there appalling even by the standards of Third World Asia. The Khmer Rouge had destroyed all the medical documents and textbooks, and although the curriculum is in French, the Hun Sen government had been unable to turn to France for help. "Western Europe didn't help my country. It only helped the Pol Pot regime," the school's director, Dr. Ly Po, told me. Studying was done from mimeographed sheets; as many as four hundred students were jammed into classrooms built for a hundred. When I visited the chemistry laboratory, the electricity wasn't working, and barren shelves contained only a few brown bottles, mostly empty, and a few yellowed glass beakers. "The students hate the Hun Sen government, because it has made the people suffer for many years," one medical student said. "Everyone in government is a rich man. They make their profits from the people."

The demonstrators out on the streets and the many other Cambodians incensed by corruption had every reason to protest. Corruption in Phnom Penh today goes far beyond the level of government ministers' taking something extra, in business transactions or in dealings with foreigners, to supplement their meager salaries. Smuggling and financial manipulation have created an entire shadow economy, robbing Cambodia of desperately needed revenues from taxation. Cambodia has so little foreign exchange that its government is essentially bankrupt, and its reserves can't cover the purchase of enough oil to maintain an uninterrupted supply of electricity. Yet ship after ship loaded with luxury goods from Singapore—motorcycles, boom boxes, fancy cars—docks in Phnom Penh daily. A wealthy Cambodian businessman I met told me how the shadow economy works. "All the business deals are using Cambodia to pass merchandise from Thailand and Singapore to Vietnam and China," he said. "It started in 1987, when overseas Vietnamese began sending money to their relatives. Vietnam has strict rules on imported products like VCRs, televisions, beer, and cigarettes. Either it doesn't allow them into the country or it levies a big import tax. The people who own the big cars in Phnom Penh are in the smuggling business. Ten percent of them are Khmer, and 90 percent are ethnic Chinese. The Chinese mafia brings in shiploads of VCRs, motorbikes, and cigarettes. Customs officials, government ministers, and army officers all get a share. Sometimes the payoff could be a million dollars a shipload. I know one guy who brought in a shipload of stuff worth seven million dollars. Pirates attacked the ship and took it all."

During my stay in Phnom Penh, I got to witness one of the more impressive schemes of manipulation. The Cambodian currency, the riel, had stood at 1,100 to the dollar when Prince Sihanouk returned, and stood at 960 when I arrived, two weeks later. Then shortly thereafter it increased in value even further, to 380. This phenomenon is the equivalent of dropping a ball from the roof of a building and seeing it rise instead of fall—it defies one of the basic laws of economics. Foreigners had been flooding into Cambodia, creating a situation in which a huge amount of new money was chasing a limited supply of available goods, and that is a certain prescription for inflation of the national currency. But instead of being worth less, the riel had increased in dollar value by 300 percent in two months—perhaps a world record. I got a hint of the explanation when I tried to acquire as a souvenir a five-hundred-riel note, the largest banknote in circulation. It took me several days to find one. Someone had clearly cornered the market, but there were only rumors about who it might be. The government could have taken advantage of the circumstances to print new currency and reinflate the riel to its former level, thereby getting enough new money to pay its soldiers, buy oil, and take care of other desperate needs. It didn't—probably because the manipulation of the riel took place with government connivance. "I heard that Thai bankers here were responsible," a friend in Phnom Penh told me. "They brought gold into the country and bought riels with it to corner the market. They have all the five-hundred-riel notes."

Corruption is not limited to such grand schemes. Patients must pay to be admitted into "free" hospitals, to receive donated drugs, to get a transfusion of blood originally donated by the Red Cross. A group based in France called Handicap International has a program in Cambodia to fit people with artificial limbs, but under the agreement that allowed the organization to come into the country the Cambodian government selects the patients. All those selected are either maimed government soldiers or civilians who are able to pay bribes to the officials who make the selection. The Indochina Project, a Washington-based research and aid group sponsored by the Vietnam Veterans of America Foundation, runs a prosthetics clinic at Kien Khleang, across the river from Phnom Penh. About a hundred and fifty amputees live at the site and receive training to enable Cambodia to be self-sufficient in manufacturing and fitting artificial limbs. "Of the thirty people who worked at Kien Khleang originally, none were handicapped," Ron Podlaski, who heads the program, told me. "Officials from the ministry of social affairs sent their families for employment. I said, 'I don't want to employ your families, I want to hire the handicapped.' Here's a ministry that graduates the handicapped from school training and then won't consider them for jobs."

To many Cambodians, the most infuriating aspect of corruption presents the extraordinary spectacle of government ministers selling off state-owned houses and other buildings and pocketing the proceeds. These transactions are made possible by the uncertain status of property ownership in Cambodia. Not only did the Khmer Rouge destroy all property records but then the Vietnam-backed government declared that all property belonged to the state. In 1989, the Hun Sen government began a privatization program. For several government ministers, a rainbow suddenly ended at whatever buildings they occupied. Stretching the concept of the free market to its extreme, they sold their buildings to foreigners and moved their ministries to smaller quarters. They also held the Cambodian equivalent of garage sales to make money on the contents: light fixtures, doors, desks, chairs. The corruption extended to factories, which were shut down and sold to foreigners, putting workers out of a job. Government officials appropriated villas and rented them at high prices to foreign diplomats and relief agencies.

Government officials are somewhat less than convincing when they say they're going to stop all this. "Corruption is happening not only in Cambodia but all over the world, and especially in countries with free-market economies," Ngoun Pen, the vice-minister of finance, told me. "Our government has set up many measures to prevent corruption, and has sent directions to all ministries to stop it." When I asked him about all the Mercedes-Benzes and BMWs on the roads, his reply was, "The cars and motorcycles being used in Phnom Penh are secondhand. In other countries, they would be gathered and put into the furnace." In November 1991, when Charles Twining presented his credentials to Prince Sihanouk as the American representative to the SNC, Sihanouk, who relishes creating controversy, told him, "If you need Cambodians to help, please pay them yourself directly. Please don't give your money to my administration. You know, in Asia we cannot avoid corruption." Over the next three months, Sihanouk seemed to be trying to prove the truth of his words, for three of his children got high posts in government. His son Chakkrapong became a deputy prime minister, his daughter Bopha Devi became deputy minister of information and culture, and his son Sihamoni in late 1992 took up the post of ambassador to the UN. Sihamoni prepared for his new position by serving as a dance teacher in Paris. As for Hun Sen, accusations swirl around his family—particularly allegations of financial dealings involving his wife and foreign businessmen.

The outrage of Cambodians over this corruption, which has the potential to destroy the peace process if demonstrators and Hun Sen's army engage in further clashes, cannot be discounted. The revulsion has been best expressed in an open letter written in elegant French by a Cambodian dissident who calls himself Sam Rainsy. I could find no one who knows who he really is, but the letter circulated widely; many journalists in Bangkok who cover Cambodia received copies. The letter was written in the midst of the anticorruption demonstrations:

> The rumblings of revolt are heard everywhere. It would be hard to imagine a more unpopular regime than the one currently installed in Phnom Penh. . . . We have a state without law, corroded by corruption, which has become totally irresponsible and is capable of anything. At the head of this system are several boorish individuals with their families and their clans. They are true brutes, who have no sense of the public good or of the national interest. From the moment that they reign in the country, they consider that everything belongs to them and that they can do what they wish with all the goods of the state and nation as if they were spoils of war. Knowing that they're threatened by the elections organized under the auspices of the United Nations, and by more competent people, who will toss them out of their command post, they are selling at clearance prices all the goods of the state, and are pocketing the sales money for strictly personal ends. We are witnessing acts that revolt the population, acts inconceivable in the West or in any civilized country. . . . The people of Phnom Penh are right to revolt. Their courage deserves our admiration and support.

With the Cambodian People's Party government tarred by corruption and by acts of repression in putting down the student demonstrations, and with the Khmer Rouge the only visible alternative, Cambodia should, in theory, be ripe for new political parties. That is exactly what the peace process is designed to bring about, through free and open discussions, access to the media, and the ability to campaign anywhere in the country under UN protection. But, next to walking through a field strewn with land mines, planning a political party seems just now to be the most dangerous activity in Cambodia. The first person to try it, back in May 1990, was Ung Phan, then the minister of communications, transport, and posts. He circulated proposals for a new political party among a few friends, and one of them apparently leaked the document. The Cambodian government accused Ung Phan and at least five associates of plotting to sabotage the state, and they were thrown into the notorious T3 prison, in central Phnom Penh, where they languished for seventeen months, until their release in October 1991. The arrests clearly represented a power play by Hun Sen's rival Chea Sim, since Ung Phan and Hun Sen were longtime friends. A month after Phan's arrest, Khieu Kanharith, then the editor of the weekly newspaper *Kampuchea*, advocated multiparty elections. The government controls all of Cambodia's newspapers, and Chea Sim immediately fired Kanharith. "I said I advocated multiparty elections for later, not then," Kanharith told me, "but they took away my right to travel out of the country."

In December 1991, with the peace agreement and the protection it at least theoretically offers already in effect, I tried unsuccessfully to get in touch with Ung Phan, who was in hiding. Through a friend of mine, I was able to find one of the associates who had been imprisoned with him. The associate agreed to speak with my friend, not with me, and only in a car while driving around Phnom Penh, so they couldn't be overheard. He allowed my friend to take notes but did not allow direct quotes. "X says his political party is operating underground," my friend wrote to me. "He says that the Khmer Rouge, Sihanoukists, and the KPNLF are regarded by the government as foreign-backed parties, and that no internal new parties will be permitted to form. He believes that the government will kill the leaders of any new opposition parties and arrest their followers. History will repeat itself, he says—the foreigners will decide, and the Cambodians will accept their decisions."

The cloak-and-dagger tactics of X proved to be prudent rather than paranoid. On January 17, 1992, Ung Phan emerged from hiding to announce the formation of Cambodia's first new party, the Free Democratic Society Party, claiming already to have the support of five thousand people for the new venture. Eleven days later, four or five men in a jeep pulled alongside Ung Phan's car and shot at him, hitting him three times in one shoulder. Ung Phan was lucky. The week before, Tea Bun Long, a senior government official in charge of religious affairs who was an outspoken critic of corruption, had been abducted outside his Phnom Penh home, again by men in a jeep; his bullet-riddled body was found near Phnom Penh the next day. Then, on March 15, one of Ung Phan's associates, Yang Horn, was, according to his family, beaten into a coma as he left a restaurant. Hun Sen seems to have had no prior knowledge of these actions. After the Ung Phan shooting, reporters saw the prime minister in the hospital weeping while Phan underwent surgery, and later he took his friend to his house to recover. While suspicion for the shootings focused on security forces allied with the Chea Sim faction of the People's Party, Hun Sen discounted this possibility, reasoning that he himself had never been the target of an attempted assassination, despite the political and economic reforms he had instituted. Bill Herod, the program director in Washington for the Indochina Project, told me, "I spoke with several politically active Cambodians. There was a suspicion they were dealing with death squads functioning from deep inside the government. But they had no real evidence to back it up."

During my visit to Cambodia, the political maneuverings, the demonstrations, and the suppression of dissent were being monitored by an American diplomatic staff that numbered just five. They had not yet set up offices and were working out of bedrooms in the Hotel Cambodiana, without a secretary and with a filing system that consisted of stacking documents on the floor. They had thought that they could communicate with the United States through a portable transmitter hooked up to a communications satellite, but as soon as they plugged in the transmitter, which was supposed to work with any kind of electric current, it burned out. Because the Cambodiana's switchboard operators had not yet mastered the alphabetizing of Western names, I found that I could reach Charles Twining, the chief American diplomat, only by walking to the hotel and leaving a message. Twining has to perform a difficult diplomatic dance as the American representative to the SNC. He must operate in Cambodia without any official contacts with the Cambodian government, because the United States has always refused to recognize the Hun Sen regime. Twining and his staff also refuse to meet with the Khmer Rouge delegates to the SNC, although the United States has maintained that the peace process could not succeed without Khmer Rouge participation. But Twining, an experienced Indochina analyst for the State Department, who speaks fluent Khmer and appears unscarred by the animosities that have long governed American policy in that area, seems to be well qualified for his task. "I have been seeing a lot of political maneuvering going on among the Cambodians," he told me. "They have to stake out positions, and we foreigners have to sit down and be patient. As long as Cambodia remains so unstable, you have all of Southeast Asia affected by this. Over the long run, you want the countries of Indochina integrated into Southeast Asia, and you've got to have Cambodia to do it. We feel a particular responsibility for this."

The United States has not always been so reasonable in its dealings with Cambodia. Blinded by hatred of the Vietnamese Communists, it looked upon Vietnam's 1978 invasion of Cambodia as unprovoked aggression, notwithstanding Pol Pot's provocation of Vietnam and the fact that Vietnam had overthrown a genocidal regime. The United States immediately blocked all humanitarian and medical aid to the Cambodian government, and by December 1981 it had succeeded in getting UN agencies to cut off most of their relief efforts as well. In January 1982, when a Mennonite relief agency wanted to send a shipment of pens and pencils to Cambodian children, the Commerce Department denied it an export license.

The remnants of the Khmer Rouge, massed on the border of Thailand, had an easier time. "My people fear the return of the Khmer Rouge the most," Prince Sihanouk said in 1980. "That is the number-one problem, but Washington is not aware of the fact. . . . The only idea that guides the U.S. is the efficiency of the Khmer Rouge." On the theory that the enemy of my enemy is my friend, the United States, China, Thailand, Singapore, and several other nations began a secret effort, which lasted through the 1980s, to insure that the Khmer Rouge remained viable as a fighting force and could serve as a counterweight against Vietnam and its ally the Soviet Union. Without this aid, the Pol Pot forces would have faced extinction. But the food and arms that flowed to the Thai border allowed them to rebuild their army and to keep enough people under their control to give a veneer of legitimacy to their claim as the true Cambodian government. "I was on the Thai-Cambodian border in early 1979," Ben Kiernan, a Cambodia specialist who is an associate professor of history at Yale, told me. "The Khmer Rouge were able to evacuate huge numbers of people forcibly into Thailand. They would shoot people in Thai territory, including Thai farmers who were passing through. The Thais gave the Khmer Rouge crucial sanctuary. The Khmer Rouge took half a million people into the hills along both sides of the border."

The United States sought to secure the future of the Khmer Rouge without appearing to support a genocidal regime, and the key to this strategy was China, then America's newfound ally and a longtime enemy of Vietnam. "I encouraged the Chinese to support Pol Pot," Zbigniew Brzezinski, who had been President Carter's national security adviser, told the American journalist Elizabeth Becker in 1981. In her book on the Khmer Rouge era, *When the War Was Over*, she writes, "The result was a policy that the United States continued to follow during the subsequent Republican administration. The United States 'winked, semi-publicly,' in Brzezinski's words, while encouraging China and Thailand to give the Khmer Rouge direct aid to fight against the Vietnamese occupation." China, with Thai connivance, funneled arms and money to the Pol Pot forces; and the UN, because the Khmer Rouge continued to hold the Cambodian seat in the General Assembly, which it had assumed in 1975, sent humanitarian aid. Beginning in 1979, America voted year after year for a decade to keep the Khmer Rouge in the UN rather than give the seat to the Phnom Penh government. In 1982, when other Western nations started to rebel against this policy, the Reagan administration's solution was to persuade the two non-Communist Cambodian factions, the Sihanoukists and the KPNLF, to form an alliance with the Khmer Rouge. As part of a broad-based coalition that included the so-called non-Communist resistance, the Khmer Rouge could be made more palatable. In the early 1980s, both Sihanouk and the KPNLF's Son Sann, the latter long a favorite of Washington, told interviewers that the United States had forced them into the coalition as a condition of their getting aid. For Sihanouk, joining the

Khmer Rouge was the bitterest of pills, for not only had the Khmer Rouge made him a prisoner in the Royal Palace during their rule but they had murdered five of his sons and daughters and fourteen of his grandchildren and other relatives.

To this day, the details of American aid to Pol Pot's partners remain cloaked in secrecy. The subject is a sensitive one because the Sihanoukists and the KPNLF combined could have fielded only a few thousand ill-trained, ill-equipped troops and had to depend on the Khmer Rouge army for their survival. Since neither of the resistance factions was able to operate independently as an effective fighting force, any military aid to them would have inevitably ended up helping Pol Pot in his effort to retake Cambodia. The United States has consistently denied supplying arms to the resistance, but when Peter Jennings, in an ABC News documentary that was broadcast in April 1990, asked Richard Solomon, the assistant secretary of state for East Asian and Pacific affairs, what the United States would do if it found that the Sihanoukists and the KPNLF were fighting side by side with the army of Pol Pot, Solomon replied, "If there was a judgment made that this violated the law, then we would have to cut off arms." He quickly claimed to have misspoken.

Although the Khmer Rouge are not normally a subject of humor, American policy has provided one moment of semi-comic relief. By the late eighties, the Hun Sen government had backed off from its rigid Communist ideology and eased up on repression. And by the end of 1989, Vietnam had completed a unilateral withdrawal of its troops from Cambodia, thereby undermining the entire rationale for supporting the Pol Pot forces. These moves left defenders of the Khmer Rouge thrashing around for new justifications. In January 1991, James Pringle, a British journalist who specializes in Cambodia, wrote in the Bangkok *Post* about a story he had been given by "Western intelligence sources along the Thai-Cambodian border," which is usually a euphemism for the CIA. The news was that Pol Pot had become an environmentalist and was calling on Cambodians to protect endangered species. "The sources said that, in areas where poaching is most serious, the Khmer Rouge is fencing off animal sanctuaries," Pringle wrote. "Anyone contravening Pol Pot's 'green' directive along the northern border of Cambodia . . . is brought before a jungle court and is normally sentenced to four days' labour on constructing fencing for animal sanctuaries, the sources add."

Critics of American policy toward Cambodia charge that in 1989, Washington sabotaged an agreement that had been worked out over two years by Hun Sen and Sihanouk, under which Sihanouk would abandon the Khmer Rouge and form an alliance with the Phnom Penh government. By creating a strong Cambodian government, with Hun Sen providing the troops and Sihanouk the international respectability needed in order to get outside aid, such an alliance could have proved the best solution for dealing with the Khmer Rouge. But at an international conference on Cambodia held in Paris in August 1989, Sihanouk unexpectedly backed off. Bill Herod, of the Indochina Project, contends that the United States played a key role in the collapse of that proposed alliance, by not offering Sihanouk support if he cut ties with the Khmer Rouge and its sponsor, China. Herod told me that he had learned from two diplomats who participated in the conference that "Sihanouk was convinced that if he moved away from the Chinese by leaving the Khmer Rouge and associating himself with Hun Sen, no one in the international community would support him—specifically, the Americans." He went on, "The Chinese had always backed him and given him a safe haven. He believed in Paris that if he left them he would be on his own. The United States opposed the alliance because it would have legitimatized the Hun Sen government. At that time, they regarded Hun Sen as a Vietnamese puppet, so whether or not Vietnamese troops were in Cambodia was irrelevant. Sihanouk looked around him in Paris and got cold feet."

The peace agreement came about two years later only because both the United States and China had changed their policies toward Cambodia. China no longer needed the Khmer Rouge as a force against the alliance of Hun Sen, Vietnam, and the Soviet Union, for the Soviets had retreated into their internal problems and Vietnam had withdrawn its troops from Cambodia. Moreover, China and Vietnam had found common ground in their struggle to preserve their anachronistic Communist systems. Embarrassed by the debacle of Tiananmen Square and eager to make a positive move on the diplomatic scene, China was now ready to back a Cambodian peace accord. As for the United States, the Bush administration did a dramatic about-face in July 1990, when Secretary of State James Baker announced that Washington was prepared to withdraw support of the Khmer Rouge for the Cambodian seat at the United Nations and would open talks with Hanoi on bringing peace to Cambodia. Bill Herod maintains that the American shift "was a direct and immediate response to congressional pressure," which had increased after a secret briefing by intelligence agencies disclosed to members of a Senate committee that the administration had known that some of its aid to the non-Communist resistance may have been funneled through to the Khmer Rouge, in violation of a law that Congress had passed in 1985.

To claim, as the State Department does, that the Khmer Rouge were included in the peace agreement because the United States, China, Thailand, and other nations felt that Cambodia would be more secure with the Khmer Rouge on the inside, as part of the election process, than with it on the border, as a guerrilla force, is perhaps to interpret events in an overgenerous light. The history of the 1980s offers another possible explanation—that of the raw exercise of superpower politics. The failed alliance in 1989 between Hun Sen and Sihanouk would have represented an internal Cambodian solution, with the United States and other major powers left out in the cold. By contrast—praiseworthy though the principle of free elections may be—what emerged successfully from Paris in October 1991 was something quite different. As Khieu Kanharith has said, "The UN plan was mapped out not for the Cambodian people but to please the superpowers." For a decade, these superpowers had used the Khmer Rouge, despite their genocidal tendencies, as a pawn in a chess game, and in Paris the superpowers showed little inclination to change the strategy.

While the Khmer Rouge, the Hun Sen government, and the Sihanoukists are all major players in the struggle for the future of Cambodia, practically nothing has been heard from the fourth faction in the peace process, the KPNLF. In the 1980s, the United States strongly supported this anti-Communist group as the great democratic hope for Cambodia. (The State Department never seemed bothered that the group's leader, Son Sann, lacked a support base within Cambodia itself.) Since the KPNLF holds two seats on the SNC, just as the Khmer Rouge and the Sihanoukists do, during my stay in Phnom Penh I began to wonder what had happened to it. When I asked a Western diplomat who should have known, he couldn't tell me. "If the KPNLF disappeared from sight, no one would have noticed," he said. Finding the group's headquarters took a bit of sleuthing, with the aid of a determined motorbike driver who took me all over the city to check out leads. Finally we located the KPNLF villa, on a busy street near the National Stadium. Son Sann was in Bangkok, I was told, but his second-in-command, Ieng Mouly, eagerly agreed to answer questions. "How did you find us?" he asked, saying that of the hundreds of reporters who had passed through Phnom Penh, I was the first to request an interview. Mouly motioned me into a big barren room. "Now there are chairs, but when we came there was nothing," he said. "We still have no telephone." He described his party's ideology as based on "democracy, liberalism, and Buddhism," but said that the alliance on the Thai border with the Khmer Rouge had been "the only way to liberate our country from the Vietnamese." I asked about an open secret: Had the CIA in fact financed the KPNLF? "You can say that," Mouly replied, "but the covert aid finished in 1988." Now the group is looking for campaign funds, and Mouly said, somewhat wistfully, "Maybe we will ask Mrs. Thatcher's party."

The village of Kompong Speu, twenty-five miles southwest of Phnom Penh, is situated on one of the few decent roads in Cambodia, and the drive from the capital takes less than an hour. Another journalist and I went there one morning without asking the Foreign Ministry's permission; the Foreign Ministry had been so overwhelmed with visiting diplomats and reporters that it no longer had sufficient staff to keep tabs on everyone. Even though Kompong Speu is close to Phnom Penh, Khmer Rouge guerrillas roam the nearby Elephant Mountains. A few days before my visit, government forces encountered some Khmer Rouge in Kompong Speu, and there was a brief skirmish, which left one of Hun Sen's soldiers shot through the stomach. From Kompong Speu, we headed west down a dirt road, and soon we were in a refugee settlement called O Koki, one of the camps for people displaced by the fighting among the Cambodian factions. This was a picture of life in Cambodia that I saw nowhere in Phnom Penh—not even in the poorest back alleys. People were dressed in dirty rags; many children showed signs of malnutrition; and goiter and disfiguring eye diseases were common afflictions. The settlement stretched on for miles, with simple huts of bamboo and thatch built in clusters along dirt roads. The landscape was completely bare, a victim of deforestation, and the nearest wood for cooking was miles away. As people walked along the dirt roads, passing vehicles enveloped them in clouds of dust.

Relief workers say that the poverty and despair that is so striking in O Koki is far from the worst in rural Cambodia. Because O Koki is so near Phnom Penh, and the road is good enough to be passable all year, relief agencies provide the camp with services that don't exist elsewhere in the country. Nevertheless, O Koki illustrates dramatically the gap between Phnom Penh and the rest of the country—a gap that will be central to any Khmer Rouge strategy to retake Cambodia. Most of the future aid that flows into Cambodia will inevitably appear first in Phnom Penh, and widen the already serious disparity with the countryside—a situation that the Khmer Rouge once before, in the early 1970s, exploited with skill. And if the first few months of the peace process are any indication, the new aid will fuel even more corruption, and more resentment on the part of those who have been left out. In December 1991, with the peace process just beginning, the appearance of the army in the streets of Phnom Penh, shooting at people who were demonstrating against corruption, brought back memories of similar scenes during the Lon Nol regime. Writing about the demonstrations in the *Far Eastern Economic Review*, Nate Thayer pointed out, "The unrest shifted the focus of anger from the murderous years of Khmer Rouge rule to the desperate economic conditions, political repression and official greed that now exist in the country. The undermining of the legitimacy of the current government could open the door to the only other group that has a sophisticated political organisation—the Khmer Rouge."

The Khmer Rouge hold no press briefings to announce their future plans. Pol Pot continues to work secretly on the Thai border, where he is under the protection of the Thai military. When Prince Sihanouk was asked at a press conference how reporters could locate Pol Pot, he replied, "Perhaps you may see General Suchinda Kraprayoon, the prestigious commander in chief of the Royal Thai Army [who achieved notoriety a few months later as Thailand's prime minister], and negotiate with him." Although the Thai military no longer fears Vietnam, it is favorably disposed toward the Khmer Rouge, because it gets a share of the profits from lucrative logging and gem-mining operations in the territory in western Cambodia that the Khmer Rouge control. In June 1991, according to several reports, Pol Pot secretly went to the Thai beach resort of Pattaya to dictate to Khmer Rouge negotiators what concessions they could offer in peace negotiations taking place there. Pol Pot's desire to get the peace process going apparently brought unexpected progress in the negotiations, resolving disputes about representation on the SNC.

The actions of the Khmer Rouge so far make clear that a central element in their strategy to retake Cambodia involves winning the support of the rural areas, where 80 percent of the Cambodians live, by capitalizing on the resentment felt toward Phnom Penh and the Hun Sen government. "The Khmer Rouge have been buying rice at twice the market price," a Western diplomat in Phnom Penh told me. "When they capture a village chief, they talk to him for a couple of days and then let him go, instead of killing him."

I asked Leah Melnick, an American photographer in Phnom Penh who speaks Khmer and has traveled widely in Khmer Rouge territory, about the tactics. "My sense is that the Khmer Rouge find support in areas where they had support in the early 1970s," she told me. "In some places, they operate by threatening people; in other places, they offer the best deal for rice and meat. The Sihanoukists and the KPNLF have a worse reputation for stealing food than the Khmer Rouge do."

When a Reuters correspondent visited Khmer Rouge areas in southwest Cambodia in January 1992, he reported that "the Khmer Rouge are earning some respect among villagers, who say their main problems are thieving government troops and land mines." He quoted the owner of a rice mill as saying, "The Khmer Rouge do not steal. They come down from the mountain and bargain for pigs, rice, and chickens. They invite us to believe in them. The military robs us." For their effort, the Khmer Rouge are well financed. Their cross-border trade in timber and gems brings them an estimated $70 million to $100 million a year, and they are reported to have been buying bulldozers, tractors, and trucks to assist villagers in the territory they hold.

The Khmer Rouge operations in Cambodia are shrouded in mystery. One of the biggest unanswered questions involves their unpredictable behavior, which often belies that of a group conducting a "hearts and minds" campaign to win the support of the rural population. In January 1992, they initiated a series of attacks on villages in government-controlled Kompong Thom Province, northeast of the capital. At least fifty civilians were killed or wounded, twenty-five villages came under mortar attack, and eleven thousand people had to flee their homes. In March, they launched another offensive in northern Cambodia, apparently to gain more territory before the UN troops arrived. Then in May they renewed their attacks in Kompong Thom; UN peacekeepers called the attacks the worst violations to date of the peace accord. Many other credible reports of Khmer Rouge atrocities have surfaced since the peace process began. At O Koki, I interviewed a twenty-five-year-old woman who had escaped from Khmer Rouge–held territory just three weeks before. No government officials were around during the interview—only some members of her family, another journalist, and a translator we had taken with us—and her story seemed genuine. She told of men from her village, including her husband on two occasions, being forced to trek to the Thai border carrying food and ammunition for Khmer Rouge soldiers; some of the men died of starvation during the journey. A cousin of hers who was listening to her story then told us that ten Khmer Rouge soldiers had barged into his house eight months before, taken his teenage son outside, and executed him on the spot. One possible explanation for this sort of behavior is that the Khmer Rouge devote their pacification program to areas where they think it will succeed and operate with traditional ruthlessness in other areas to instill fear.

The Khmer Rouge have not changed their leaders and have not changed their tactics since the early 1970s. Every Cambodian knows of their genocide, and it's likely that most Cambodians fear them. Yet I left Cambodia with a conclusion that I found inescapable: the Khmer Rouge could eventually come back to power through the peace process. During my interviews, I heard outlined again and again a scenario according to which they could emerge victorious. It begins when the alliance of Hun Sen and Sihanouk sweeps the forthcoming election, with the Khmer Rouge getting perhaps 20 percent of the votes. The UN troops and administrators withdraw, removing the one check on corruption. With foreign aid and new investment flowing into Cambodia, opportunities for corruption abound, and the government takes full advantage of them. The Khmer Rouge exploit this—in the words of one Western diplomat, "they play up the corruption, the night clubs, the fat cats in Phnom Penh while the rest of the country suffers"—and lead the rural population to revolt against Phnom Penh. In the following election or the one after that—the Khmer Rouge have always been patient—they win at the ballot box. Or, alternatively, their army is lying in wait at the Thai border. "It's a worry," I was told by another diplomat in Phnom Penh, who is the ambassador to the SNC from a Western country that played a major role in the peace process. "I think the Khmer Rouge honestly expect to lose the elections, but they also expect the successor government to fall apart of its own dead weight," he went on. "They think they can come to power peacefully, which would be a horrifying prospect. They go out in certain areas that have never been given anything by a government in Phnom Penh, and win support by providing services."

I asked this ambassador, who agreed to the interview on the condition that he not be identified, if their plan could work. "Sure, why not?" he replied. "If the rich become very rich and ignore the problems of the countryside, it's very feasible someone could take advantage of that discontent. You can't be absolutely confident that the Sihanoukists and Hun Sen can run the country."

If this is the eventual hope of the Khmer Rouge, it makes clear what is otherwise inexplicable—why they have been so eager to participate in the peace process, making compromises during the negotiations, and ignoring such provocations as the attack on their headquarters and the move by Sihanouk to ally himself with Hun Sen. Throughout the 1980s, despite the flow of arms and money from China through Thailand, the Khmer Rouge were unable to achieve military gains. In 1989, after the withdrawal of the Vietnamese troops from Cambodia, the imminent collapse of Hun Sen's army was predicted. Bill Herod says, "It was widely assumed by many analysts, including me, that the Khmer Rouge would make significant progress after the Vietnamese left. But this wasn't true. In one instance Phnom Penh was able to hold its ground on three different fronts." If Pol Pot looked at those failures realistically, the prospect of the peace process must have seemed like a gift from heaven.

In Phnom Penh, I began to understand why the Khmer Rouge, after what they had inflicted on Cambodia, could still have hopes for support. By positioning themselves as the only true nationalists, they have tapped into a deep vein of resentment against the foreign powers that for this entire century have dominated Cambodia—rule by France, occupation by the Japanese, bombing by the United States, and, finally, invasion by Vietnam, their historical enemy. The Cambodians' hatred of the Vietnamese cannot be overstated. In 1989, Prince Sihanouk said, "The Khmer Rouge are tigers. But I would rather be eaten by a Khmer Rouge tiger than by a Vietnamese crocodile, because the Khmer

Rouge are true patriots. Oh, they are vicious, they are cruel; they are murderers. But they are not traitors like Hun Sen." Even if this statement reflected nothing more than the expediency of the moment, it accurately depicts how many Cambodians feel about the Hun Sen government, particularly now that the resentment over its former association with Vietnam has been exacerbated by its current corruption. When I met with the seven students from Phnom Penh University, I asked them why they hated the Vietnamese, since Vietnam had liberated Cambodia from the Khmer Rouge tyranny. "For many thousands of years we have been enemies," one student replied. "Vietnam wanted to help the Cambodian people only so it could take things in return— timber, fish, rice, rubber, oil." I put the same question to the Cambodian businessman who had told me about the shadow economy. His reply, coming from an educated man who had given persuasive answers to previous questions, was jarring. "The Vietnamese want to take over this territory so badly they'd do anything," he said. "The Vietnamese people like to steal. Anything they can sell they'll steal. Even the telephone cord— one day they climbed a tree to cut my telephone cord. If you take your shoes off to go into a house, they'll steal your shoes. They have some smoke they blow toward your room that makes you faint, and then they steal everything in your house."

If there is even a remote chance of an eventual Khmer Rouge victory—an occurrence several Western countries, including the United States, have said would be intolerable—why were the Khmer Rouge included as participants in the peace process? The official American answer came in October 1991, from Assistant Secretary of State Richard Solomon. "Continuing warfare would give the Khmer Rouge their best chance at a return to power," he told a congressional panel. "The settlement agreement obliges the Khmer Rouge to turn from the battlefield, where they have particular strengths and experience, to the ballot box, where they can be held accountable by the Cambodian people for their bloody record." Solomon's statement casts much too rosy a glow on the Khmer Rouge military, which failed in the 1980s under far more propitious circumstances than they would encounter today. But the Khmer Rouge participation has also drawn more objective supporters. Elizabeth Becker, whose book chronicled the Khmer Rouge atrocities, wrote in the Washington *Post* that the peace plan "eliminates the conditions the Khmer Rouge have always needed to win a war: foreign arms (Chinese), foreign sanctuary (Thailand), and that horrible isolation from the rest of the world that has made the people vulnerable to Pol Pot's party and army."

Some other analysts of Cambodia, however, see a different picture—that of a military organization, unsuccessful for thirteen years in its attempt to gain more territory, suddenly getting a new lease on life. Bill Herod said to me, "Including the Khmer Rouge in the peace process gives them political legitimacy they haven't earned. They will have access to the airwaves and the ability to run a campaign in public. It gives them the advantage of being able to play in the political arena as a legitimatized party. I would fully expect the Khmer Rouge to continue to function in the jungles, in remote areas, no matter what happens in the peace process. There is no reason to believe they will respect the political process in areas where they don't win in the election."

Ben Kiernan, the Yale Cambodia specialist who has written extensively on the Khmer Rouge, also calls into question the idea that Cambodia is safer with the Khmer Rouge on the inside. He maintains that the peace process has actually made them more of a military threat, not less, because they are getting "a chance to improve their military position by hiding their troops and arms while the other factions lose seventy percent to demobilization by the UN." In an essay on the making of the peace agreement Kiernan writes, "Few UN or other monitors will risk mines and malaria to comb the Cardamom mountains, or the jungles of northern Cambodia, to uncover hidden Khmer Rouge camps and caches. Further, the UN plan is ominously weak on procedures for locating hidden arms depots." And a *New York Times* article by Philip Shenon, published only nineteen days after the signing of the peace accord, reported that the Khmer Rouge had already begun hiding troops and weapons, in violation of the agreement's disarmament provisions. The article stated, "According to intelligence reports and accounts from Cambodian refugees crossing into Thailand, the Khmer Rouge has put aside enough weapons and ammunition in the Cardamom mountains of western Cambodia and elsewhere to allow it to fight on for years. Khmer Rouge soldiers are also being told to hide in remote base camps to prevent their detection by UN inspectors."

I asked Kiernan why many Cambodians supported the inclusion of the Khmer Rouge in the peace process despite all these dangers, and he replied that they were reacting to the fact that the peace plan was promoted by the five permanent members of the UN Security Council. "It's quite understandable why Cambodians in Phnom Penh think they can't just throw off the Khmer Rouge if the five superpowers tell them they can't," he said. "They're realistic people and quite pragmatic in their acknowledgment that, whatever the Permanent Five does, it would certainly be dangerous to oppose it."

The five superpowers had another feasible alternative to inviting the Khmer Rouge back to Phnom Penh or leaving them on the border as a guerrilla movement. They could have done what the Allies did with the Nazis in the Second World War: secure their defeat and begin war-crimes prosecutions. Already too weak militarily to challenge the Cambodian army successfully, the Khmer Rouge would have been decimated if the United States and other Western nations had persuaded China and Thailand to withdraw their support. Since China, having resolved its differences with Vietnam, had no further use for the Khmer Rouge, and since Thailand, where military decisions often have a dollar sign attached to them, was eying the business opportunities in Phnom Penh, a little arm-twisting might well have gone a long way. But the United States did not insist, nor did it show any interest in war-crimes prosecutions, despite Pol Pot's record. In his 1990 documentary, Peter Jennings said to Assistant Secretary of State Solomon, "You were at the Cambodian peace talks. You sat not far from a leading member of the Khmer Rouge who, I assume, you accept is guilty of genocide. Why didn't you try to have him arrested?" Solomon replied, "What does that lead to in the way of a settlement of this conflict? You arrest one man, that doesn't solve the problem." Jennings persisted, asking, "Are there not new guidelines which say we can go to other countries, even without their permission, and arrest people we deem guilty of international crimes?" Solomon's answer was that the United States was working for "the creation of a political process . . . where people like Pol Pot could be brought to justice." In other words, leave the war-crimes prosecutions to the fragile Cambodian government that will emerge from the elections, which can somehow be expected to carry out an action that the United States and other international powers didn't have the fortitude to undertake. The result, Representative Chet Atkins of Massachusetts wrote in the Washington *Post*, is that "if Pol Pot wished to enter Phnom Penh tomorrow, by virtue of the Paris accords the full power and prestige of the UN would have to be marshaled for his protection," and he added, "A man who should be on trial for genocide is instead now a protected ward of the international community."

The Khmer Rouge operations have been enveloped in such secrecy that even today the American press uses widely divergent figures for the number of victims during their reign of terror: they range from several hundred thousand to more than three million. One figure, however, has an impressive amount of research behind it. In 1979 and 1980, two experts on Cambodia, who speak fluent Khmer, independently conducted interviews with hundreds of Cambodian families, asking them about family members who had died during the Khmer Rouge period, and extrapolated these findings to the population as a whole. Ben Kiernan, who was then teaching in Australia, and Steve Heder, an American researcher with long experience in Cambodia, came up with the same estimate for the number of dead—one and a half million. "I did about a thousand such interviews, and then broke the population down into broad social categories," Heder, who now works for UNTAC, told me. The percentage who died, he said, ranged from a seventh of the rural peasants to half of the ethnic Chinese in the cities. A third of the urban dead and half the rural victims were actually executed, he concluded, and the remainder perished from starvation and disease brought about by Khmer Rouge policies. Someday, these analysts may be contemplating a new set of figures, for the Khmer Rouge are giving every indication of planning to add to their toll. In anticipation of regaining power, they have apparently already selected their first two hundred thousand victims—the ethnic Vietnamese who live in Cambodia. The families of many of these Vietnamese have lived in Cambodia for generations, their forebears having been recruited by the French to fill administrative posts. In a 1991 interview, Khieu Samphan said that the Vietnamese were "brought into Cambodia by Vietnamese troops and are part of the Vietnamese forces' occupation of Cambodia," and that "these Vietnamese settlers are occupying the land and rice fields of our peasants."

Barring some process of born-again conversion that would inspire the Hun Sen government to stop enriching itself and start working for the good of Cambodia, there is little ground for optimism about the future of the country. If the very effective intimidation of independent candidates by death squads persists—for several months after the shooting of Ung Phan not a single new candidate or new party came forward—Cambodians will be left to choose in their first free election between debilitating corruption and genocide.

The United Nations faces a herculean, if not impossible, task in administering the peace process. With funding for the $2 billion operation still a big question, the UN proposes to clear enough land mines to make repatriation of 330,000 refugees on the Thai border possible; to resettle these refugees; to demobilize 70 percent of the four warring armies; to monitor the cease-fire and block all illegal shipments of arms; to oversee the operations of five key ministries of the Hun Sen government; and, finally, to hold free elections. They must do this in a nation with primitive communications, with roads that are impassable during the June-to-October monsoon season, and with jungle-covered, malaria-ridden mountains that make the hiding of soldiers and the smuggling of arms relatively simple. The repatriation of the refugees alone is posing staggering problems. Bjorn Johansson, who was planning the repatriation effort for the UN, ticked the problems off for me when I visited him in Phnom Penh. Although he was running an operation as complex as that of any corporation president, he was working out of a small office reached by a third-floor balcony of a former colonial villa, with no secretary or staff to screen visitors. "We will start off with four staging areas," he said. "People will be moved in a day before, so they can assert that their repatriation is voluntary. Then they will go by convoys of buses and trucks to six reception centers, five in the northwest provinces and one near Phnom Penh. The convoys will transport as many as five hundred people and we will have seven days to take them to where they want to settle. To get started, they'll need food for two months, a package of tools, mosquito nets, and plastic sheeting. Then we'll have drop-off points where they can pick up bamboo, poles, and planks to build their houses. The same drop-off points will resupply them with food. We'll have to feed them for eighteen months, until the first successful harvest." Johansson was worried about raising the $110 million needed for this effort. When I remarked how small the sum seemed compared with the billions spent just for the American bombing of Cambodia two decades ago, he replied, "We should remember that there's always plenty of money to make war, but when it comes to peace, funding dries up quickly."

The arranging of free elections might seem to be of minor complexity compared with the repatriation of the refugees, but here, too, the problems could prove insurmountable. To an illiterate peasant in a Cambodian village, the idea of a secret ballot to choose a government without fear of repercussions is probably a concept from another world. That peasant, now and historically, has followed the dictates of the village leader, in the hope that the leader will provide protection in return. "Even the meaning of voting in the Cambodian language is very different from what it is in English," Seanglim Bit, a former Cambodian government official who fled in 1975 and now works as a psychologist in Oakland, California, told me. "The literal meaning is almost like buying a lottery ticket. In a lottery you cannot select." Nor can UN officials easily establish an independent press to provide impartial election coverage. "The official government newspapers get newsprint and subsidies from the state," Khieu Kanharith told me. "A newspaper now costs two riels. If I wanted to launch an independent newspaper, I'd have to sell it for a hundred riels to break even"—and a hundred riels can amount to half a day's wage for those Cambodians fortunate enough to have a job. I asked Kanharith if he thought that the UN could protect an independent newspaper. "No," he replied. "If people in the government want to close my newspaper, they will try to find some legal argument. They won't say it's because they don't like my political position. Or they can organize a demonstration to destroy the facilities, as they did with Khieu

Samphan. This is Asia, and freedom of the press in Asia is the exception, not the rule."

Finally comes the most difficult question of all: How could the UN, even if it chose to run the day-to-day affairs of the Interior Ministry, protect independent candidates against death squads? The shooting of Ung Phan has sent other dissidents into hiding, fearful that they might be next. After that attempted assassination, Prince Sihanouk said, "I am told by the Cambodian parties that they cannot now run for election because those who dare to support them are disappearing. I am told that the regime here kills, but there are no photos. They simply disappear. I don't know the truth, but morally I suffer. . . . The truth is there is no neutral political environment now."

BURMA

A Rich Country Gone Wrong

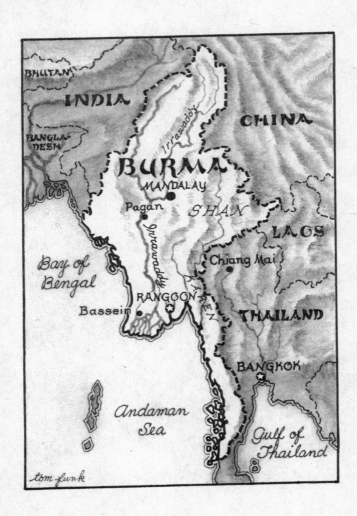

BURMA IS A NATION that does not have to worry about air pollution, because it has little industry. The country also avoids the plague of traffic congestion, because there are few cars. No one complains about urban overcrowding, because in Burma— a country the size of Texas, with 40 million people—there are no jobs in the cities to attract migrants. No one needs to organize a historic-preservation movement, because hardly a new building has gone up since the British withdrew, in 1948. Rangoon and Mandalay, the only large cities, boast not a single skyscraper, and in the entire country there are just a handful of elevators and one escalator, which is boarded up. Since 1962, Burma has stood isolated in the world, governed by a brutal and xenophobic military dictatorship, which, though it has maintained diplomatic relations with all major nations and has not refused foreign aid, is as suspicious of anything Russian or Chinese as of any- thing American. In the 1960s, the government, to guard against the taint of foreign ideas, limited visitors to a stay of one day. That limit gradually grew with the need for hard currency, jump- ing to fourteen days. But this liberalization came with a signifi- cant catch: all tourists must now hire an official government guide, whose duties include restricting contacts with the Bur- mese people.

For many years, the few visitors who came had been fascinated by Burma—a nation that for three decades had shut itself off so tightly from the modern world, it had all but faded from view. Then, during the summer of 1988, an uprising of unprecedented scale propelled Burma onto the front pages of American newspapers. A people's movement arose with what seemed like total spontaneity. Without any identifiable leadership, without a program or a platform beyond a demand for freedom, students and Buddhist monks took to the streets daily. They rallied their countrymen to the point where even government workers and policemen left their posts to join the demonstrations. By September, the entire nation stood allied, opposed only by the government and the army. America—a remote nation whose wealth and liberty people could only dream about—became a symbol of what the protesters wanted for Burma. Each day in Rangoon, the capital, crowds gathered downtown in front of a former bank building that houses the American embassy. Hundreds of thousands of Burmese—many of whom did not understand English—marched under English-language banners calling for "DEMOCRACY."

But on September 19, in an action that now seems almost a blueprint for what happened at Tiananmen Square in Beijing nine months later, soldiers took to the streets and the roofs and gunned down anyone in sight. At the American embassy, frightened employees huddled on the floor as troops outside fired into groups of demonstrators. At Rangoon General Hospital, the bodies of the dead and the wounded piled up in corridors. The government decreed that from that day on, outdoor political gatherings of more than four people would be fired upon. It kept its word. Life in Rangoon changed in many other ways as well, with the closing of all schools, a 10:00 p.m. curfew, and thousands of political arrests—arrests so numerous that in July 1989, the jails were emptied of most common criminals to make room for new political prisoners.

In January 1989—with Burma's rulers discredited, foreign

aid cut off, the population openly discontented—the Burmese government made a move that defies Western logic. For months, there had been government pronouncements about eventual elections and about liberalized investment policies. Now—for the first time since 1962, when its present dictator, General Ne Win, seized power—the government invited the foreign press in to observe Burma's new, "open" society. General Saw Maung, the head of state, who had been installed by Ne Win in September 1988, announced, "We have a teaching from the Buddha: Welcome to see for yourself and to see the truth." In 1985 and again in 1986, I had visited Burma as a tourist, since that was the only way a reporter could enter the country; on my visa application I had listed my occupation as teacher. Shortly after the January announcement, I applied as a journalist. The Foreign Ministry approved my visa request in mid-March and told me that I might enter Burma on April 17. (In mid-July, the government abandoned the policy of inviting foreign journalists to visit.)

Visitors to Burma are not allowed to go to the towering mountains that ring the country like a horseshoe, because for decades the mountainous areas have been controlled by ethnic minorities rebelling against the government. Nor can visitors enjoy the country's magnificent beaches, because they lack tourist facilities. But just the visitor's standard itinerary—Rangoon, Mandalay, Inle Lake, and the ruined city of Pagan—offers experiences hard to find elsewhere in Asia. Rangoon was laid out by the British as a colonial capital beginning in 1852, and it exists today almost exactly as the British left it, with the seediness of decades of decay somehow adding to its charm. It has two and a half million residents, but because it also has vast parks, lakes, and fields, and tree-lined boulevards on which there is almost no traffic, it is marked by none of the manic bustle that characterizes so many Asian capitals. Singapore and Bangkok must have felt before the Second World War the way Rangoon feels today. Far to the north of Rangoon, on the great central plains of Burma, is Mandalay, a city of five hundred thousand people. The center of Burmese culture and religion, Mandalay is a jumble of buildings and pagodas fanning out from massive walls that once surrounded the royal palace of King Mindon, who founded the city in 1857. Inle Lake, in Shan State, to the east, is surrounded by farming and fishing villages. Spanning the Irrawaddy River west of Mandalay is Pagan, one of the most magnificent ruins on earth. Spread out for miles across a flat plain, Pagan consists of more than two thousand carved and decorated pagodas and temples, which were built in the twelfth century.

The Burmans—the ethnic group that makes up two-thirds of the Burmese population—are an extraordinarily handsome people, often tall and willowy, their skin the color of light coffee. Men and women alike wear *longyi*—ankle-length skirts tied at the waist with a huge knot. During my previous visits, Burmese who knew English had seemed eager to talk to foreign visitors, and they often displayed an uncanny knowledge of the language and life of America. In other Asian countries, my conversations had tended to be superficial, little more than exchanges of amenities. But a Burmese—once he had looked around and convinced himself that no police informers were present—plunged with zeal into any subject. Meeting people in Burma posed little problem then; you needed only to walk into a teashop. Teashops are the center of Burmese social life, and the Burmese will sit for hours in a teashop on shin-high stools that quickly prove to be alien territory for American legs. Strong black tea mixed with sweetened condensed milk is served. You take the cup, pour a little of the tea into the saucer, and then hold the saucer to your mouth and drink; if you drink from the cup, people at nearby tables will stare at you. Afterward, you get a pot of weak Chinese tea to wash it down—and you drink that from a small cup. In the past, a Westerner sitting in a teashop alone quickly found himself engulfed in conversation. One day in 1985, while I was waiting out a rainstorm in a Mandalay teashop, a young Burmese man came in, shook the water off his hat, walked directly to my table, and said, "It's raining cats and dogs." He then launched into a conversation whose every sentence was filled with American idioms. I finally asked him why he was using all those idioms. Without a second's hesitation, he replied, "To keep up with the Joneses."

In this same teashop, also on my first visit to Burma, I met U Myint Thame, who became a close friend. (The "U" that precedes a Burmese name is an honorific, but much more important than the equivalent "Mr." A Burmese wouldn't mention even his worst enemy without using the "U" before every reference.) U Myint Thame came up to me, asked if I was an American, and then, looking pleased with himself, said, "Tell me everything about Rambo-mania." He turned out to be a free-lance magazine writer from Rangoon who read American books and magazines voraciously, often in the United States Information Service library. He was paid nine dollars for each article he wrote for a Burmese magazine; he had turned down fifteen dollars to write about American rock stars, because he considered that assignment "selling out." He supported a wife and child on $250 a year, and they lived in part of a tiny wooden house; their part was filled with cartons of books and was separated from the living quarters of other tenants by a sheet of paper tacked to the support beams. U Myint Thame had a broad knowledge of American politics and culture, but the next year, when we traveled together to Mandalay and the former British hill station of Maymyo, I had to show him how to use a flush toilet, and when he saw steam from a hot shower he thought the hotel was on fire.

U Myint Thame demonstrated to me one of the characteristics of Burmese culture that make the country so attractive to Westerners who know it well: when you reach a certain point in your friendship with a Burmese, you become part of his family. One day, I told U Myint Thame about the American practice of putting aged parents in nursing homes—a concept beyond the imagination of most Asians. He looked sad and troubled and said, "When you get old, I want you to come to Burma to live. The door to my house will always be open for you. We'll take care of you." Shortly before leaving the United States for my most recent visit, I sent word to U Myint Thame that I was coming to Burma and asked him to serve as my interpreter, but only if he felt that doing so was entirely safe. I told him not to reply but to meet me at the Rangoon airport if he could.

Why was Burma inviting foreign journalists to visit the country at that time? My passport carried a clue to the answer. The Burmese visa stamp I got in Bangkok read "Socialist Republic of the Union of Burma," but "Socialist Republic" had been crossed out with blue pencil; in 1988, the country officially changed its name to the Union of Burma. (And in June 1989, possibly on the theory that a new name would help erase memories of the political repression and the economic ruin that had come to be associated with Burma, the name was changed once again, this time to Myanmar, which is what the country had always been called in the Burmese language.) The Burmese government was seeing the cause of democracy advance all over the world. On Burma's northern border, China had transformed itself from an isolated nation with a moribund economy into a promising member of the world community; now its students were demanding democracy as well. The repression that was to come at Tiananmen Square was still nowhere in evidence. China advancing, Burma crumbling: the contrast could have provided little comfort to the Burmese rulers. Burma had succeeded in putting down with bullets a manifestation of people power, but what was to come next? The government clearly had no solution, but admitting journalists seemed to be a symbolic gesture—a tiny opening to the West.

Ne Win had somehow withstood all the forces that provoked major changes in so many other countries: discontent with the economy, a rebellious student population, a growing outrage at the tactics of a tyrannical government. He had crushed a national uprising, and I wanted to find out how he had succeeded.

U Myint Thame was at the Rangoon airport to meet me, along with his wife and their eleven-year-old son. We embraced, then piled into the back of a Japanese pickup truck for the drive to my hotel. (Such trucks, which have benches in the bed and a canvas top above it, can be used as taxis, buses, or private vehicles. They have replaced a group of rusty old De Sotos as the basic transportation in Rangoon for people who can afford not to take a city bus.) As we pulled away from the airport, U Myint Thame said, "I know you didn't want me to be your interpreter if there was risk involved. Well, there is some danger. But I had to do it anyway. You're like part of my family, and I couldn't desert you."

On my previous visits, Rangoon had looked as if no one had used a paintbrush since the British pulled out, but now virtually every exterior surface had a fresh coat of whitewash, and the whole city seemed dazzlingly bright. Several Burmese told me that the government had distributed the whitewash to the owners of buildings and houses in a "beautification campaign" motivated by its desire to cover up political slogans written on the walls during the democracy demonstrations. I was also told that people had diluted the lime with additional water so they could sell the excess on the black market, and that when the summer monsoons came the whitewash would probably flow into the gutters.

Rangoon had new pedestrian overpasses, too. After putting down the democracy demonstrations, the government decided to build footbridges spanning some of the major downtown streets. Now, a worker in Rangoon would earn a maximum of about twenty kyats a day, equivalent to forty cents, and a gallon of gasoline costs seventy kyats. (All currency translations mentioned here are translated at the black-market rate of fifty kyats to the dollar; the official government rate is six and a half to the dollar.) Since hardly any workers can afford to buy gasoline, to say nothing of a car, traffic is sparse; when I first saw one of the overpasses, during a morning "rush hour," a dog was sleeping on the roadway beneath it. The explanation for the overpasses seems to be that the army found it inconvenient to fire on demonstrators from roofs. Lining up on a footbridge would be much more efficient.

There are constant reminders that the army is in charge of the country. Trucks filled with soldiers rumble through Rangoon. Armed soldiers are to be seen everywhere in the Shwedagon Pagoda, the revered symbol of Burmese Buddhism whose golden dome and spire tower over Rangoon. At some major traffic circles, concrete blockhouses with loopholes for guns have recently been built, painted the same reddish-orange color as a wall erected a year ago around the compound of the Ministry of Defense. When the curfew begins, at 10:00 p.m., the streets are abandoned to the army. For the first few months after the massacre of demonstrators in September 1988, a civilian appearing on the street after curfew risked being shot by a soldier; these days, anyone violating the curfew would more likely be hauled in for interrogation. (The curfew was dropped in September 1992.) While regular taxis won't take the chance of violating curfew, in Burma anything can be bought for the right amount of money. One night when I wasn't ready to eat dinner until 8:30, I stood on the street and waved at passing cars until one stopped; the driver took me to a restaurant, sat at a nearby table and kept looking at his watch nervously while I hurried through the meal, and then drove me back to my hotel. The charge for this service was 150 kyats, or three dollars—a small fortune in Burma.

Rangoon had a very different feel now. The teashops were jammed with students, because the government had closed the universities and no jobs of any sort were available, but when I walked into a teashop I didn't find the smiles and curiosity that had usually greeted me in the past; this time, many people averted their eyes when I looked at them. I was successful in making contact with people only when I jogged around Royal Lake, a mile north of downtown Rangoon, early each morning, wearing running shorts with an American-flag pattern. Several Burmese would call out "America" or wave; one day, a young man standing on the street motioned to me to stop and handed me a flower.

Those Burmese who were courageous enough to talk with reporters told frightening stories of life in Rangoon. Particularly shocking were accounts of men being snatched off the streets to serve as porters for the army in its campaign against the rebelling ethnic minorities. During the student uprising, the army had transferred to Rangoon some of the troops battling the Karens. About five hundred thousand Karens, who are largely Christians and animists, live in rebel-held territory near the Thai border, occupying a third of Burma's Karen State and some adjacent areas. They have been fighting for their independence since 1949. The Karens took advantage of the troop withdrawals to seize additional land. In October 1988, with the demonstrations repressed, the army turned its attention to regaining that land. The Karens had protected it by laying mines, and the army forced some of the porters taken from the streets to march ahead of the troops and act as human minesweepers.

Before I left for Rangoon, a friend in the United States gave me the name of a Burmese professor in Rangoon who spoke fluent English and had many contacts with Americans. It turned out that this professor had been temporarily detained in one of the sweeps to round up porters. "I was waiting for a bus near the Shwedagon Pagoda," he told me when I got in touch with him. "An army truck suddenly pulled up, and soldiers started grabbing every man at the bus stop. Everyone started to run. A woman fell and was trampled in the rush, and as I tried to help her a soldier grabbed me. They pushed me into the back of a truck with about twenty-five other people. They took us to a police station and recorded our names, addresses, and occupations. By then, you could bribe the police to set you free if you had an expensive watch or were carrying enough money. I had very little cash on me, but I always carried letters from American friends. I told the police that I was working with Americans and that I wanted to call the U.S. embassy. They checked me by asking me the phone number. I had memorized it, and I think this was what saved me. A police captain went away, made a couple of telephone calls, and, after half an hour, set me free. He warned me not to say a word about it to anyone."

How did Burma reach the point where the government would build pedestrian overpasses to be used for the shooting of demonstrators and the military would snatch men from the streets of Rangoon to become human minesweepers? The answer to this, as to all questions involving the government and the military of Burma, revolves around the eighty-one-year-old General Ne Win, who ostensibly retired in July 1988, when he resigned as chairman of the Burma Socialist Program Party, but who clearly still makes all the major decisions. Ne Win, an intensely private man, shuns all trappings of a cult of personality; you will never see his picture displayed in a government office. A notorious womanizer who has been married seven times, he has imposed a strict code of morals on Burma, outlawing night clubs and banning photographs of people kissing. While he is said to be capable of extreme kindness and generosity, he has also had close friends in the government thrown into jail, and he has allowed his army to commit unspeakable atrocities upon the rebellious ethnic minorities and, most recently, upon student demonstrators. Ne Win is so intensely xenophobic that he has sought to purge Burma of foreign influence, yet he has often left the country for months at a time—to seek medical care in London, to patronize health spas in Switzerland, and, according to an account that came from a friend of his, to undergo psychoanalysis in Vienna. He sets the tone for life in Burma in every respect. When his daughter Sanda Win failed an English-language examination while seeking to attend a medical school in Britain, he restored English instruction to a place of prominence in Burma's schools. When he decided to take up golf in the early 1960s, the whole country took up golf; today, there are more than a hundred golf courses in Burma, and the courses are the key places for Western diplomats to meet Burmese officials.

Ne Win leads a reclusive life in a three-house compound on the edge of Inya Lake, in northern Rangoon. He's an avid reader; a librarian from Rangoon University once took three weeks to catalogue his library. At least two thousand soldiers are garrisoned near his home. Behind the compound are a steel fence and land mines, to keep out any intruders who might come by way of the lake. When I asked my driver to drive toward his compound, we had little success; rolls of barbed wire blocked the street, and troops with submachine guns motioned to us to turn around. While Ne Win rarely appears in public, stories of his exploits circulate widely in Rangoon. Some of the stories have enough witnesses to be credible. Two Western diplomats independently gave me identical accounts of Ne Win's running after a Burmese man on a golf course about fifteen years ago and trying to hit him with a golf club; the man was accused of having slept with Ne Win's wife. (Both diplomats are friends of the victim.) In 1975, Ne Win, with his armed bodyguards, invaded a party at the Inya Lake Hotel where people were dancing to Western music. He beat up a drummer and kicked in a drum; apparently, the music was loud enough to be heard at Ne Win's house, across the lake. Western music and dancing were thenceforth banned in Burma.

Among Ne Win's more interesting foreign visits was a secret five-day trip to Oklahoma City in April 1987, made on a whim to visit a wealthy American woman named Ardith Dolese, whom he had first met in London soon after the Second World War. Ne Win chartered a World Airways DC-10 and instructed other top officials, among them the foreign minister, the defense minister, and five high-ranking military commanders—forty-five people in all, including some members of his family and his doctor—to come along. On this trip, which the American press did not find out about when it took place, Ne Win remained in his hotel room most of the time, reading American magazines and technical journals on oil exploration. The next month, Ne Win invited Mrs. Dolese and some friends and family to Burma. "We were on a floor of the Inya Lake Hotel all by ourselves, with guards," she told me. "No one else was staying on that floor. Wherever we went, the guards went with us. Everyone couldn't have been more polite, but we didn't have much of a chance to see things. I don't know why we were guarded; I guess that's what happens when you visit General Ne Win."

Despite Ne Win's fondness for visiting the West (Hammersmith Hospital in London has a Burma Suite in honor of the fact that he is one of its best clients), he lost little time expunging foreign influences from Burma when he seized power, in 1962. He nationalized industry, banks, import-export operations, and most retail businesses without compensation, including all businesses owned by foreigners. He stripped Indian and Chinese residents of their property; two hundred thousand of them, some of whom had lived in Burma for decades, were forced to leave the country without their assets. He ended all the activities of the World Bank in Burma. In foreign affairs, Burma has maintained a rigid neutrality; in 1979, it withdrew from a conference of nonaligned nations when it sensed a tilt toward the Soviet Union.

The roots of Ne Win's xenophobia aren't hard to grasp. Starting in 1886, when England conquered what remained of the Burmese kingdom, the British ruled Burma as a province of India. They assumed all the high government offices, and they appointed Indians to the lower-level positions. Indian merchants, moneylenders, professionals, and laborers came to dominate the economy, and the army troops, too, were largely Indians and minorities of the northern hill tribes. Burmans were frozen out. By the start of the Second World War, the typical Burman was a landless laborer drifting from village to village. Rangoon, the capital, was in large part a city of foreigners: before the Second World War, there were 250,000 Indians, 40,000 Chinese, and 160,000 Burmese (Burmans and other indigenous ethnic groups). George Orwell, who was a police official in Burma in the 1920s, captured the racism of the British occupiers in his novel *Burmese Days*. One of the characters, talking about the "damn black swine who've been slaves since the beginning of history," pleads,

> No natives in this Club! It's by constantly giving way over small things like that that we've ruined the Empire. This country's only rotten with sedition because we've been too soft with them. The only possible policy is to treat 'em like the dirt they are. . . . We've got to hang together and say, "We are the masters and you beggars. You beggars keep your place."

Ne Win, who was later to act so ruthlessly to suppress student dissent, was himself part of a nationalist uprising, called the Thakin movement, which started with a group of students at

Rangoon University in 1930. They called each other *thakin*, which literally means "my owner" and was the title by which Burmese addressed Europeans. After the Second World War, two of the movement's leaders, Thakin Aung San and Thakin Nu, became the most important figures in the move for Burma's independence. In 1941, Aung San and Ne Win were among the so-called Thirty Comrades—young Burmese nationalists who secretly left the country to be trained by the Japanese in guerrilla warfare. They re-entered Burma with the Japanese invasion in December 1941, and organized the Burmese into the nationalist Liberation Army. But in 1945 Aung San, convinced that the Japanese would not carry out their promise to grant Burma independence, transferred his army of ten thousand men to the Allied side.

After the war, Britain's new Labour government, led by Clement Attlee, quickly agreed to General Aung San's demand for Burma's independence. National elections for a Constituent Assembly were held in April 1947, with Aung San's party, the Anti-Fascist People's Freedom League, winning a majority of the seats, and Aung San set up an interim government. But on July 19 two men with submachine guns, who had been hired by an opposition, right-wing politician, burst into a session of the executive council of the interim government and opened fire. Aung San, who was then thirty-three, and six of his ministers were killed, and Burma lost its only genuine national hero. The British asked U Nu, the oldest and wisest of the Thakin group, to form a new executive council, and the interim government continued. U Nu became prime minister when Burma achieved its independence, on January 4, 1948, at the astrologically auspicious hour of 4:20 a.m. (Astrology has always played a significant role in Burmese beliefs. The day you were born determines your name and your character, for instance.)

U Nu presided over a parliamentary democracy for most of the years until Ne Win's 1962 coup. But his tenure as prime minister was plagued with problems. In 1949, several dissident groups, including the Karens and two Communist organizations, took up arms against the government and almost overthrew it; the Burmese army, by then under the command of Ne Win, saved the day, eventually forcing the dissidents to seek refuge in the border areas. U Nu also failed to resurrect Burma's economy from the ravages it had suffered in the Second World War. In addition, he faced problems within his own political party; the Freedom League split in two in 1958, virtually paralyzing the government. U Nu decided to transfer power to a caretaker government headed by Ne Win, with the mandate of restoring order and stability so that elections could be held. By all accounts, Ne Win was completely scrupulous in working within the constitution, and was very effective in revitalizing the government and bringing about needed reforms.

The 1960 elections brought U Nu back to power; he won decisively over a faction of the Freedom League supported by the army. In February 1962, he attempted to resolve the vexatious problem of the ethnic minorities by calling the minority groups to Rangoon for a conference. Early on the morning of March 2, while the conference was still going on, General Ne Win and his army moved in, with a quick and efficient coup d'état, which cost only one life. Ne Win apparently feared that U Nu was about to grant some minority groups independence—a move that in his eyes would have gutted the Burmese state and, not incidentally, deprived the army of the threat it needed to legitimatize its powerful role in Burmese society. U Nu was arrested in his bedroom by a lone lieutenant waving a revolver, was kept in prison for four years, and then was exiled; in 1980, at Ne Win's invitation, he returned to Burma.

Ne Win's coup provoked virtually no opposition. But under his rule the Burmese economy was dragged down to depths that made the U Nu years look like boom times. In the British colonial era, up until the Second World War, thanks to the rich farmland of the Irrawaddy delta, Burma was the world's leading exporter of rice, producing 3.5 million tons a year for export—half the rice traded on international markets. In U Nu's final years in office, rice exports were still at the level of 2 million tons a year. But by 1988 they had dropped to 20,000 tons, and, in a country blessed with a relatively small population and large amounts of fertile land, there were for the first time reports of food shortages. Under British rule, Burma was a major supplier of crude oil to other Asian nations; now it can't produce enough oil to meet its own needs. The government-owned factories, run by bureaucrats from the army, who reject any foreign expertise and technology, all operate at a loss. An economist in Rangoon told me the story of one such factory, in the southern city of Bassein. "It was a glass factory built in the early 1970s," he said. "Although there's no sand near Bassein, they located it there because someone had promised Ne Win there would be a factory in Bassein. Then, in June 1988, they finally ran out of raw materials. But it's more expensive to close down a glass factory temporarily than to recycle its output of glass back into the furnaces, and that's what they did for a while. Finally, the factory did shut down, with 500 million kyats of unsold glass in its inventory. They can't sell the glass—no one has the money to buy it, it would cost too much to ship, and, besides, it's a cheap sort of glass that no one wants."

In early 1987, the Burmese government swallowed its pride and asked the United Nations to put it in the category of "least-developed country," or LDC, which would qualify it for additional aid. Making the request must have been humiliating for the military government, because it was in effect admitting that it had brought this once-rich country, with its fertile farmland and vast resources of oil, timber, and gems, down to the level of a pauper state. Burma ended up qualifying for the LDC designation, since its per-capita income amounted to $210 a year. But it almost missed out because of its high literacy rate, another factor in the LDC calculations: Burma's literacy rate is estimated at 66 percent overall and 85 percent in the cities.

Burma's situation is not like that of many of the forty other least-developed countries; there are no matchstick limbs, no swollen stomachs, no people dressed in rags. There are fewer beggars in Rangoon than you see on the streets of New York City. "You look at this country and you compare it to any country in Africa and you see that this isn't a poor country—it's a rich country gone wrong," a diplomat in Rangoon told me. But no one can be certain that mass starvation won't appear in the future. Rice prices have soared; by September 1989, a condensed-milk can filled with rice (the ubiquitous pint-size condensed-milk cans in Burma do double duty as measuring devices) cost five kyats, more than double the price of the year before and more than four times what it cost before the demonstrations began. One day in Rangoon, I walked through Thaketa, one of the poorest areas—a district of rickety wooden shacks along the bank of the Pazundaung Creek. I spoke with an elderly pensioner living in two tiny rooms with his wife, his son, his daughter-in-law, and three grandchildren. He earns an army pension of $3.20 a month, but that isn't nearly enough to live on, so all seven go out to sell fruits and vegetables on the street. They bring in a combined daily income of between 28 and 60 cents. "We never have enough rice to eat," he said.

Given the situation in Burma today, it is hard to believe that Rangoon once stood out as a hub of manufacturing, trading, and transportation in southern Asia. "Rangoon is known for its excellent airport, where three major lines converge," *National Geographic* reported in 1939. "So many around-the-world aviators and air-minded travelers come this way that it has been predicted that Rangoon will become to the air lanes what Singapore is to sea lanes—a 'crossroads of the East.'" In 1952, Supreme Court Justice William O. Douglas wrote, "Burma today is one of few bright spots in all of Asia. . . . If Burma has freedom from attack, she will show feudal Asia an alternative to Communism." From the British period until the early 1960s, Rangoon was the place to go to escape from the backwaters of Bangkok and Singapore. It had the best bookstores in southern Asia, wonderful food and entertainment, and all the Western magazines.

The answer to how Ne Win brought Burma to economic ruin begins with *The Burmese Way to Socialism*, his astonishingly muddled blueprint for Burma's future, which was published in 1962, less than two months after he seized power. Ne Win's socialism bore a vague similarity to Eastern European Marxism, combined with the xenophobia that demanded the expulsion of the Indian and Chinese managerial class and the rejection of Western investment and expertise. Ne Win called upon his fellow officers to run Burma's business. "Army officers gave up their ranks and became civilians," John Badgley, who is the curator of the Southeast Asia collection at the Cornell University Library and an expert on Burma, told me. "As they took over manufacturing and trade, they got the perks—the house, the car, gasoline, a telephone. But nine times out of ten they didn't know what they were doing. The Burmese were having enough trouble making their industry operate without having this intervening layer. Your boss was always someone from the military, and he was in it for the plunder, building on Ne Win's premise that you couldn't trust the Burmese Ph.D.'s, who had been educated in the West."

Making a living in Burma today is an enormously complicated task, generally involving several jobs, not all of them legal. One man in Rangoon, outlining all the business dealings that he was involved in, told me, "You need ten to fifteen kyats a day to buy rice for your family. But a clerk in a government office, depending on his rank, earns between 210 and 400 kyats a month"—the equivalent of about four to eight dollars. "So his salary probably isn't even enough for rice alone. People need three or four jobs to survive. They may work in government offices, but they will also smuggle and sell things on the streets at night. You don't do anything in your government job—you just sit there. Nothing happens in government offices; there's nothing to export, nothing to import, no raw materials for factories." This man, like most of the economists, diplomats, students, and others I interviewed in Rangoon, agreed to be quoted only if I didn't use his name. With a few exceptions, Burmese view the appearance of their names in a Western publication as the prelude to a jail sentence.

Because of the faltering economy, a flourishing black market exists in Burma today, and it operates with government connivance. Mingala Bazaar, in Rangoon, offers ten acres of smuggled goods—including clothes, gourmet food, and stereos. The aisles are jammed with shoppers. At Bogyoke Market, in downtown Rangoon, a woman pulled me aside and told me in English about her selection of imported wines. She took me behind the counter and showed me bottles from the United States, France, Australia, Yugoslavia, and Germany. A 1985 Mouton-Cadet from Bordeaux and a 1985 Beaulieu Chablis from California were selling for only $4.50 each, indicating the vitality of a black market that could come up with goods for about what they cost in their home countries. Even prescription drugs are now widely available from black-market stalls. Three years before I had seen only a few prescription drugs on the black market—the only place where they could be found at all—and most of them had yellowed labels and expiration dates that had long since passed. Now there are entire pharmacies, well stocked with Western medicines. Many of the pharmacies are said to be selling foreign-donated medical supplies that were supposed to go to Burma's hospitals, which had run dangerously low on medicine while treating wounded demonstrators. For instance, in September and October of 1988, the United Nations Children's Fund sent eighty-three tons of supplies and medicine to Burma, but Dr. Tin Myo Win, who had worked at Rangoon General Hospital until December of that year, told me, "We heard about big shipments of drugs supposedly coming in from overseas, but nothing ever arrived."

There are signs that the government sees the black market as an important safety valve; both government employees and the armed forces freely participate in it. One day, I was about to take a trip to a farming village, and my driver stopped to get gasoline directly in front of the entrance to the compound of the army unit assigned to protect the leaders of government. A woman pulled out from under a counter several gallon canisters of gasoline that had been siphoned from army vehicles. Soldiers walked past all around us, giving the transaction not even a glance, as my driver poured the fuel.

Outright pilferage from the government is common among holders of government jobs. Buses and government vehicles in Rangoon have locked hoods so that drivers can't steal engine parts to sell on the black market; if you need access to the engine, you have to call a special number to have a government service vehicle dispatched. "The Burmese are ingenious at making things run, but only when it's for the family," John Badgley says. "No one makes things run for the state. The tradition of bureaucracy is an alien tradition." The difference between working for the family and working for the state became abundantly clear when I decided one night to have dinner at my hotel, the Kandawgyi, a state-run enterprise on the shores of Royal Lake. My previous dinners had been at Rangoon's privately owned Chinese restaurants, where the menus offered dozens of choices, service was excellent, and the food was both good and bounteous. (There's not a single Burmese restaurant in Rangoon—a reflection on the extent to which the ethnic Chinese continue to control parts of the economy despite Ne Win's efforts. If you want Burmese food—an interesting cuisine based on mild, aromatic curries—you have to buy it from a sidewalk vender or get invited to someone's home.) I chose to try my hotel for dinner because of what I had witnessed each morning at breakfast. All the cooks—about a dozen—would change to chef's whites, put on their toques, and march single file through the dining room to the kitchen. Since the cooks seemed to outnumber the hotel guests, and looked so dazzlingly professional, I presented myself for dinner. I asked the waiter for a menu, but he said there was none; I could have fish, pork, chicken, or beef. I selected fish, and he went away, but soon came back to ask what I had ordered. Five minutes later, he appeared with a plate bearing a small piece of beef, accompanied by French fries and vegetables, which both tasted of rancid oil. I would probably have done far better at the chefs' homes, for that was in all probability where the fresh cooking oil ended up.

The complexity of some of the black-market activities is so impressive that it is easy to imagine how prosperous Burma could become if the government allowed the entrepreneurial talent to be directed into legal channels. "These chaps are really organizational geniuses," a Western diplomat in Rangoon says. "If they could be brought into the legal fold, they'd have this country going in short order." Smuggling goods over the border—rice goes to Bangladesh, and teak, minerals, and gems go to Thailand and China, while consumer goods and hard currency come in to Burma—is such an efficient operation that the smuggled goods sell on the Burmese black market for little more than they would cost in Bangkok. One economist calculates that the black market must be at least as big as Burma's entire official economy.

Then there's the opium trade. The State Department has calculated that Burma now produces almost half the world's supply of opium. Opium production and opium smuggling today are largely in the hands of the Burmese Communist Party—it has found drug running a far more profitable activity than promoting an ideology—and of a Shan State army that is a private enterprise of a notorious drug lord, Khun Sa. (The Karens and the Kachins, two of the other largest minority groups, aren't involved in the opium trade. They get their revenues by taxing goods being smuggled into and out of Thailand.) The mountainous Shan State, in eastern Burma, provides some of the world's best terrain for the cultivation of opium poppies. Khun Sa—who has a vacation house in Chiang Mai, Thailand, complete with turrets and barbed wire, that occupies an entire city block—has enraged the Burmese government on several occasions by inviting foreign reporters for interviews and press conferences, at which he announces that he would be willing to sell his entire opium crop to the United States government, which could then destroy it.

American efforts in this area have been the subject of considerable controversy. In the 1950s, the CIA armed Kuomintang troops who had fled to Burma after the Communist victory in China, the idea being that they could make border raids back into China. Instead, the troops used the American arms to protect the Nationalist Chinese opium-smuggling trade. In recent years—from 1985 until the cutoff of American aid after the September 1988 massacre—the United States had been supplying the Burmese army with helicopters, planes, and herbicides for a program of aerial spraying of poppy fields, but supporters of the minority groups charged that Rangoon was unwilling to risk flying those planes to the major opium-growing areas and instead used the herbicides to poison vegetable crops in the villages of the ethnic minorities fighting the government.

Recently, with the economy in disarray and foreign-exchange reserves desperately low, the Burmese government has been making some moves to reform the economy. But very few deals are being concluded, in part because the reforms haven't gone nearly far enough. There is still no private banking system, and the government—at the insistence of Ne Win, according to one report—sticks with the ludicrously low rate of six and a half kyats to the dollar for official transactions. The only suggestion of economic progress so far is a trade agreement with Thailand, which was negotiated in December 1988 when Thailand broke an international boycott of Burma and sent its top military officer, General Chavalit Yongchaiyudh, to Rangoon. The benefits from that agreement are dubious at best. Logging concessions were sold to Thai companies for a pittance, according to most reports, and the sale of fishing rights caused more than a hundred Burmese fishing vessels to lie idle as the Thais moved in with their sophisticated equipment. But the agreement was to prove much more profitable for both Thailand and for General Chavalit personally. According to a high-ranking diplomat familiar with the transaction, Chavalit's wife owned a share of one of the logging companies that would benefit from the deal, while his son had an interest in one of the fisheries affected. In January 1989—after Thailand had locked in these valuable concessions for Burmese teak—the Thai government announced that for environmental reasons it was banning all logging in Thailand. A Western economist told me the price of teak quickly shot up from $1,900 a metric ton to $10,000. In return for the logging and fishing concessions, the Burmese government got more than $10 million in badly needed hard currency that could be used to keep its army supplied. It also got an agreement on Thailand's part to repatriate many of the students who had fled from Burma. "The Thais have already raped their own environment," a Western diplomat in Rangoon says. "There's not a fish left in the Gulf of Siam. Now you're going to get that here. And you're not going to have a stand of timber left in Burma within ten years."

Ne Win may have led the economy into ruin, but until 1988 he was more successful politically. He transformed Burma into an oppressive military dictatorship, but it was a police state with a relatively quiescent population. The people certainly had reason to rebel, almost from the beginning of Ne Win's rule. All forms of communication—books, magazines, plays, movies, music—were under strict government control and censorship. Anyone criticizing the government in public or in private was subject to arrest. The government abolished almost every kind of entertainment, and political meetings were the only way for people to get together. Civil liberties were unknown. In 1988, Amnesty International protested the long-term detention of thirty-four Muslims of Bengali origin on suspicion of being illegal immigrants; for this crime, some of them had been in jail for thirty-one years. The organization also issued a 71-page report titled "Burma: Extrajudicial Execution and Torture of Members of Ethnic Minorities," which said, "Victims were shot in the head or heart most commonly, also stabbed to death, had their throats cut, drowned, strangled, hanged or beaten to death . . . farmers [were] shot down for being in their fields tending crops; the Burmese wanted them to stay in the villages. Often their eyes were gouged out." Arrests could come at any time, for any reason or for no reason at all, and no one was immune. Shortly after I returned from Burma, I had dinner at a Burmese restaurant in San Francisco and fell into conversation with the owner. He had been an architect in Burma, he said, and in the 1960s he had gone to a city in the Irrawaddy delta to design a headquarters building for the local military commander. Just at that time, the commander fell out of favor with Ne Win and was arrested. The authorities decided that they might as well arrest his architect, too; the architect was thrown into jail and held for two and a half years—seven months in solitary confinement—and during that time his family was not informed of his whereabouts.

Despite the government provocations, before late 1987 there were only two major disturbances in Burma. The first came in 1962, just four months after Ne Win's coup, when students demonstrated against strict new regulations at Rangoon University. Ne Win responded in a manner that became characteristic of his rule: he sent the military in to shoot students. Some reports say that hundreds were killed. The following day, the army blew up the student-union building on the campus, which had been an important symbol of Burmese nationalism since the 1930s.

The second and more severe uprising came with the funeral of U Thant, in Rangoon, in 1974. U Thant, the most famous of all Burmese, was actually a relatively minor figure in his country until he rose to prominence at the United Nations. He was the headmaster of a provincial school before the Second World War, and in 1954 he became the chief of staff and close confidant of U Nu. Three years later, U Nu appointed him Burmese ambassador to the UN. Since Burma was probably the most neutral country on earth, he was the perfect compromise candidate to head the UN, and in 1961 he became secretary general. His fortuitous presence in New York no doubt saved him from being jailed along with his friend U Nu when Ne Win seized power. U Thant died in New York in November 1974, and his family brought his body to Rangoon for burial. His grandson Thant Myint-U, who was then nine years old, remembers what happened. "When we went from the airport to the Turf Club grounds, where he was to lie in state, there were tens of thousands, maybe hundreds of thousands, lining the roads," he told me. "That scared the government. They wanted to get the funeral over with as quickly as possible. But the people wanted a monument, not just burial in a cemetery. The day of the funeral, thousands of students and monks surrounded the coffin, lifted it from the hearse, and put it in a taxi, and they took it to the campus of Rangoon University. There were flowers all over the place. Women were taking off their jewelry and donating it for the construction of the monument. Four or five days after we arrived, the military attacked the university, at four in the morning. Hundreds of students were bayoneted, many to death. U Thant was buried under ten feet of concrete near the Shwedagon

Pagoda. There were riots for the next few days, but they were suppressed under martial law, and the government asked our family to leave the country."

U Thant got a monument, of sorts. I visited his mausoleum— a depressing concrete building with a steel grating through which one can see the thick concrete slab that serves as his grave. The ceiling is near collapse; the floor is filthy; the grounds are strewn with rubble. In contrast to the rest of Rangoon, this structure was left unpainted after the massacre in September 1988.

Ne Win's ability to impose three decades of tyranny on Burma, interrupted by so few protests, can be explained in part by the tenets of Burma's form of Buddhism. "The word I use to explain people's respect for Ne Win is 'thrall,' or 'awe' in the classic sense, referring to God," John Badgley says. "The Burmese believe that the power a ruler exercises is a function of the merit he was born with. Ne Win has accumulated merit from a previous existence—people know he has, or he couldn't have held power for so long. There's a great fear of doing damage to him. The basic perception of power is that power is used more frequently for bad things than for good things. The primary purpose of life is suffering; the reason people want to get to Nirvana, the after-life, is to avoid this suffering." But while there is reverential respect for Ne Win in the armed forces, he has never left any-thing to chance. He has given enormous power to subordi-nates—particularly the heads of the secret police—and then suddenly removed them, often to jail.

In 1983, Brigadier General Tin Oo, who was once the head of military intelligence and Ne Win's heir apparent, was unex-pectedly ousted and put in jail. His alleged crime was misusing government money. Today another powerful military-intelli-gence chief, Brigadier General Khin Nyunt, waits in the wings. The fifty-four-year-old Khin Nyunt has been given enormous power to pry into the affairs of influential generals many years older than himself; such is a typical Ne Win tactic for keeping subordinates off balance.

In view of the presumably untouchable status of Ne Win, it seems strange that the entire nation would turn against him, as it did in 1988. But the year before that, an event took place so devastating and so bizarre that even the long-suffering Burmese could suffer quietly no longer. In September 1987, the government suddenly declared that the three highest-denomination banknotes—75, 35, and 25 kyats—would thenceforth be worthless and would be replaced by 90-kyat and 45-kyat bills. You couldn't cash in the old notes; you couldn't exchange them; overnight their value was reduced to that of scrap paper. The decree eliminated 56 percent of the money in circulation and wiped out the entire savings of many Burmese. Almost no one in Burma keeps money in banks; to withdraw money from a bank account you have to stand in line half a day, and if the withdrawal is more than the equivalent of $200, you must see the authorities and convince them that you have a good reason to want your cash. Not surprisingly, most savings accounts in Burma have long consisted of banknotes hidden at home, often buried in locked boxes. Now there were no more savings: students had no money to go to school; people squirreling away an occasional bill for a radio, a TV set, or a fan were back to zero overnight. No one had advance word of the change—not even the army. When I interviewed a retired army colonel in Rangoon, he said that he himself had lost the equivalent of $1,600. A Western diplomat in Rangoon said, "Ne Win caught everybody—his ministers, everybody. The army got an extra month's salary, but that was it."

Three explanations for the change have been offered, but two of them—to control inflation and to punish black marketeers—make no sense. While wiping out more than half a nation's money supply should, in principle, prove deflationary, in Burma it had the opposite effect. Because no one trusted money any-more, every kyat earned from then on went into land and tangible goods, and prices soared instead of dropping. "The result was that the urban dweller would buy anything—land, rice cookers, whatever—fearing another demonetization," one economist says. "So if it was an effort to control inflation, instead Ne Win created more." As for punishing black marketeers, the demonetization created such a frenzy for material goods that the black market actually prospered. The third is the most likely explanation, in that it seems characteristic of Ne Win: he re-placed the largest bills with notes worth 90 and 45 kyats because he is fascinated by the number nine. Ne Win has had a lifelong infatuation with numerology, and much of what happens in Burma turns out to be closely related to the number nine. The army takeover of the puppet civilian government, which led to the massacre of the students the next day, occurred on September 18, the eighteenth day of the ninth month. Armed Forces Day is celebrated on March 27. When the government allowed political parties to register in preparation for the parliamentary election planned for 1990, the parties in the ninth, eighteenth, and twenty-seventh slots were affiliated with the government. Why the number nine? A Western diplomat who speaks Burmese says, "The number nine is not just lucky. It is a powerful number, which has to be conquered. Otherwise it's a danger to you."

Few Burmese proved willing to conquer the number nine by holding 90-kyat and 45-kyat notes; they were afraid to accept them, fearing another demonetization. I saw many people in Rangoon pay their checks in restaurants with huge wads of small-kyat notes. One man I spoke with needed to take a hun-dred thousand kyats with him on a train trip to buy smuggled gems; he carried a big shopping bag full of small-denomination bills onto the train. An economist told me that he knows people who need large sums of money and now devote an entire room of their house to the storage of cash.

For the Burmese people, who had suffered one indignity after another over the years, the arbitrary decree that wiped out their savings was too much. Demonetization marked the first time in Ne Win's rule that people spilled out into the streets at regular intervals to protest. If Ne Win's fascination with the number nine was the original cause, an equally unusual event in March 1988 added to the trauma. At a teashop near the Rangoon Institute of Technology, students began arguing with workers about which music tape to play, and the two sides came to blows. The police were summoned and reacted savagely, clubbing both male and female students to the ground and killing one. Some students placed under arrest were crammed into a police van. It sat for hours in the heat, and forty-one students suffocated.

These deaths apparently shocked even Ne Win, for he apologized publicly for them. (There is some debate, however, about whether Ne Win was disturbed more by the deaths or by the fact that the news of the suffocations had been kept from him.) They also produced more rioting on the streets of Rangoon, and during these riots the death toll rose into the hundreds. Diplomats reported that the police brutality in March was a key factor in the extension of the students' base of support to other elements of society. Then, on June 21, came another battle between students and police; this one started when a thousand students marched to downtown Rangoon after a political-protest meeting in front of Convocation Hall, on the Rangoon University campus. According to a State Department report, several hundred students may have been killed by the police, and "in one instance, police drove three trucks into a group of peacefully demonstrating high-school students, killing four or five." The government responded to this protest by shutting all the universities in the country; a few weeks later, it closed all the schools.

On July 23, 1988, Ne Win spoke to a special session of his Burma Socialist Program Party in Rangoon. "Since I am indirectly responsible for the March and June affairs, and because of my advanced age, I am resigning from the party chairmanship and also as a member," he told the delegates. He said that a referendum would be held within two months to determine whether the people wanted a multiparty system, and that if it was found that they did, elections would follow. "Whatever the results of the referendum and whatever the new government, I will completely retire from politics," he said. These remarks were not to be taken at face value, as they would be if they were made in a Western country. Instead, they represented the start of an elaborate charade. It was what John Badgley calls Burmese theatre—a play that cost thousands of lives, plunged Burma into chaos, and resulted in a police state more repressive than anything ever before seen in the country. Ne Win directed the drama from his "retirement" home on the shores of Inya Lake.

Any possibility that Ne Win's presumed retirement was meant to be a conciliatory gesture was immediately shattered when people learned that his successor as head of state was to be General Sein Lwin, perhaps the single most hated man in Burma. Sein Lwin, who is nicknamed the Butcher, had directed the three most repressive acts of Ne Win's regime: the blowing up of the student union in 1962, the bloodbath after U Thant's funeral in 1974, and the putting down of the demonstrations in March 1988. Within two weeks of his ascension, tens of thousands of Burmese took to the streets in Rangoon, Mandalay, and other cities. A State Department human rights report describes what happened between August 8 and August 13 of 1988:

> Troops opened fire on peaceful, unarmed citizens protesting Sein Lwin's ascension to power. Numerous eyewitness accounts confirm that troops chased and killed fleeing demonstrators and fired indiscriminately at onlookers and into houses. On August 10, troops fired into a group of doctors, nurses, and others in front of Rangoon General Hospital, killing or wounding several doctors and nurses, who were pleading with troops to stop shooting. . . . Four

separate eyewitness accounts of an August 10 incident in North Okkalapa, a working-class suburb of Rangoon, describe in detail how soldiers knelt in formation and fired repeatedly at demonstrators in response to an army captain's orders. The first casualties were five or six teenage girls who carried flags and a photograph of Burma's assassinated founding father, Aung San. All four eyewitnesses reported large numbers of dead and wounded and estimated several hundred casualties on the scene. Eyewitnesses report similar incidents throughout Rangoon during the August 8–13 period. Deaths probably numbered over two thousand, but actual numbers can never be known. In many cases as soon as they finished firing, troops carted off victims for surreptitious mass disposal in order to mask the extent of the carnage.

During this period, Dr. Tin Myo Win was working as a surgeon at Rangoon General Hospital; he had earlier been a leader in a move by doctors and nurses to protest the government's shooting of demonstrators. He agreed to see me during my visit to Rangoon and actually insisted that his name be used. Dr. Tin Myo Win, who is forty, has never been outside Burma, but he speaks fluent English in a brisk, professional manner. This is how he described one of the incidents he witnessed during the demonstrations against Sein Lwin: "It was eleven at night on August 12, and two trucks came up to the hospital, driven by soldiers. There were bodies of students piled in the back. Some had been shot at two or three in the afternoon, and they were being brought to the hospital only now. The soldiers wouldn't listen to my protests about the delay; they said they knew nothing about it and were only following orders. So I asked my interns to go out to the trucks and check if anyone was alive. It was a grisly scene searching through dead bodies to find a live one. Some people had been shot in the stomach and their guts had spilled out. The interns would pull at a leg and try to find what body it was attached to. Out of forty people, twelve were still alive. We managed to save four of them."

The hospital was badly understocked then, and the situation only got worse as the demonstrations continued through mid-September. "I worked at Rangoon General Hospital nearly ten years," Dr. Tin Myo Win said. "In all that time, in every area—drugs, facilities, books—we didn't have enough. There was a shortage of anesthetic gases, so we had to use spinal anesthesia. There weren't enough scissors for surgeries. There weren't enough knives. The X-ray machines had no film, and we had to go to the black market for it. The only antibiotic the hospital stocked was penicillin. If a patient needed drugs, we had to send the family out to the black market to buy them. If they didn't have enough money, the patient had to suffer; sometimes the surgery was successful but the patient died for lack of drugs. There were no textbooks for medical students; they had to depend on lecture notes. For four hundred students studying surgery, there were just four clinical tutors to take them on rounds at the hospital. Some of my students are now working as specialists at the two military hospitals. They have all the drugs and equipment they need." Shortly after, Dr. Tin Myo Win left Rangoon General Hospital to practice surgery at a private clinic. "Many of the doctors were forced to resign, nurses also, because they had participated in peaceful demonstrations," he told me. "I knew they would kick me out, so I resigned first. Now many of the professors of medicine and the medical specialists are leaving the country."

Sein Lwin's tactics to end the demonstrations had failed, and on August 19, 1988 (the sum of the digits 8/19 is divisible by nine), Ne Win ordered another change of government. Sein Lwin, the hardest of the hard-liners among Ne Win's associates, was replaced by U Maung Maung, the most conciliatory. Maung Maung, who had been attorney general in Ne Win's cabinet, was unique in the government in that he had had a Western education. He had studied law in London and Holland and had taught for two years at Yale. He was the author of a biography of Ne Win and had also written for magazines, including the American magazine *The Nation*. Maung Maung now offered a plan for elections within three months, and the Parliament named several elderly men connected with the government to supervise the voting. The opposition leaders turned down the election proposal, demanding that instead Maung Maung resign and appoint an interim government to oversee any elections. No one trusted Maung Maung, who had so long been a close and loyal Ne Win associate, and no one seriously believed that Ne Win wasn't still in control.

During Maung Maung's tenure, which lasted just a month, something extraordinary happened to Burma, and no one really knows why. As demonstrators took to the streets to demand democracy, the government slowly stopped functioning. At first, lines of soldiers looked on at the protests but took no action; after a few days, the soldiers rolled up the barbed-wire barricades, drove away in their trucks, and were no longer to be seen. The students and the monks, who had bravely borne the army's clubs and bullets all year, now found themselves joined in their demonstrations by doctors, lawyers, film stars, journalists, and, most important, masses of workers. And then government officials left their offices and marched in the parades. Finally, some policemen and personnel from the air force and the navy came over, to the cheers of the crowd. Half a million euphoric Burmese paraded through the streets of Rangoon, passing deserted government offices. The center of the demonstrations was the American embassy. When the ambassador, Burton Levin, rode in his official car, with American flags flying on the fenders, the crowds would applaud; as the Burmese knew, the United States had been the first nation to condemn the brutal killings under

Sein Lwin. Every day, speeches were made on the street in front of the embassy. The theme of the speeches was democracy, and America became the symbol of everything the Burmese wanted and lacked. Some demonstrators carried the American flag, and at one point a group of students came to the front door of the embassy and recited the Gettysburg Address word for word in English.

And suddenly, after three decades of strict censorship, Burma had a free press. Springing up out of nowhere were dozens of newspapers, which offered a stark contrast to the solemn gray *Working People's Daily*. Previously, the *Working People's Daily* had had on its front page stories like "PRESIDENT U SAN YU SENDS FELICITATIONS TO EGYPT." (The presidency of Burma became a figurehead position when Ne Win gave it up, in 1981.) Now, people were reading very different sorts of news. The newly liberated journalists lost no time in taking advantage of the unprecedented opportunity to attack Ne Win. "KING OF THE WOMANIZERS," said a headline in one paper, and it noted in an accompanying article that "he married a little girl the same age as his daughter." A comic strip showing Ne Win at a lectern, first smiling sweetly and then firing a gun, bore the captions "Sincerity and kindness are very good," "Love and friendship are the way of human beings," and "But my hobby is killing." One newspaper was entirely in Burmese except for a huge English-language headline: "WANTED DIE OR ALIVE NGA MYAING." U Nga Myaing is Ne Win's astrologer, and many Burmese blame his advice for prolonging Ne Win's life. Even the official *Working People's Daily*, which each day publishes one issue in English and one in Burmese, started covering news more objectively. It was running headlines like "PEACEFUL DEMONSTRATIONS CONTINUE WITH CALLS FOR DEMOCRACY."

But below the euphoria lay a threat. If the government had stopped functioning, the secret police—the Directorate of Defense Services Intelligence—hadn't got the message. "The

DDSI had people everywhere," a Western diplomat says. "There were lots of signs that they were very concerned about what everyone was doing. They would interrogate people for hours. They were at the airport supervising customs; they were suspicious of what the diplomats were bringing in." A second bad sign was an absence of leadership among the protesters. The students were the force behind "people power," but now that they were getting some freedom they had no idea what to do with it.

In April 1989, I discussed this with Yuzana Khin, who, as treasurer of the All-Burma Federation of Students' Unions, was by then one of the highest-ranking student leaders not dead or in jail. A second-year psychology student at Rangoon University, she was in hiding in Bangkok when I saw her. (Somewhere between a thousand and two thousand Burmese students fled across the border to Thailand, and several hundred ended up in Bangkok. Six thousand took refuge with the Mon and Karen ethnic minorities, in rebel-held territory adjacent to the Thai border.) "We knew that no constructive change could come under this regime," she told me. "But we felt that we had little knowledge of the outside world. We wanted to overthrow the government and hand power over to those who could create a new government. We held meetings all day, but the meetings were just to plan the overthrow of the government." The opposition, however, was far too fragmented: when U Nu, by then eighty-two years old and in poor health, attempted to organize an interim government, the idea got nowhere. Aung San Suu Kyi, who was later to become the leading opposition figure, didn't achieve a power base until after the September massacre. It was only on August 26 that she made her first public appearance. As for the students, they operated under a dream—that the United States would intervene to save Burma. "We hoped to form an interim government and get arms and ammunition, or even troops, from America," Yuzana Khin said.

In September 1989, I was able to meet Yuzana Khin once more, this time in a very different atmosphere. After a nine-month effort and the vigorous help of Representative Stephen J. Solarz and Senator Daniel Patrick Moynihan of New York, she finally got a visa to the United States, and I saw her at San Francisco Airport, where she was on her way to a new life as a student in Washington, D.C. A week before she arrived, the *New York Times* had published an editorial about the hostility the United States was showing the Burmese students who had fled to Thailand; in some cases, the American embassy in Bangkok was recommending that they go back to Rangoon to get the necessary documents—advice that could possibly lead to their execution. "While the Bush Administration provides sanctuary to endangered Chinese democrats, it cold-shoulders those from Myanmar," the *Times* said. "Washington rebuffed student pleas to prevent Thailand from sending them home. Why? Is it because Washington wants Burmese Army cooperation in drug interdiction? Rampant corruption makes that army a dubious partner. There are even reports of Noriega-style links between officers and drug kingpins. Or is the State Department worried about offending Thailand, which has new and lucrative business links with Myanmar?"

The students in Rangoon during the summer of 1988 seized on every scrap of hope that the United States would intervene. Representative Solarz, then the head of the House Subcommittee on Asian and Pacific Affairs, became something of a national hero in Burma when a resolution he sponsored in support of the students passed the House. A false story that circulated widely in Rangoon described an attempt by Ambassador Levin to deliver a gift of medical supplies to Rangoon General Hospital: a student told me in elaborate detail how Levin had risked his life facing down a hostile soldier at the hospital's gate. And a headline in one underground newspaper said "AMERICAN FLEET STARTS INVADING BURMESE WATERS."

Refreshing as the rebellion must have seemed to the students and to others, it lacked a strong ideological foundation. The students had only the vaguest idea of what democracy meant; they hadn't traveled in the West, and they had experienced nothing for their entire lives but Burma under Ne Win. They knew what they were against—socialism and Communism, because the economic systems of both smacked too strongly of Ne Win's Burma. They knew what they wanted—freedom, as exemplified by the United States. And that was enough. "I'm surprised that you come from America and ask why I want democracy," a seventy-year-old rice miller in a farming village said to me with disdain. "Everybody knows the difference between democracy and socialism: in socialist countries, you get only guns and bullets. It's not only city people; we country people know it." On a table in his house was a book translated into Burmese and distributed by the United States Information Service—the autobiography of Lee Iacocca.

Besides the increase in activity of the secret police, another unsettling event occurred in Rangoon during this month of freedom. Over the week of August 21, the government emptied the nation's prisons; doors were unlocked, and the prisoners were free to leave. Those who maintain that the events of this month were scripted by Ne Win cite the release of prisoners as a prime piece of evidence. The intent, they say, was to destabilize Rangoon to the point where calling in the troops would be a necessity. If that was the plan, it proved entirely successful. In order to survive, the prisoners, lacking jobs and money, did the one thing they knew how to do: they committed crimes. Looters plundered government warehouses and factories; thieves were seen carrying air conditioners and office equipment away from the Rangoon headquarters of the United Nations Food and Agriculture Organization. Nor did only prisoners participate in such activities. A student who witnessed the lootings told me, "People had been struggling for survival at the same time that government officials had got privileges at special shops. So now that they had the opportunity, they destroyed the shops and sold the goods along the road. The first day of the lootings, I saw a twenty-inch television set on sale for seventy-five dollars and a liter of Johnnie Walker for one dollar. People called the area where they were selling the stolen goods the Sein Lwin market." For protection from the criminals, neighborhoods blocked the streets with bamboo barricades. Each block had its own committee, which organized patrols. The market in *jinglees*—sharpened bicycle spokes that are shot from slingshots—boomed. Angry crowds in neighborhoods set upon suspected government informers, and some were beheaded.

During this period, with Burma closed to journalists and tourists, news was reaching the outside world largely from the Western embassies in Rangoon; the diplomats were interviewed over the telephone each day by reporters stationed in Bangkok. But there was no news at all from Mandalay. The fact is that Mandalay—through the efforts of its monks, who have always had a vast influence there—completely escaped the looting that was plaguing Rangoon. The monks demonstrated that the "law and order" that Burmese authorities have always talked about is possible without repression. I discovered what had happened in Mandalay when I was able to track down an American graduate student who had been in Burma to study Buddhism on a visa that lasted until October 1988. From June through October, he lived in a monastery in Mandalay; fluent in Burmese, he had participated in the demonstrations. On the condition that I not use his name, since he wants to return to Burma, he agreed to meet with me and tell his story.

Well before Maung Maung took over the government, on August 19, he said, the demonstrators had seized control of Mandalay, and the city had been largely able to escape the army killings that swept Rangoon during the period in August Sein Lwin was in charge. "Before August 8, the vast majority of the protesters were students and monks," he said. "But on August 8 a general strike was declared. It's the custom in Burma for poor people to be cared for to a far greater extent than in other impoverished countries, and people out of work often wind up in monasteries doing odd jobs for room and board. The monks spread the word that people who joined the general strike would be taken care of if they lost their jobs. People poured out into the streets; a few were killed. The next day, hundreds of thousands marched, offices were closed, and that was it. The army withdrew to the walled fort in the center of the city, and the police to their barracks. There was a tacit agreement with the monks that if the demonstrators left those places alone, the army wouldn't interfere with the protesters. It was the monks who kept order—particularly the Red Eagle Brigade. This was named after the abbot who headed it; 'Red Eagle' is the English translation of his name. They were the local militia; they pirated government vans and trucks, and they armed themselves with staves and samurai swords. A cottage industry making these swords sprang up overnight. If there was a problem, armed monks would come up in a van. People feared the monks, especially the Red Eagles. Also, every neighborhood formed a local strike unit and a local defense unit, and set up barricades. I had friends who lived on the other side of town. We'd talk politics, and then on the way home I'd be stopped at every barricade, and I'd always get into a conversation, so it took hours to go home.

"The pagodas, the monasteries, and the universities were used as meeting places of the de-facto government. Forty newspapers sprang up. They ran pictures of government informers and said that if you saw any you should report them to the information booths. These were kiosks manned by students, doctors—whosever turn it was. Since rumors were sweeping the city, the idea was to have places to go where the facts could be learned. Local news was posted at them, like the places and times of speeches.

Meanwhile, the Red Eagles made all the merchants agree not to raise their prices. Prices of goods from China actually dropped precipitously, because there were no soldiers on the route to collect their payoffs. The price of bicycles dropped by half. Everyone was participating—providing food for the poor, collecting money for medicine for the wounded. No one went hungry. Every day, there were demonstrations. One day, six hundred thousand people marched—more than the population of the city. I've never seen anything like it. Support was almost one hundred percent.

"In Rangoon, people were desperate. The prisoners had been released; goons were running around. People were going crazy, so they'd catch suspects and maul or behead them. But in Mandalay the prison was in the walled fort surrounded by a moat, so you could catch the prisoners as they came across the bridge. As soon as prisoners were released, the monks would apprehend them and take them to pagodas. They were fed, clothed, given necessary medical care, and then turned over to the local neighborhood groups to be watched."

While Mandalay was being governed by monks and Rangoon was falling into chaos, the soldiers, except for some well-publicized defections, remained in their compounds, under the control of Ne Win. The army and the government leadership were effectively holding out against the entire populace. Why didn't the armed forces crumble? The answer is that, in effect, Ne Win was reaping the rewards of having established the military, from the lowliest soldier on up, as a separate, privileged class. The military had its own schools; its own hospitals, with unlimited medical supplies; special stores, stocking goods unavailable elsewhere; and even its own golf courses. For the foot soldier, an army career represented security in a country where not even a university graduate could get a job unless his parents had ties to the military or the government. For the officer, there was the opportunity to retire to a high position in a government-owned industry. In Rangoon, the son of an army captain told me, "There's free housing on a military base. If you're sick, you go to a military hospital—and that applies to all your relatives. There are big rations of food, and special items like Nestlé condensed milk instead of the local condensed milk, which smells like garbage. The sons and daughters of an army officer can get good jobs in Burma, or they can go abroad to work in embassies."

Therefore, when September 18 came—the eighteenth day of the ninth month—the army was ready to move. At four in the afternoon, the Burmese radio stations ominously started broadcasting martial music. A rapid series of announcements followed: The government of Burma was dissolved and replaced by a nineteen-member military council, the State Law and Order Restoration Council. The council ordered striking workers back to their jobs, outlawed demonstrations, imposed a nighttime curfew, and banned gatherings of more than four people. Many American newspapers the next day called the action a military coup, but the description was hardly accurate, for the military was taking over from a government that it already ran. What had really happened was that the military had stripped the civilian façade from the government. The cabinet, the Parliament, and other government ruling bodies, right down to the township level, were abolished, and military officers began exercising direct control. At the top stood yet another close associate of Ne Win, General Saw Maung, who had been the defense minister for the past two months and the army chief of staff since 1985. In addition to his military titles, Saw Maung now held those of prime minister and foreign minister.

On Monday, September 19, 1988, the bloodbath started. In the early-morning hours, before any demonstrators appeared, soldiers took up positions on the roof of the building across from the American embassy. Student demonstrators started gathering around 9:00 a.m., and soon three thousand protesters filled the street in front of the embassy. At about 10:30 a.m., the troops on the roof opened fire on the crowds. The front hallway of the embassy filled with frightened students; Ambassador Levin immediately gave orders to let them past the guard booth and into the embassy proper. Other demonstrators weren't so lucky. Although most of the embassy's employees were huddled in inner hallways, one diplomat remained at a window, gazing in horror at students who lay on the street covered with blood; he later took me to that window and described the entire scene. At least two people were killed directly in front of the building, and many were wounded. Those who tried to escape were pursued. "It was an ambush, nothing but an ambush," the diplomat told me. "There was no attempt to scatter crowds other than by shooting to kill. And once they ran, the army followed them. As the soldiers chased students, they fired at random into nearby buildings. They killed the son of one of our drivers that way— he was lying in bed."

In some instances, soldiers wouldn't let Red Cross workers come to the aid of people who had been shot; on at least one occasion, a Red Cross employee was shot attempting to do so. Bodies were thrown into military trucks and taken off for disposal. In Bangkok, Thant Myint-U spoke to a man who had been present when the trucks arrived at Kyandaw Cemetery, in a residential area of Rangoon about a mile and a half south of Inya Lake. The man reported hearing screaming and shots as live students were cremated along with the dead ones. "Such reports are solid enough to believe," Thant Myint-U told me. According to the State Department, possibly a thousand people were killed in Rangoon alone over a three-day period.

In Mandalay, the army was more disciplined, inflicting far fewer casualties as soldiers tore down barricades and moved through the city slowly over four days. But brutality was still evident. "They started grabbing people, particularly monks," I was told by the American student, who was an eyewitness during the entire period. "They humiliated the monks by kicking them and making them take down barricades. They marched into monasteries and pagodas with their boots on, carrying weapons. The abbot of one monastery confronted the soldiers at the entrance and told them, 'If you want to come into my monastery, you have to shoot me first.' Finally, he reached an agreement with them: they could enter if they took their boots off and left their weapons outside. By that time, the student demonstrators inside had been spirited out."

How could soldiers in a deeply religious country, where monks are so greatly revered, desecrate monasteries?

"The soldiers are recruited as teenagers," the student explained. "The army is isolated from the rest of society. The soldiers were told that these monks were Communists, and therefore not monks at all."

Two other circumstances helped explain the brutality. First, the soldiers, I learned in Rangoon, had been given alcohol before they moved in. "We saw officers order their troops to drink alcohol, early in the morning and again at night," one student told me. "The alcohol was very strong, what you call in the United States moonshine. The soldiers had red eyes; they did anything they were ordered. They couldn't decide in their own minds what was right or wrong." Second, the Burmese army didn't have tear gas in its arsenal; its recent method of crowd control has been to go in shooting.

To what extent were the events of August and September planned by Ne Win? Probably what happened during this time represented more than blundering by a rudderless government. The constant presence of the secret police while the government had supposedly dissolved into chaos suggests as much. So does the nature of the approach to the students: first the brutal Sein Lwin, then the conciliatory Maung Maung. But the conciliation was illusory: Maung Maung's election proposals never had the remotest chance of acceptance without an interim government in place. Meanwhile, the release of prisoners—not to mention incidents of poisoning of the demonstrators' water supply—was clearly meant to be disruptive, and to provide a pretext for army intervention. And when the army did move in on September 19, the action was far from spontaneous. Machine guns were already in position on the roofs, and after the shootings trucks came out to collect the bodies and fire engines hosed down the streets. Military officers almost immediately took over from civilians in both business and government.

Why, if the whole thing had been planned, didn't the military intervene immediately instead of withdrawing and allowing several weeks of turmoil to pass? I posed that question to Yuzana Khin.

"Everyone knew that Maung Maung was a Ne Win associate," she said. "No one believed in him from the start. We sensed that the army was playing for time during the Maung Maung period. They played these games because they wanted to know the strengths of the students, who they were, what the threats to the government were, before they moved in."

On the other hand, some see evidence that two events in the days just before the military crackdown were what provoked it. Students had laid siege to the Ministry of Defense and the Ministry of Trade, raising grave fears in the army that it, too, might be vulnerable. At the Ministry of Defense, students were actively urging soldiers to come over to their side, and some of the soldiers were listening. At the Ministry of Trade, soldiers on the roof opened fire and killed one demonstrator. The troops guarding the building ended up surrendering to the protesters. According to this theory, these incidents increased the paranoia of the army and prompted it to act. "A lot of the military really believed that the Communists were going to take over," one diplomat notes.

Whatever the explanation for the withdrawal of the army in August, followed by the massacre in mid-September, Ne Win was clearly the one who had made the major decisions. Any doubt that he was continuing his role during his "retirement" disappeared on March 27, 1989—that day divisible by nine, which was also Burma's Armed Forces Day—when he attended a dinner for foreign envoys; it was the first time he had appeared in public since his resignation as head of the Burma Socialist Program Party the previous July. On March 28, the *Working People's Daily* devoted its lead article to the dinner, listing all the guests, but it never mentioned Ne Win. Then someone must have sent word that Ne Win was once again to be treated as a public figure: the March 29 issue carried a huge front-page picture of him sitting at a banquet table and laughing. And a week later came the banner headline "PATRON OF THE WAR VETERANS ORGANIZATION GENERAL NE WIN (RETIRED) VIEWS THE 44TH ANNIVERSARY ARMED FORCES DAY EXHIBITION." Another big photograph showed Ne Win smiling broadly and looking fit. While I was in Burma, I read through nine months of the *Working People's Daily*, and this was the only time the paper devoted its entire front page to one subject.

Early one morning in Rangoon, three students came to my hotel. The day was hot and humid, but they were shivering with fear, and although we sat in the dining room, they had no interest in eating breakfast or in being interviewed; they kept looking over their shoulders, as if they expected to be snatched away at any moment. They had taken this risk because they wanted to suggest that I speak with Aung San Suu Kyi. When I told them that I would be attending a press conference she had scheduled the next day and had already arranged to interview her afterward, they looked relieved and quickly left. "Aung San Suu Kyi is our only leader," said the student who spoke English best. "She's the only one left. There is no one else."

Aung San Suu Kyi, the daughter of the assassinated hero of independence, Aung San, arrived in Burma from England in April 1988, with her husband and their two sons, to visit her mother, who had suffered a stroke. (Her given name is Suu Kyi, pronounced "sue chee"; she added her father's name.) She was an infant when her father died and has spent most of her forty-four years outside Burma. She holds a degree from Oxford and is married to Michael Aris, a scholar at Oxford who is a well-known expert on Tibet. At the time she came to Burma, she was working on a doctorate in Burmese nationalist literature and writing a biography of her father.

Upon her arrival in Rangoon, Aung San Suu Kyi was swept into the turmoil of events. The opposition was desperately searching for a leader, and she alone had been untainted by any previous connection to Ne Win. Like Benazir Bhutto and Corazón Aquino before her, she made a magnificent symbol: the daughter of Burma's great assassinated hero, come back to lead a pro-democracy movement that was trying to wrest her country from the clutches of a dictator. But she was more than a symbol: a student of politics and economics, articulate, a brilliant speaker in both Burmese and English, she immediately became a persuasive leader in her own right. Her husband and two sons eventually returned to Europe, while she stayed on to lead what has proved a lonely and dangerous fight.

Amid all its brutality, the military government of General Saw Maung that took over in September 1988 insisted that it would eventually hold elections. It had at least to talk about elections, if there was to be any chance of its getting foreign aid restored. The three big donors—Japan, with $278 million in annual grants and loans; West Germany, with $80 million; and the United States, with $14 million—had cut off their aid, and the government's foreign-exchange reserves were perilously close to zero. Almost immediately, the Saw Maung government allowed political parties to register, but it set no timetable for elections. By the time registration closed, at the end of February 1989, 233 political parties had signed up. Many of these were little more than groups of friends who, once they had registered as a party, could legally meet to discuss politics without fear of being arrested or shot. Two parties stood out as the powerful ones: the National Unity Party, which was the government's (before September, it had been called the Burma Socialist Program Party), and the National League for Democracy, which was Aung San Suu Kyi's.

Originally, the National League for Democracy had three leaders: Suu Kyi; U Tin Oo, a former defense minister (he is not related to the ex–intelligence chief of that name, who is now in jail); and U Aung Gyi. U Tin Oo, dismissed by Ne Win in 1976 and jailed for four years, represented what could have been an important tie between the army and any new government. Aung Gyi, who was then seventy, has proved to be the mystery man in Burmese politics. An associate of Ne Win's in the army, he resigned after Ne Win seized power and began steering the country toward a socialist path. He was jailed for three years, starting in 1965, and again, briefly, in July 1988; in between his jail terms, he ran a popular chain of Rangoon teashops. Aung Gyi has nearly always been a critic of Ne Win; in June 1988, he wrote a forty-one-page open letter to Ne Win, criticizing Ne Win's economic policies. Yet in an interview in October 1988 with the magazine *Asiaweek*, he said of Ne Win, "I have been associated with Ne Win for the last forty years, and we are very close to each other . . . he is like my godfather." His affection for the man who twice threw him in jail naturally makes him suspect in the eyes of students, and their suspicions were strengthened when, in January 1989, he broke with the League and accused Suu Kyi and Tin Oo of being associated with

"Communists"—a charge that was quickly picked up by government officials. (They said that they weren't making the allegation, merely repeating it.) In short, there is some merit to the view that Aung Gyi might have been planted by Ne Win to discredit the opposition.

In March 1989, the government issued a draft election law that set up rules for running for Parliament. Although military officials left themselves plenty of escape hatches, their published timetable had the election taking place by May 1990. But even before a wave of arrests wiped out Suu Kyi's opposition effort in July 1989, the campaign had been held on a dramatically uneven playing field. The opposition got no access to state-controlled newspapers, radio, or television. The notorious government order known as 2/88 (the second order issued by the military government installed in September 1988), which prohibits gatherings of more than four people, technically outlawed all outdoor political activity. (The three numbers add up to eighteen, which is divisible by nine.) And Aung San Suu Kyi's campaigns in the countryside had encountered every sort of government harassment: loudspeakers warned people not to come into the street to see her; the authorities banned displays of campaign signs; soldiers distributed crudely drawn cartoons alleging that she and her husband engage in "foreign" sexual practices; and on April 5, 1989, she came close to being murdered by an army captain.

That threat to her life was very much on reporters' minds as we gathered on April 19 for her press conference, held in a thatch-roofed outbuilding with a dirt floor on the grounds of her family compound, in northern Rangoon. April is the hottest month of the year in Burma, and under the midday sun the room was sweltering. But Suu Kyi—an impressively handsome woman, wearing a purple *longyi* and a matching long-sleeved silk blouse—looked cool and composed. Self-assured and witty, she handled the press conference with such skill that many of the reporters burst into applause at its conclusion. Her responses to questions tended to be both dramatic and highly quotable. For example, when she was asked about government harassment of her campaign, she noted that "on some occasions people were prevented from greeting me, even told they shouldn't smile at me." She paused, looked up at the reporters, smiled broadly, and added, "This should be one of the last human rights of the Burmese people."

Suu Kyi seemed to realize that there was only a slim chance that the election would take place, and to be taking care not to imperil that chance by appearing to pose a threat to the army. As she had already done a number of times, she went out of her way to be propitiatory. "One of the tragedies of this country is that there is a big brick wall between the army and civilians, and neither understands the other," she said. "The main obstacle to achieving democracy is the lack of cooperation between the authorities and the political parties. The constant clashes could have been avoided if there had been cooperation. The forces of democracy are not out to destroy the army. We're not interested in splitting the army; we know very well that a split would pose even more problems for our country. If they refuse a dialogue, we'll just keep calling for one, because it's the right thing to do." She did comment with some cynicism on the soldiers who followed her around Rangoon, supposedly for her protection. "I fail to understand why they need clubs wrapped with barbed wire for my protection," she said. And she also said, "So many of our party members have been arrested; so many more expect to be arrested. What I say to the authorities is this: It might hurt to have people say things against you. But it doesn't hurt nearly as much as a bullet, and the people have had to face bullets."

Suu Kyi saw some negative omens for Burma. One was the reappearance of Ne Win in public at the Armed Forces Day dinner. "There have been many who thought he was pulling the strings," she said. "I tend to agree with the people who think this. His appearance is not what we would call the most encouraging sign in the world." Then, there was Japan's decision to break with the foreign-aid donors' boycott and resume aid to projects that had been begun before the 1988 repression. "For a country as rich as Japan to put profits before human rights is really shocking," she remarked. "It's not that they would starve to death if they placed human rights before economic considerations."

Speaking almost casually, as if her courage were no big deal, Suu Kyi talked about what had happened at Danubyu, a town in the Irrawaddy delta, on April 5. As she was walking down the street with some followers during a campaign visit, six soldiers under the command of an army captain jumped down from a jeep, assumed a kneeling position, and took aim at her. She motioned to her followers to wait on the sidewalk, and she herself walked down the center of the road toward the soldiers. "It seemed so much simpler to provide them with a single target than to bring everyone else in," she told us. "It was at this point that a major ordered the captain to revoke the shooting orders."

After the press conference, I walked with Suu Kyi to her house, a rambling old structure without air conditioning, comfortable but clearly in a state of disrepair. We took off our shoes at the front door and went into the living room to talk. Her responses to questions were short and direct, just as they had been at the press conference, and she revealed nothing of the anxiety that must have been haunting her, away from her family and facing a military government that more than once seemed on the verge of murdering her. "The campaign has made me rather thin and weather-beaten," she said. "It's quite exhausting tramping around the countryside. It's not excitement—it's grinding hard work. I don't have time to think about a previous life."

Suu Kyi quickly dismissed the notion that she deserved credit for her courage at Danubyu. "It's not bravery," she declared.

"It's a question of doing what you have to do. You can go ahead with what you're doing or you can run away." Her boasting was reserved for the students who were working so hard to build her campaign organization around the country; talking about them brought the only display of emotion she allowed to cross her face. "These young people were very brave," she told me. "They said everything that people had wanted to say for twenty-six years but had been afraid to. There are no professional politicians in our party; we learn on the job, as it were. We've grown far too quickly; our membership is two or three million after just a few months. Because of that, we're not doing as well in organization or discipline as we want to. But now the students have a framework in which to work. By working with older people, they've matured so much more quickly. They were teenagers in August; they're young men and women today."

The opposition politicians and the dissident students proved far easier to find than leaders of the Burmese government. The government, having invited eight reporters into the country that week in April 1989, the first major test of the open-door policy for the press proclaimed in January, apparently had no idea what to do with us. We determined later that military intelligence had been attempting to learn whom we spoke with, but that was all. No one met us at the airport, no one dropped off propaganda packages at our hotels, no one got in touch with us to suggest people we might interview. I tried phoning U Kyaw Sann, who held the title of military spokesman, but his line was always busy. Finally, I set out, with a Burmese interpreter—not my friend U Myint Thame, since I didn't want to take him into a military building—to find him. We went to the area of Rangoon where the Defense Ministry buildings are clustered, and started asking for him. At each building, we were greeted by soldiers who pointed rifles with bayonets at us and, when we had posed our questions, gave us directions to another building. At last, we found the right place, but the soldiers wouldn't let us in; they told us that the building was closed for lunch. It was 10:40 a.m.

That afternoon, thinking that I might have to leave Burma without so much as laying eyes on someone in the government, I started calling a list of government phone numbers I had been given. Telephones aren't easy to use in Burma: a call from my hotel to a hotel a mile away would generally take half an hour and result in a connection so poor I had to shout every word. But eventually a person answered at the Foreign Ministry, and I asked to talk to someone who spoke fluent English. A man came on the line speaking perfect, British-accented English. As soon as I told him my name, he said, "Ah, yes. From San Francisco."

"How do you know that?" I asked.

"We know more about you than you think," he replied.

"If that's the case, then you know how frustrated I am at not being able to talk to anyone in the government," I said.

He asked me to hold the line, and within thirty seconds he was back with the news that I could interview the head of the Foreign Ministry the next afternoon.

U Ohn Gyaw is the director-general of the Foreign Ministry; he's not called foreign minister, because that is one of the titles that Saw Maung appropriated when he became head of state. Wearing a purple *longyi*, a white Nehru jacket, and sandals with no socks, Ohn Gyaw took a seat in a room furnished entirely with overstuffed chairs and couches upholstered in yellow cloth. With heavy brown-rimmed glasses, a loud and forceful voice, and hands constantly moving to punctuate his remarks, he makes a powerful impression. His words sounded oddly anachronistic in 1989 as he made it clear that to his mind the nationwide demonstrations were part of a Communist conspiracy. "Rangoon is a city with many satellite towns," he told me in speaking of what happened in August and September of 1988. "Activists of the Burma Communist Party were present on the outskirts. Why were there so many people on the streets of the city? The people on the outskirts came in waves, some by coercion. They were coerced by a group the government analyzed as cells of the BCP. The busloads of people coming in, the slogans, the way of organizing—it was quite obvious there was someone behind this." He added, "The BCP is not like the Russian or Chinese Communists. Its members are very much dogmatists, resorting to extreme actions, believing that nothing can come without revolution." In reality, according to all analyses outside the Burmese government, the BCP lost the backing of Beijing years ago, and now exists almost exclusively as an opium-smuggling operation.

While Ohn Gyaw's theory about a Communist conspiracy was not to be taken seriously, his answer to my question about Aung San Suu Kyi and the incident in Danubyu struck me as chilling.

"Even assuming she was violating the government's order against outdoor campaigning, aren't there other ways to deal with that besides shooting her?" I asked. "Couldn't you negotiate with her, use tear gas, arrest her, or do something short of killing her?"

Ohn Gyaw was unmoved. "The captain was asking the group not to hold the flag in front of the march," he replied. "The point is that demonstrations are not allowed. This was a demonstration: holding the flag and shouting slogans. The captain designated a lamppost and said, 'If you pass this, we'll be compelled to shoot.' At that moment, the major came. This is a land of law and order. Be it Aung San Suu Kyi or a passerby, if people didn't listen to the authorities, what would happen? This is not the West. Here they can express themselves inside some hall."

Ohn Gyaw confidently predicted that the elections would indeed take place no later than May 1990. "The responsibility of the armed forces is to hold the elections," he said. "Beyond that, they will go back to the barracks. We will hand over power when the next government is formed."

I said I wondered how there could be elections if a candidate gets shot for campaigning outdoors.

He answered that campaigning would be allowed for three months preceding the election. "If law and order are threatened, of course, any drastic ban could be enforced," he said. He also said that I wouldn't be able to interview General Saw Maung— he was much too busy—or Ne Win or Maung Maung, since both were retired. "The retired people are retired," he stated. "We let them have their own time."

Later in the week, however, the government did grant a request by the American reporters visiting Rangoon to interview the Information Committee of the State Law and Order Restoration Council. That committee is made up of four high-ranking military officers and three civilians who run the Burmese media and disseminate official propaganda. We were seated at a long table, with waiters serving finger sandwiches, eggrolls, and tea. There were microphones, tape recorders, and photographers. It had all the earmarks of a government-sponsored propaganda extravaganza, the full text of which would appear in an issue of the *Working People's Daily*. That newspaper has the habit of printing critical questions from press conferences, or critical comments from Western publications or the Voice of America, and then telling the "truth" about the subject by giving the official government position. No Burmese, of course, believe the answers, but they avidly read the criticisms—criticisms that would get people executed if they appeared on a political poster.

But not a word of our press conference ever appeared in print. In retrospect, I wasn't surprised. The Information Committee was used to giving commands to the Burmese media, not to being questioned by Western reporters. And some of our questions were so unsettling that we threw its members into an uproar. On several occasions, they seemed to forget about us and argued loudly among themselves in Burmese.

One of our questions was what the army's response would be if the government that took power after the elections started prosecuting military officers for murder.

"Everything that was done was done according to the law," a member replied.

That was actually a much more diplomatic response than Ohn Gyaw's earlier answer to the same question. "Nothing like that will happen in Burma," he had told me. "You're thinking of the West. It won't happen here."

The committee members told us they were going to clear up all our misconceptions about Burma. (They spoke as a group rather than as individuals; they would reach a consensus to answer a question, and then one of them would deliver the answer in English while the others nodded in agreement.) "Certain foreign journalists do not write things in our favor," they said. "Now we are giving you the right news."

What was the right news?

"Ne Win does not have any control whatsoever." The army is loved by the people, particularly in rural areas. "In Burma, eighty percent live in villages. You have to go to a village to hear what people say." Although the law forbids outdoor gatherings of more than four people, you can have a wedding or a funeral and not get shot (presumably an indication of the government's flexibility). Stability must come before democracy, or "this could be a little Lebanon." Finally, don't underestimate the Communist threat: "We think we know more about our Burmese Communists than you do."

The interviews with Ohn Gyaw and the Information Committee left serious doubts about Burma's future. The responses in each case allowed no room for compromise, and their views about students and Communists seemed to bear no relation to reality. Can such people allow free elections and willingly turn the government over to civilians? In July 1989, the Burmese authorities answered that question. July 19 is Martyrs' Day, the anniversary of the day Aung San was assassinated, and Suu Kyi planned to lead a rally. The day before, the government issued an edict allowing military officers, even those of junior rank, to arrest political protesters and administer one of three sentences on the spot: three years at hard labor, life imprisonment, or execution. Thousands of troops flooded into Rangoon, setting up barricades and broadcasting warnings against demonstrations from trucks with loudspeakers. Fearing a bloodbath, Suu Kyi called off the rally. On July 20 (the sum of the digits 7/20 is divisible by nine), the troops surrounded her compound, putting Suu Kyi and former defense minister Tin Oo, the other leader of her party, under house arrest. Then came a wave of arrests of Suu Kyi's supporters, including, as I learned in late August, the students who had come to my hotel that morning in April, and also Dr. Tin Myo Win, the surgeon at Rangoon General Hospital whom I had interviewed. The arrests numbered in the thousands, virtually eliminating the leadership of Suu Kyi's campaign organization. "The Burmese government never bothered to try to justify the arrests," a diplomat told me. "They never even formally outlawed her political party, which to this day is still legal." To make space in the jails for the political prisoners, the government released more than eighteen thousand common criminals. On August 21, Ambassador Levin cabled the State Department that "we now have credible, first-hand reports that torture, beatings, and mistreatment [of the new political prisoners] are commonplace, and that in some instances death has resulted." In mid-September, the Kachin Independence Organization, an ethnic group fighting the government from northeast Burma, reported that the army was using several hundred of the new prisoners as porters in their fight against the Kachins, roping them together, marching them with almost nothing to eat, and beating to death those who stumbled or fell. By September 20, there were reports that an average of twenty people a night were being hauled away in Rangoon, some jailed and others executed. The arbitrary nature of the arrests was setting off a mass exodus of young Burmese toward the Thai border, and Thai authorities were threatening to deliver them back into the hands of the Burmese army.

Why did the Burmese government so brutally sabotage its own move to restore respectability through elections? The most likely explanation is that the dictatorship had originally envisioned a Guatemalan-type solution for Burma—with the military pulling the strings behind the scenes and a powerless civilian government creating a façade that would allow the resumption of foreign aid and investment. But Suu Kyi wasn't following the script: she was turning into a national hero with broad-based support that threatened the military leadership. In the summer of 1989, her political rallies were routinely drawing between ten thousand and fifteen thousand people, and for the first time she had begun to criticize Ne Win by name, urging the army to support the Burmese people instead of the entrenched dictatorship. There were indications that at least some of the troops were listening; the government kept rotating the soldiers who were posted at Suu Kyi's rallies.

With all the top political opposition in jail, it's now the army that holds Burma's future in its hands. In August 1989, I was given the opportunity to submit questions through an intermediary to a high-ranking army officer who now opposes the government. "There is a great deal of discontent within the army," he said. "For the soldiers and their officers fighting the ethnic minorities, conditions are very difficult, and this is where the discontent begins. To enjoy real privileges, you have to be based in Rangoon or have personal connections. Many of us in the army realize that things cannot go on like this." Will the split in the army, or perhaps the growing discontent from soaring food prices and a deteriorating economy, bring on another uprising? That's one possibility. Continued shootings and repression as Burma falls apart is another.

THE ONLY THING predictable about Burma is the lack of predictability. After the harassment of the candidates from the National League for Democracy and the arrest of their leader, Aung San Suu Kyi, few outsiders could imagine that the Burmese junta would allow the parliamentary elections to proceed. But, then, no outsider is privy to the extraordinary delusions and self-deceptions that must occur in the minds of the Burmese leaders. On May 27, 1990 (a date that is divisible by nine), the elections took place. Moreover, they were free and fair elections, the first in three decades. The junta must somehow have convinced itself that its candidates could win, but the results instead were a sweeping victory for the forces of Burmese democracy. The National League for Democracy took 392 of the 485 seats at stake, even winning the vote at several military bases.

The Burmese military leaders were hardly ready to acknowledge their sins and to step down. Instead, they simply ignored the results, making no concessions and even increasing the level of repression. A year after the election, all the democracy leaders and one-quarter of the elected representatives were in jail. In 1991, when Buddhist monks in Mandalay demonstrated against the arrests, Burmese troops, according to some accounts, killed six hundred of the protesters. Continuing its campaign against minorities in the border areas of Burma, the government in

1991 and early 1992 expelled more than two hundred thousand Burmese Muslims from Arakan state into neighboring Bangladesh. And the junta continued selling off the country's rich natural resources to provide badly needed foreign exchange for the purchase of arms.

In October 1991, still under house arrest, Aung San Suu Kyi was awarded the Nobel Peace Prize for what the Nobel committee described as "one of the most extraordinary examples of civil courage in Asia in recent years." The award put tremendous international pressure on the Burmese leaders, but they responded with only one small concession. In the spring of 1992, the junta allowed Michael Aris to visit his wife, and he reported that Suu Kyi's spirit was "indomitable" and that she was prepared to remain in detention until freedom comes to Burma.

In 1991, Aris put together into a book a collection of Suu Kyi's essays. One of these essays contains what will someday be a fitting epitaph for the Burmese military leaders. "It is not power that corrupts," she wrote, "but fear. Fear of losing power corrupts those who wield it."

BORNEO
Logging the Rain Forest

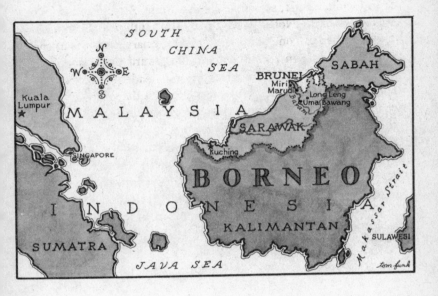

MARUDI, the last major trading post along the Baram River before the vast tropical rain forest of Borneo begins, has no doubt proved a disappointment to many of its visitors. Those tourists who associate the island of Borneo with a fearsome primitive existence, a land once dominated by ferocious head-hunters, would hardly expect a quiet and well-scrubbed little town of trim houses, Chinese restaurants, and late-model Japanese cars. Four blocks of shops along the main street offer nothing more exotic than plastic buckets, T-shirts with English-language slogans, and cases of Coca-Cola. The restaurants serve the pork, chicken, and fish dishes that are found in Chinese restaurants all over the world, and not wild game and bitter greens from the jungle. Nor is it possible to distinguish the natives of the rain forest who come to Marudi to stock up on clothing, canned goods, and other enticements of a steadily in-truding modern-day civilization from the ethnic Chinese who dominate the town's retail trade; the natives, with their almond-shaped eyes and skin color ranging from near-white to light brown, resemble Chinese, and most have adopted Western-style dress. The constant stream of cars and motorcycles—the vehicles have to be brought up the Baram by boat, and people can drive only nine miles from Marudi before the road ends and the rain forest takes over—especially speaks of the modern

Malaysian state of Sarawak rather than the Borneo of a travel writer's fantasy. (Borneo, the world's third-largest island, after Greenland and New Guinea, straddles the equator and lies four hundred miles east across the South China Sea from peninsular Malaysia. The northern third of the island is divided into the Malaysian states of Sarawak and Sabah and the oil sultanate of Brunei. The southern two-thirds, Kalimantan, is part of Indonesia.) In Sarawak, a tourist can find a Hilton or a Holiday Inn far more readily than a jungle-style wooden dwelling on stilts. Even the first leg of a trip to some of the most remote parts of the rain forest—the voyage from Miri, on the South China Sea, up the Baram River to Marudi—is made aboard a big air-conditioned river taxi, which blasts videotaped kung-fu movies from a television set at the front of the passenger cabin.

Yet one day in Marudi I glimpsed a very different side of life in Sarawak. Most of Marudi is flat, but a good-sized hill rises from one bank of the river. On the hill stands a stately white wooden building, a ninety-year-old fort that now serves as the administrative headquarters for the Baram district, which starts at Marudi and extends through the rain forest to the Indonesian border. Underneath the steps leading up to the main entrance is a little unmarked door that looks as if it might be the entrance to a storage room; instead, it opens into a small, windowless courtroom. In that courtroom, I attended a trial that could perhaps qualify for a unique status in the annals of jurisprudence. Five members of the Penan tribe, wearing nothing but loincloths, stood rigidly at attention in the dock, listening to proceedings that could put them in jail. The proceedings were taking place in English—a language they couldn't understand—because English is the language of the Sarawak courts. But the prosecutor spoke it so poorly that when I interviewed him afterward he couldn't follow many of my questions. The magistrate was a Malay woman from Sabah, and the lawyer for the Penan was a Sarawakian of mixed British and Penan descent. Against a background drone of two air conditioners and several fans, this polyglot group was participating in a trial conducted under the arcane rules of the British legal system. The five Penan, the youngest of whom was just fourteen, were from a tiny settlement called Long Leng, and the charge against them was that three years earlier, in 1987, they had burned down four small wooden bridges across creeks on a logging road.

The court-appointed translator for the Penan was of scant help. Every few minutes, he would interrupt to summarize in a sentence or two what was happening, but for a people whose universe is confined to the rain forest—many of them are still not aware, for instance, that they live on an island—the court proceedings could just as well have been taking place on another planet. At the first recess, I spoke with their lawyer, Wendel Crocker. Everyone had gone outside, and, since the formality of the British-style court system doesn't take the weather into account, both Crocker and the prosecutor were suffering through a hot, steamy day in dark wool suits, white shirts, and ties. Crocker speaks perfect British-accented English, fluent Malay, and one of the rain-forest dialects, but he and his Penan clients could communicate only through interpreters. "It's a challenging case, because they have such a different sense of time," he told me. "You can't ask 'What were you doing last October 28?' because they wouldn't know what you were talking about. If you want them to meet you in ten days, they'll put ten knots in a piece of rattan and untie one every sunrise."

The facts of the case are these: On the night of August 27, 1987, the four bridges, on a road not far from Long Leng, were torched. Although there were no witnesses to the burnings, the police received a report that the five Penan had been in the area, and went in and arrested them. The five confessed under interrogation, one signing a confession and the others, who can't write, putting their left thumbprints on the papers. The defense claimed that the confessions were beaten out of them. For three days, the testimony was devoted to one of the five confessions, and the magistrate ended by throwing that confession out, saying that there were doubts about whether it had been made voluntarily. But she could devote no more time to this trial, because she had a huge backlog of cases stacked up in Marudi—cases involving everything from parking tickets to felonies. Twenty-six Penan—the defendants, their families, and some of their friends—had made the arduous journey from Long Leng, and now they were told that the proceedings would be adjourned for months.

The real issue, however, was the logging of Sarawak—a controversy that has reached into the most remote areas of Borneo. Although more than half the rain forests on earth have disappeared in the last fifty years, and although large-scale logging has been a subject of dispute in the Amazon, in Africa, and all over Southeast Asia, logging has hit Sarawak so rapidly and with such drastic consequences that many environmentalists attempting to save the world's rain forests consider it their most urgent problem. Since the logging of Sarawak began, it has spurred a boycott of Malaysian timber in several countries of Europe and has caused Prince Charles, in a speech he made in England in February 1990, to direct a slashing attack against Malaysia, one of Britain's closest Asian allies. He noted that in the past, developed countries had treated their tribal people as "total savages," and went on, "Even now, as the Penan in Sarawak are harassed, and even imprisoned, for defending their own tribal lands . . . even now, that dreadful pattern of collective genocide continues." The words were strong, but, then, the issue is dramatic: one of the largest, oldest, and richest rain forests in the world is being logged at such a rate that most of it could be gone within five years. The politicians and the wealthy timber merchants of Sarawak, who receive a large percentage of the revenues, are the beneficiaries. So are the Japanese, who are the leading buyers of the logs and use them mainly in their construction industry. The people of the rain forest come out considerably less well: their food supplies are disrupted, their rivers polluted, and their homes destroyed.

Marudi, an otherwise sleepy town of four thousand, has more than once become embroiled in this controversy, as natives arrested for blockading logging roads or engaging in other protests have ended up in its jail. But nothing could underscore the starkness of the issue more graphically than the five Penan standing in their loincloths in the alien atmosphere of the Marudi courtroom. The Penan are the shyest, least aggressive, and most isolated of the Borneo peoples—the last of the hunter-gatherers. They are one of the few tribes on earth that still depend for survival on what is to be found in the forest rather than on crops grown or animals raised. A gentle people, they are always quiet-spoken, they never punish their children, and they are so reticent that for some of them it seems positively painful to meet a stranger. They are extraordinarily generous. Eric Hansen, a young American adventurer who walked across Borneo in 1982 and wrote about his experiences in a book called *Stranger in the Forest*, describes a conversation with two Penan. He asked what would be a serious crime in the Penan community. "They conversed for a minute, as though they were having difficulty thinking of any crime," he writes. "Then Weng explained the concept of *see-hun*, which means to be stingy or not to share."

Although, as hunter-gatherers, the Penan of the Borneo rain forest represent some of the last survivors of a pre-agricultural age, to call them "primitive" would be a mistake, since they are impressively sophisticated in their methods of navigating the jungle, in their use of its products to provide their basic needs, and in their means of preserving the rain forest for future generations. Now their future is threatened by an invasion from another civilization, acting in the name of profit—a concept as alien to the Penan as the rules of British law. I wanted to go to Long Leng and learn more about their life, and, on the first day of the trial, it was my good fortune to meet a man who offered to serve as my interpreter and guide in the rain forest. His name was Jok Jau Evong, he was a member of the Kayan tribe, and he lived in Uma Bawang, half a day's boat ride up the Baram. Jok, a leader of the Kayan in the battle against logging, was a skilled linguist; he not only spoke fluent English, Malay, and Kayan but also knew enough Penan to make himself easily understood.

After dinner on the day we met, Jok took me to call on the five Penan who were on trial. They were staying in a guesthouse that the government had built for natives who had dealings with the Baram district administration—a simple house of large, unfurnished rooms. Because the Penan live far inland—not near any of the big, navigable rivers, like the Baram—they have been little influenced by Western styles. Unlike the people of other tribes, many of the Penan still dress in loincloths regularly, and not just on ceremonial occasions. Loli Mirai, the headman of Long Leng, who appeared to be in his late forties, was wearing a blue loincloth with bright-red flaps on the front and the back. He also had decorative bands of beads around his forearms and calves, and was wearing the traditional Penan haircut, which, like the loincloth, is rapidly vanishing from the jungle: the hair ends in a perfect circle about an inch above the ears except for a small area in back, where it reaches the shoulders. Two big, circular earrings hung from his distended earlobes. Distended earlobes, which sometimes reach halfway down the chest, have traditionally been considered a mark of beauty for both men and women, but the tradition is now almost universally rejected by those below middle age. Loli readily agreed to my request that Jok and I come to visit Long Leng. Jok would first take me by commercial river taxi to his home in Uma Bawang for a few days. Then we would travel back downriver in one of the community's longboats—a boat that had been carved from a tree and had an outboard motor attached to the back—and dock at a logging camp called Temala. Jok had a friend there with a four-wheel-drive truck, who would transport paying passengers on the network of logging roads; he could get us to within an easy walk of Long Leng.

In 1841, a young British adventurer named James Brooke, supported by ships of the Royal Navy, rescued Sarawak from the clutches of the Brunei sultan, who had plundered its villages. Brooke founded a remarkable dynasty; he and his descendants ruled the country for a hundred years—until the Japanese invaded, in 1941—as the White Rajas of Sarawak. The family governed judiciously, bringing peace, suppressing headhunting, and protecting the people from exploitation. In 1946, Sir Charles Vyner Brooke, the son of James's nephew, ceded Sarawak to Britain, and in 1963 Britain gave up control of both Sarawak and North Borneo, as Sabah was then called. These two states merged with Malaya, which had been independent since 1957, and with the former British colony of Singapore, which had been self-governing since 1959, to form the federation of Malaysia. Newspapers speculated at the time that the main contribution of Sarawak and Sabah was to provide enough Malay peoples to make certain that the Chinese would never reach a majority in Malaysia, so the Malays could continue to dominate the country. Singapore was expelled from the federation in 1965, as a result of such Malay-Chinese tension, and relations between the federal government and the two Borneo states have never been completely smooth. Sarawak, under the federation agreement, controls its immigration, and requires even a Malaysian citizen to get a visa when he goes to Kuching, Sarawak's capital. In part because of British fears that the federation would imperil native land rights, Sarawak was accorded the power to set its own land policies. That arrangement proved no insubstantial irony twenty years later, when state officials began to plunder the forests.

In 1933, long before the rain forest was in danger of large-scale exploitation, the Sarawakians made a hard-and-fast rule: no logging would be allowed unless the area had sufficient stock for regeneration. An exhibit in the Sarawak Timber Museum, in Kuching, illustrates the leisurely pace of logging in those days. "Up to 1961, hill forest logging operations were very limited," a caption says. "Timber harvesting was limited to a very few species which were mainly consumed by the local building industry. In the early days, logging was carried out with simple tools— axes and saws—while elephants and water buffaloes were used for log transportation." Then, the exhibit notes, there came a change: "From 1962 onwards, logging operations steadily increased. This was largely due to the entry of Japanese buyers." The demand for hardwoods sent the Japanese from one South Asian country to another to find them. When a country's forests were largely consumed, as had happened in the Philippines by the eighties, or when a country reacted to the logging by enacting restrictions, as Indonesia did in 1985, the Japanese simply headed somewhere else. In this peregrination, Malaysia—and, in particular, Sarawak—proved to be an accommodating host. As early as 1966, a Malaysian government official in charge of timber wrote, "It is incumbent upon us to open an area for exploitation irrespective of whether this area is adequately stocked with the requisite regeneration or not. . . . Inadequacy of stocking before felling should not be allowed to hinder the progress of exploitation." In time, however, Malaysia, too, was forced to enact restrictions. In 1978, realizing that the peninsula's timber supply was rapidly running out, the government announced sharp limitations on logging, to reduce the annual rate of cutting by more than 60 percent in six years. Today, these restrictions include a ban on the export of raw logs, since a country can get substantially more revenue for a tree if the milling takes place locally.

The state government of Sarawak, however, has always been free to control logging in its own forest—a resource so vast that it must seem to loggers like a bottomless pot of gold. Indeed, the astonishing size and complexity of Sarawak's rain forest have inspired scientists of many countries to devote their lives to studying it. "It can be said without any reasonable doubt that the northwest part of Borneo, including the whole of Sarawak, is the richest forest in terms of trees in the world," says a professor of dendrology who lived in Sarawak for several years and still visits frequently. (He prefers not to be named for fear that he won't be allowed back into the country.) This rain forest, occupying most of Sarawak's nearly fifty thousand square miles—an area slightly smaller than New York State—has been found to encompass some twenty thousand species of flowering plants, several thousand species of trees, hundreds of species of butterflies, 180 species of mammals, and more than a hundred kinds of fruiting trees. Thirty birds, 39 mammals, and a third of all plant species are endemic to Borneo. In a 25-acre sample plot, the Royal Geographical Society identified nearly eight hundred species of trees—twenty times the number of native species in all of Britain. Sarawak's several thousand tree species, in a rain forest that may be ten million years old, include some that are 150 feet tall. Borneo is the last spot on earth in which substantial growths of dipterocarps remain. This family of trees, sometimes called Philippine mahogany, yields very durable wood for the construction of houses and furniture, and for other objects. Dipterocarps have provided half the hardwoods used worldwide in the last thirty years.

Now, for all its vastness, large parts of the Sarawak rain forest have fallen to chain saws and bulldozers. A visitor doesn't have to consult statistics, or even travel to remote areas, to sense the scope of what has happened; the two-and-a-half-hour boat ride from Miri, an oil and timber boomtown, to Marudi is in itself sufficient. For the first hour, for mile after mile, logs were piled on either side of the river—tens of thousands of logs, in stacks sometimes twenty feet high. They had been left there to rot.

They were logs that had been brought downriver, inspected by the Japanese buyers, and rejected, either because they were the wrong species or because they were marred by defects. Why cut down trees only to let them rot? In Marudi, I put this question to Harrison Ngau, then the head of the Sarawak office of Sahabat Alam (Friends of the Earth) Malaysia, known by the acronym SAM, which has been battling the logging for almost a decade. "The government says it has a very efficient management plan, yet you see this happening," he replied. "We ask a lot of the workers who do the felling. They say they are never given instructions about what to cut, so anything of a good size they just cut away. Whatever they think can be sold is cut down."

When I continued up the Baram with Jok, I saw a different type of intrusion. The riverbanks were dotted with logging camps; the entire length of the Baram had about a hundred of them, I was told. At the camps, the logs are transferred from trucks to barges, to be transported to Kuala Baram, a harbor at the mouth of the Baram, and picked up by ships. Each camp extended for several acres and had been gouged out of the jungle, creating a sea of mud and raw red earth. Huge earth-moving machines, logging trucks, and other equipment, all splattered with mud, rumbled back and forth. Later, when Jok and I switched from boat to truck at Temala for the trip to Long Leng, I was able to get a closer look at a logging camp. Temala was quite a substantial one, with dormitories, shops, and restaurants, yet no one had bothered to build a walkway or a boat dock to make life easier for the workers and their families. When we got off the boat, we had to step directly into slippery ankle-deep muck and slog through that muck to an area where trucks were parked. As we left the camp, with Jok's friend, I got my first glimpse of the network of logging roads that now crisscrosses the Sarawak jungle. A road may sometimes extend for more than a hundred miles into the jungle, and all the roads seem to be much wider and better maintained than anything I've seen in an American national forest; they allow logging trucks to hurtle along at frightening speeds. What was formerly one of the most impenetrable jungles on earth—accessible only on footpaths, to tribespeople who knew it well—had been conquered and dramatically changed by the giant machines. The logging roads cut across contours, creating barren hillsides and deep ravines. As fast as the daily downpours wash these roads away, bulldozers show up to grade them again. Every few minutes on the trip to Long Leng, logging trucks, sometimes in convoys, would roar by, carrying full loads. On the three-hour journey, I didn't see a single tree as big as the ones coming out in the trucks. The landscape was made up mostly of skinny little trees, ferns, and brush. Everything was green—with the daily rains and a hot climate, it doesn't take long for vegetation to return—but in the context of what once existed here it would not be much of an exaggeration to speak of a forest without trees.

Scenes like the one I saw on the trip to Long Leng—multiplied by thousands, since more than two-thirds of Sarawak's remaining forests are licensed for logging—make the overall statistics comprehensible. The annual timber cut in Sarawak soared from 2.5 million cubic meters in 1975 to 12 million a decade later, and to 18 million in 1990. From 1963 through 1985, 30 percent of Sarawak's total forest area was logged. Despite the vast rain forests in the Amazon, Africa, and Indonesia, which are still in the process of being destroyed, Sarawak now accounts for almost half the world's export volume of tropical logs.

At this rate of logging, how long can the Sarawak rain forest last? Except in the myopic vision of state officials, the debate is not about whether the timber will run out; it is about how soon. In a May 1990 report on logging in Sarawak, the International Tropical Timber Organization, or ITTO, which is a forty-three-nation consortium of tropical-timber producers and consumers, estimated that Sarawak's primary forests would be logged out in eleven years. I quoted this estimate to Martin Khor, the coordinator of the World Rainforest Movement—which is based in Penang, Malaysia, and acts as a secretariat for the world's rainforest groups—and asked him if he agreed with it. "Sarawak was cutting 12 million cubic meters a year in 1988," he said. "The ITTO report, which is very conservative, was based on that figure. But the next year the cut rose to 18 million. I would say there are from five to ten years left. This is primary forest. Then the companies would have to go back to forests already logged for a second cut, but this would mean very low productivity. Sabah will have no more primary forests by 1995. Our estimate is that Malaysia—including Sarawak and Sabah—which now supplies two-thirds of the world's tropical raw-log exports, will be a net importer of wood in ten years."

From offices in Kuching, Sarawak state officials boast about their system of selective logging. It harvests only the largest trees, they say, and leaves the others to grow and the forest to regenerate around them. "We cull the trees," one official told me. "We take only two or three trees an acre; that's not much. There's no clear-cutting, as in America." True, the logging is selective, but people outside the government say that what is selected is every tree with commercial potential, and that the remaining forest is seriously compromised in the effort to get at those trees. Last year's ITTO report came under severe criticism from environmentalists; ITTO has its headquarters in Yokohama, and critics feel that this fact symbolizes the domination of the organization by timber-consuming nations. Even so, the ITTO report reads as a harsh indictment of Sarawak's logging practices. It speaks of a state forestry department too understaffed to enforce regulations, of widespread violations of rules to safeguard watershed areas, and of untrained logging workers who, gaining their experience on the job, ignore selective-cutting regulations. Concession owners and logging companies, it concludes, "plan their operations so as to get the maximum possible output with the minimum possible fixed investment in plant, roading, training, safety, or infrastructure."

Many who have witnessed the logging operations come away shocked. "There is no management of the logging procedure in the upland forest of Sarawak that I'm aware of," says an American botanist who has spent considerable time doing research in Sarawak. "The road building and the methods of extracting the logs are said to be extremely damaging. The people who man the bulldozers are paid piece rates. They're given no map; they just go into the forest looking for suitable trees. When the trees are cut down, they don't cut them in any particular direction. Then the skidders go in and look for these cut trees with no idea where they are. There's no plan. The companies just go in and take what they can as quickly as they can." Skidders are four-wheel tractors with grapples that drag the logs down to logging roads. The combination of bulldozers plowing their way to each tree that's going to be cut and skidders dragging the tree out—not to mention the haphazard felling of the tree, which takes others with it when it falls—means that ten trees can be lost for every one actually logged. These damaged, crushed, or buried trees add to the damage previously created by the bulldozing of roads, skid trails, log-storage areas, and logging camps, which together can occupy up to 40 percent of the area to be logged. Then, day after day, come the heavy rains, sometimes in torrents. The thin layer of topsoil from the skid trails and other bulldozed areas washes away, eventually turning the rivers muddy brown and—along with pollutants from the logging camps and diesel fuel from barges and other operations—killing the fish. With the tree cover gone and the topsoil washed away, the sun bakes the bare earth, making it inhospitable for all but scrub growth.

The destruction of rain forests is, of course, by no means

unique to Sarawak. Tropical rain forests once covered 14 percent of the world's landmass and now occupy just 6 percent, most of the loss having taken place since the Second World War. In those four and a half decades, the acceleration of the process has risen steadily. The Rainforest Action Network, an environmental group based in San Francisco, estimates that 125,000 square miles of tropical rain forest are now being lost every year—an area almost as large as Germany. This represents an increase of almost two-thirds over the area lost just a decade before. Where the great teak forests of India once stood there is now desert. The Philippines has lost more than 90 percent of its forest cover in the last five decades. Logging in Thailand reduced that country's forest cover from 53 percent in 1961 to 18 percent in 1988; in that year, devastating floods linked to deforestation left hundreds dead, and only then did the government ban logging. Forests throughout Asia are being treated like veins of ore—as a non-renewable asset to be exploited at will.

There is nevertheless something special about the deforestation of Sarawak, which puts it toward the top of the agendas of many environmental groups around the world. In Sarawak, there are no mitigating factors: no hordes of jobless are migrating into the jungle as their last hope for survival; no population pressures force the clearing of vast amounts of land for farming or the cutting down of large numbers of trees for firewood. Here the issues are starkly black and white, with the forest dwellers— twenty-four ethnic groups make up almost half of Sarawak's population, of 1.7 million—the obvious losers. "Sarawak is the belly of the beast in a couple of different ways," Randy Hayes, the director of the Rainforest Action Network, told me. "It's the oldest rain forest on the planet. Its situation is so desperate that if we can turn it around we can perhaps save a significant part of what's left of the world's rain forests. At some point, you've got to draw your line in the sand and say 'Don't cross this line.' Borneo is that line in the sand."

·   ·   ·

When I first arrived at Uma Bawang, I could see only one clear indication that all was not tranquil—the presence of a logging camp almost directly across the river. Other indications followed. One involved a constant stream of visitors to Jok's house each morning and night. They would sit in a big room furnished with a beat-up old desk, a blackboard, and rattan chairs made by Jok himself. They talked to him with worried looks on their faces, never laughing, or even smiling. Jok, who is forty-one, has light-brown skin and a wiry build. He is among the tallest of Uma Bawang's five hundred residents, although in America his height would be only average. His teeth, like those of most of his fellow tribesmen, are badly stained from the chewing of betel nuts. In a place where almost everyone speaks in a near-whisper, his voice is surprisingly loud, and it carries force and conviction. Jok was eager to translate the conversations for me, and I learned that they constituted a whole litany of problems: expropriation of part of the community's farmland by the logging company, injuries to Kayan working at low-level logging jobs, the loss of young people to the cities, pollution of the Baram, and a shortage of fish and game that is turning a once self-sufficient community into one dependent on a cash economy.

Walking around Uma Bawang, I found it hard to realize that all these problems existed. There were flowers everywhere, magnificent jungle foliage, bright-colored butterflies, and the songs of birds and cicadas. Whenever I took a walk, people would invite me into their quarters, even if they spoke no English, and would offer me food and drink, and show me their possessions. The most impressive was the blowpipe. A formidable hunting weapon ranging from four to seven feet long and with a sharp-pointed iron head so that it can double as a spear, the blowpipe is carved from a light but rigid piece of wood, then bored out with an iron rod. Darts are about ten inches long and are poisoned with tree sap. A skilled user can hit a target the size of a coin from a distance of seventy-five yards; the poison, which has no known antidote, takes effect in anywhere from ten to thirty minutes. When I tried blowing a dart into the side of a cardboard box a few feet away, just a small breath caused the dart to shoot out and penetrate the cardboard with a loud thwack.

In social situations, the Kayan were touchingly shy. One evening, Jok gave a party in my honor; about twenty people attended, many bringing jars of homemade rice wine—a milk-colored liquid, which I found unusually tasty. Jok had placed his rattan chairs in a line along the walls, and everyone sat down and spoke softly, only to his or her neighbors. After the rice wine took effect, a few of the braver guests rose, one at a time, to do a dance with a ceremonial hat, shield, and sword. Kayan gatherings end in a way that Westerners find strange: anyone ready to leave simply gets up and walks out, without so much as a nod; there isn't a word for "goodbye" in the Kayan language. The blowpipes, the betel nuts, and the dancing all made me feel immersed in another culture, but the sense of isolation in the forest evaporated quickly one evening when a family invited me for dinner. At dusk, the community's generator came on, and at 7:00 p.m. my host and hostess, with big smiles, turned on their television to surprise me with CNN news in English.

Uma Bawang has a tiny general store, whose owner has done well enough to afford a color television and a videocassette recorder, and one night he invited me over to his living quarters to see an hour-long Australian documentary about the logging of the Sarawak rain forest and the plight of the natives. In a longhouse, which can be described as a horizontal apartment building with a communal veranda, an invitation to one person is an invitation to the community, and the big room was jammed with people watching, although only Jok knew enough English to understand the narration. At one point, with the camera showing sunlight streaming through the trees as monkeys swung from branch to branch, the narrator described the forest as "paradise." To many Westerners, the forest represents man at peace with nature, as the abundant land provides food, shelter, medicine, and all other needs. But when I heard the word "paradise" I thought of a very different vision—a scene described by Eric Hansen in the account of his walk across Borneo, which concerned his meeting with a group of nomadic Penan. Hansen noted that the nomadic Penan would occupy a base camp for several weeks to several months. "This base camp is for the very young and the very old people," he wrote. "Forty is old for a Penan. . . . They age quickly because of the harsh environment, and few live to reach fifty."

The romanticizing of the rain forest—the feeling that paradise will return if only the loggers go away—does the natives no service. It ignores endemic problems in many longhouse communities—problems of poverty, disease, and lack of education—and it precludes the possibility of solving these problems by continuing the logging operations but making them environmentally sensitive and using the proceeds to help the people whose lands are being affected. It also assumes that modern civilization offers the natives little more than tarpaper shacks in squatter camps, with women selling their bodies to support their families. But in reality—except among the Penan, where the cultural gap has in most areas been too broad to bridge—the modern world has already come to the longhouses, bringing with it what the natives clearly see to be advantages. Many parents are happy to send their children off to towns or cities for schooling, even though they realize that some children will succumb to the attractions of urban life and never return to the longhouse. Evelyne Hong, a Malaysian anthropologist who has written a book about the threat to native culture in Sarawak, acknowledges the benefits of education and at the same time sees the damage it has done to longhouse life. "Starting in the 1970s, the government in a big way built boarding schools in cities and secondary schools in semiurban areas," she told me. "They subsidize some of the costs for poor children, who can bring rice as payment if they can't afford school fees. The government meant well. Even the people themselves wanted this. They knew education was a ticket to a better life, because their children would earn a salary and wouldn't have to work so hard. But the people didn't realize that it would destroy the culture of the longhouse community. Now some longhouses have only the very old and the very young." Jok himself, although he is an untiring advocate of the native way of life, has sent his two young sons off to school in Long Lama, a town downriver on the Baram.

And even the remote Penan have adopted Christianity, which all through the forest either has displaced or coexists with the forest people's traditional animist beliefs. Their animism—centering on omens from birds and animals, which were thought to be messengers of good and evil—inflicted severe hardships on everyday life. The Penan could not fell large trees for their shelters, because they believed that such trees contained spirits. This belief enshrined in religious dogma the preservation of the forest, and thus their own future, but it gave them no choice except to continue their nomadic existence, since without wood they would have no permanent housing. And their animism complicated that existence as well. If they set out on a journey and the first birdcall omen came from the left, they would have to return.

Sidi Munan, a member of the Iban tribe who now heads a political party in Kuching, told me about growing up in a longhouse in the 1950s. "We believed that any birdcall was from God through the bird," he said. "The missionaries said our traditions were a hindrance to our progress; you can't plant enough rice if you stop because of birdcalls. The priest said, 'You disobey the birdcall and nothing will happen,' and it turned out to be true. They told us that education was the fundamental thing—you could get a job and come back with new clothes and feel the hero of your village. Back then, we didn't have to worry about meat or fish; we would just go out and we'd be sure to catch something. But without education there was no improvement in life. Your father was a hunter and you became a hunter yourself. Christianity and education are the root causes that are leading to the destruction of the longhouse."

The notion of the rain forest as paradise doesn't take into account how hard the natives must work for no reward beyond basic subsistence. I was able to observe this when I went with Jok and his wife, Minah, to spend a night at their farm. Except for the Penan, who rely almost entirely on the forest for food, the people of Sarawak grow rice, the basis of their diet. They practice swidden agriculture, which is also called "shifting cultivation" but is best known by the pejorative term "slash and burn." Jok told me that the community's farmland was directly across the river, but distances in the forest are often a question of one's own perspective. In this instance, "across the river" turned out to be a grueling two-hour trip.

Accompanied by half a dozen other Uma Bawang residents who were on their way to their farms, we got into a longboat, attached a small outboard motor, crossed the Baram, and headed up a tributary, but soon the river became so shallow that the motor proved useless. In a scene that reminded me of *The African Queen*, one of the men got out of the boat to drag it through the water, a second hacked away at the branches and vines with his *parang*—a machetelike knife that is ubiquitous throughout the forest—and a woman stood up in the back of the boat and pushed it along with an oar. Then came an hour-long hike that mostly involved slogging through muck and crossing streams on slippery logs. When we reached the farms, the difficulties involved in getting there paled beside the backbreaking work of weeding the rice fields, which were on hills so steep that it was hard to get a firm footing; furthermore, we were alternately baked by the fierce sun and drenched by downpours. The farmhouses were crude one-room wooden huts on stilts, and insects inside them cut short any attempt to take a nap. Jok and Minah sometimes spend several days at a stretch working on their farm, and they visit it frequently. For this laborious work—clearing the fields, planting, weeding, harvesting, and milling, with all tools and supplies carried in on people's backs—Jok gets a yield of a year's worth of rice for him and his family; that amount would cost $1,200 if it were bought in a store. This is in a good year, in which rainfall is adequate and no disease strikes the plants.

"Slash and burn" calls up images of vast stretches of forest being torched for inappropriate uses like cattle ranching and abandoned after a couple of years, when the soil gives out. But along the Baram River and in most of Sarawak it's a far different story—of a stewardship of the land that displays remarkable environmental sensitivity. The natives call their system *adat*, an unwritten body of rules and principles that extends to all relationships. Under *adat*, the longhouse community clears nearby land to grow rice; the land, called *temuda*, is enough to provide each family with a few acres. The community owns all that land, but each family gets the right to use its own plot and pass it on to the next generation, provided that family members continue to farm it. "Your existence, your identity, is built around the land," Hong, the anthropologist, told me. "The land is more than a piece of earth that gives you food; it's a link between the past and the future. If you lose it, you have nothing. You're reduced to nothingness."

The key to swidden farming is to leave most of the land fallow much of the time, so that the soil can regenerate; otherwise, the longhouse would eventually have to move, because there would be no fertile land nearby. Jok himself uses a ten-year rotation cycle, growing rice on 10 percent of his land one year and moving to another 10 percent the next. Dispersing the rice plots through fallow land also means that the danger from pests is far less than it would be if the plots were concentrated on one site. When long-fallow plots are cleared by the burning of trees that have grown back, the layer of ash fertilizes the soil and increases its alkalinity. The rice is planted with a dibble, a stick that punches holes in the soil for seeds; by not disturbing the soil, this method leaves it resistant to erosion. S. C. Chin, who until recently was a professor of botany at the University of Malaya, in Kuala Lumpur, has studied shifting cultivation in Sarawak, and he estimates that it intrudes on only nine thousand acres of new primary forest each year—a tiny fraction of the acreage destroyed by logging. But swidden farming has provided a convenient scapegoat for government officials. In 1988, Mahathir bin Mohamad, the prime minister of Malaysia, wrote in a letter to a New Zealand environmentalist, "You are wrong if you think giving the forests to the indigenous people will save the trees. The indigenous people practice slash and burn cultivation, and vast tracts of forests have been completely obliterated by shifting slash and burn practice. Logging of selected mature trees allows the forests to regenerate quickly. But, of course, it will not sound noble to condemn the tribal people. It is much more romantic to fight for their rights against the Government."

To get another evaluation of the controversy, I asked Y. S. Rao, the regional forestry officer in Bangkok for the United Nations Food and Agriculture Organization, for his opinion. "In some situations, shifting cultivation is an ecologically harmonious practice, provided that the people are not numerous and the fallow period is long," he responded. "In Sarawak, shifting cultivation is not a danger. It's beneficial deforestation—beneficial to the people."

On March 22, 1987, bulldozers and trucks belonging to a company called Marabong Lumber appeared across the river from Uma Bawang, on the community's *temuda*. They began the construction of a base camp, a log-collection depot, and logging roads—all on land being farmed by Kayan families. Nine days later, a group of Uma Bawang residents filed a complaint with the police, to no avail. The logging company claimed that it was there legally, because the land had been "gazetted" in 1951. Under this system, the Sarawak government has the power to take away tribespeople's customary land rights by publishing a fine-print announcement to that effect. The tribespeople don't have to be notified personally; often, they learn about gazetting only when the bulldozers and the chain saws show up. In this case, however, there apparently had been notification. Thayalan Muniandy, a lawyer for SAM, the Malaysian environmental group, told me that in 1951 a British colonial officer had come to Uma Bawang and "told them this would be the Uma Bawang Protected Forest," and he went on, "The natives helped him mark the boundaries. People didn't realize that the term 'protected forest' meant that it was protected for the purpose of logging. If a native cut a tree, he would be technically guilty of an offense. The gazette notice was published in English, in an official government publication in Kuching, and the Kayan didn't see a copy until 1987."

In Sarawak, logging activities are governed by a network of political connections that is often called the Ali Baba system, because the right word will open a storehouse of riches. The logging concessions, granted by the state's chief minister, frequently go to friends, relatives, and other politicians, generating many millions of dollars in profit. But little or none of this money finds its way to the people whose farmland was seized. Under the law, compensation procedures are vague—supposedly a matter of negotiations between the timber company and the longhouse community. In some cases, the loggers resolve the issue simply by paying off the headman, or by bulldozing the fields with no compensation at all. "Sometimes the loggers will pay to pacify the community," Harrison Ngau, the Marudi anti-logging activist, says. "But in every instance they are the ones who determine the rate of compensation, not the owner of the property. It's like walking into a store and deciding how much you will pay for something you want to buy." The timber companies hold the ultimate weapon: if the natives aren't satisfied with the compensation offered, the bulldozers just go to work anyway; the government never interferes.

When some of the Uma Bawang residents went to the logging company and asked for compensation, they were refused; the company cited the right of access that had been granted by the state in the 1951 gazetting. So in April 1987 a hundred men, women, and children set up a barricade of tree limbs and wooden posts on the logging road and sat down in front of it. This wasn't the first logging protest in Sarawak, but it was the best organized and the best publicized, and it galvanized the native communities into erecting blockades throughout the Baram region. The Uma Bawang protest escalated over the summer, and by October 29, when special forces of the Malaysian army and the police swept in by helicopter, more than four hundred people were manning barricades. Forty-two Kayan were arrested, put on an express boat chartered by the timber company, and taken to jail in Marudi. They were detained for fourteen days, the maximum "investigation period" under the law, and released. Since then, there have been at least fifty other logging blockades in Sarawak, many of them ended by police action and arrests. Ngau says that almost a thousand people in the Baram region have been arrested over the years, with hundreds put in jail for the full two weeks. "It's mostly harassment to kill their spirit," he says. "In our society, if you're even questioned by a policeman you're looked upon as a criminal or troublemaker. But now people have respect for you even if you go to jail. Jail has stiffened the protesters' spirit and moved others to join the protests." A month after the Uma Bawang arrests, the Sarawak state legislature passed a law spe-

cifically making obstruction of a logging road an offense pun-
ishable by up to two years in jail. But while a number of cases
have gone to trial, not a single person has been convicted. The
charges against the forty-two Uma Bawang protesters were finally dropped in April 1989, because there was insufficient
evidence that they were the ones who had actually set up the
barricades.

The Malaysian government, however, has remedies that go
beyond the courts. While Malaysia is nominally a democracy,
democratic practices extend only so far. Most of the press is
controlled by the governing coalition of political parties, and
these newspapers have scrupulously avoided any mention of
logging blockades. The Sarawak state government, which is allied politically with the national ruling coalition, doesn't hesitate
to use its power over immigration to keep out foreigners with
opposing viewpoints. When United States congressional staff
members, under the auspices of the House Foreign Affairs
Committee, went to Sarawak to investigate the logging controversy in March 1989, they arrived in Kuching accompanied by
an official of SAM; she was detained at the airport and deported
the following day. The Lonely Planet Guide to Malaysia, one of
a popular series of travel guidebooks, warns, "The Sarawak state
government is touchy about unannounced researchers, journalists, photographers etc., so remember, you're a tourist, nothing
more." I myself entered as a tourist and never applied for the
permit that the Sarawak government requires for visits to longhouse communities in the rain forest; I feared being turned
down and barred from Sarawak.

The most potent weapon for the Malaysian government is the
Internal Security Act, used in the sixties to counter an armed
insurgency by the outlawed Communist Party of Malaysia. Under the act, the minister for home affairs—a second portfolio
held by Prime Minister Mahathir—can detain anyone indefinitely without a trial. In October 1987, Mahathir used the act to

jail more than a hundred prominent politicians, trade unionists, community workers, environmentalists, and religious leaders, but no specific charges were ever brought against them. One of those arrested was Harrison Ngau. I visited Ngau in SAM's Marudi office—several cramped rooms reached by a dingy stairway behind some stores. The rooms were crowded with forest people who had come to Marudi to tell SAM staff members about encroachment on their lands by loggers and to seek advice. Ngau, a small, slight Kayan with light skin and delicate features, grew up in a longhouse, in a family of seven living in three small rooms. He started the SAM office in 1981, when he was about twenty-two years old. (Many Borneo people aren't certain of their age and arbitrarily adopt birthdays.) Ngau speaks perfect English, though in a voice so soft that it's often hard to hear him. He is strong-willed, however, and is determined to remedy the harm done to the natives. "Bulldozers will take the shortest route possible, even if rice is growing in the fields," he said. "That is what happened at Uma Bawang. They go in first and talk later. The Penan used to be able to hunt for three hours and find meat; now they can hunt for days and catch nothing. Do you sit back and suffer or try to protect your land? It's not just a question of landslides and pollution; it involves human survival."

While Ngau was working in his office on the afternoon of October 29, 1987, a dozen policemen appeared. "They told me I was under arrest under the Internal Security Act," he said. "They handcuffed me, and after they searched my office they went to my home. I was brought by a police plane to Miri, and they locked me behind bars for three days. From Miri we went by Land Cruiser to Kuching, and I was handcuffed the whole way; they were the type of handcuffs that tighten up and cut into you if you move your hands. I was kept in what was called a holding center. I was put in a locked, windowless room; I couldn't tell whether it was day or night. For two weeks, there was nothing to do, just sitting in the room. But then the guards gave me books to read. One fellow brought me a Bible, another a book that described the history of bead-making. After sixty days, I was released on a restricted-residence order: I was confined to Marudi unless I got police permission to leave. They never charged me with a crime."

In April 1990, Ngau was one of six recipients of the first annual Goldman Environmental Prizes; each recipient received $60,000, awarded by a family foundation in San Francisco. Fifty-seven leaders of various nations had endorsed the award program, and one of those leaders was Prime Minister Mahathir, so the Malaysian government had little choice but to allow Ngau to travel to the United States to accept his prize. Members of the SAM staff in Penang told me that they had had to persuade Ngau to stay away from Marudi an extra day to go to Washington with the other recipients and meet President Bush. I asked Ngau about his reluctance to leave his work. "This was my second trip to the United States," he replied. "I was there for one week in 1985, for the World Rainforest Movement conference. But I don't really like to go outside Malaysia. I'm not good at meetings; I can contribute more here. Sometimes, at meetings, there are so many ideas that you get confused and forget your objectives. You talk to a Penan who has never read a newspaper or seen television, and he can tell you the problem. The Penan are simple, direct people who care for everybody, and they are more precise and more practical." When Ngau arrived in Washington to meet the president, he had to borrow a jacket and tie; the jacket was several sizes too large. "I'm not used to all these things," he said. "We don't have these formalities here." When he returned, an English-language newspaper in Malaysia interviewed him and took his picture, but no article about him ever appeared. Nor had any of the peninsula's daily papers carried news of the award.

Shortly before I left Borneo, the Sarawak *Tribune*, in the guise of a front-page news story, launched a bitter attack against SAM, saying that it was "alleged to have instigated the rural people against development brought by the government." The paper said that the environmental group "was recently reported to be creating racial issues," which are code words of the Malaysian government when it wants to threaten its opponents. The article represented the government's initial attack on Ngau's impending candidacy for the Malaysian Parliament, which he announced a few days later. But although the parties aligned with Mahathir overwhelmingly swept the elections held in October 1990, Ngau, running as an independent, won the seat from the Baram district. He ousted Luhat Wan, Malaysia's deputy minister of works, who had held the seat for twenty-five years and had had the strong support of the logging companies.

Ngau's victory over a well-financed incumbent backed by the government indicated the depth of the opposition to logging in the Borneo rain forest. Studies have found that the logging has frightened away game and destroyed jungle plants used for food, and thus has greatly increased the incidence of malnutrition. In some areas, the logging operations, by intruding upon native farmland, have led to a collapse of the traditional crop-rotation system and subsequent exhaustion of the soil. The congressional staff members who visited Sarawak in 1989 released a report that September and summed up the damage:

> The people are faced with decreased clean water and food supplies . . . often resulting in malnutrition and disease. Other products on which they depend have also diminished, such as herbal medicine, rattan, and other essential materials. . . . As the resources are depleted, the need for, and dependency on, cash and tradeable items by the tribal people becomes more acute. The tradeable goods and cash are generated from the now disappearing forest produce.

It's a snowballing process of degradation and loss of dietary and other staples which jeopardize their traditional culture and even survival.

The militance of the Sarawak forest people's opposition to logging indicates how highly they value their land, for the timber operations have brought material gains to at least some of the longhouses in the form of jobs—jobs whose income allows the native communities to participate in Sarawak's cash economy and acquire possessions like television sets. About 23,000 tribespeople work in the timber industry, mostly in the lowest-level positions. They pay a fearsome price in terms of death and injury, because no job training is available and safety regulations are not enforced. The jobs open to them are frequently classified as being offered by independent contractors, so that the logging companies won't have to provide medical coverage or compensation for accidents. Ngau explained to me how it works. "Most of the people injured or killed are called hookmen," he said. "They hook the cables onto the trees so that the trees can be pulled away. They're employed by the drivers themselves. If I'm a truck driver, I'll get perhaps five dollars a ton and give my assistant one dollar. We also have a few friends who work in timber camps as boat drivers, and they say that every week there's someone killed—they're bringing out bodies all the time."

Wade Davis, who has worked as a logging engineer in British Columbia, and who now holds research positions in ethnobotany at the New York Botanical Garden and the Smithsonian Institution, writes in a recent book on the Sarawak rain forest: "Though less than 5% of the Sarawak workforce is employed in logging, the industry, in 1983, accounted for 67% of all fatal occupational accidents in the state. Over the last 17 years more than a thousand workers have been killed, 94 in 1989 alone. In 1980, one in five workers suffered injury and one in four hundred was killed. . . . These figures indicate a rate of accidents twenty-one times higher than what has been reported for the logging industry in Canada."

Logging has severely taxed the social structure of the long-house communities, which have traditionally operated on the basis of consensus. But—except in the case of the Penan, whose culture is so different that they have stood together—consensus is no longer possible, because the government and the logging companies have set out to buy support. In 1988, SAM charged in a report released to the public that in trying to break up the logging-road blockades, "the authorities told the people not to try to stop the timber companies from continuing with their logging activities." The report continued, "Cooperate with the companies, they were urged. Negotiate for a 'commission,' they were told." There have been frequent instances of headmen being put on retainer in return for backing the logging operations, and some of the headmen have signed away the community's land rights, agreeing that the longhouse wouldn't lodge any complaint about the pollution of drinking water or the loss of wildlife and forest products. Because a headman needs an official letter of appointment, the government can control who is chosen and try to oust any headman who opposes logging.

"It used to be that the headman was chosen by consensus," Ngau told me. "Today, it's more political. Even if ninety-nine percent of the people want to change their chief, it can't be done if the chief is close to the local politicians. Ninety percent of the longhouses in the Baram district want to get rid of their chiefs. Some headmen get around a hundred dollars a month. Others are employed by the logging company."

Today at Uma Bawang, with some families receiving monthly compensation for their land and others holding jobs for the logging companies, the community is split, with fifty of seventy-six families on record as opposing logging. Opponents of the timber companies say that the compensation being paid isn't adequate, and that it came about only because the timber operators wanted to avoid future blockades. Supporters of logging argue that the compensation would increase if the majority of each longhouse were to change its stand. The congressional staff members visited Uma Bawang as part of their 1989 trip, and noted in their report, "We were informed that the chief and others who supported the logging firms had been adequately compensated."

During my stay in Uma Bawang, the headman wouldn't see me. Jok told me that when I arrived the headman had gone by boat to the nearby timber camp and used a radiotelephone to call the police in an attempt to have me arrested. "The headman tries to stop journalists; he claims that the outsiders are trying to instigate us," Jok said. The fifty families who oppose logging have organized as the Uma Bawang Residents' Association, and Jok is their chairman. He refuses to bow to the loggers' demands. "The timber company camp manager constantly came to see me to break the blockade," he said. "At first, the company promised me $160 a month; then they went to $240. All that the politicians in Kuching do is divide up the map into logging concessions. They want to be rich in five years, before the next election. They say they're doing selective logging, but what you see is a far different thing. Day and night they're working; that's why there's such a high accident rate. They don't care about lives as long as the money is coming in. We oppose logging because we get our food supplies from the jungle. Now we eat from tins—there's no alternative. Where else can we get food? We oppose logging because we have lost all our resources."

The problems at Uma Bawang soon faded in comparison with what I witnessed at Long Leng. The truck let us off along the main logging road, and Jok and I walked downhill for about a mile on a rutted, muddy forest track. Suddenly we came upon a clearing, and I saw the sort of longhouse I had read about in books on the Borneo rain forest. Constructed of rough-hewn wooden planks and standing on stilts, it was about eighty yards long and had none of the Western touches that gave the Uma Bawang longhouse a motel-like appearance. To enter the longhouse, we climbed a set of steep wooden steps to the veranda, along which were eighteen doors, each opening into the quarters of an extended family. While everyone who lives at Long Leng knows the number of doors—to a Borneo forest dweller the word "door" is synonymous with "family"—the individual apart from the family counts for so little that no one could tell us the community's population. When I put the question to Loli Mirai, the headman, he looked startled, as if he had never thought about it before, and said he guessed that the correct number was somewhere between eighty and a hundred. The rooms at Long Leng were bare; the rattan mats, pillows, and rickety furniture I had seen at Uma Bawang would strike a Penan as unbelievable opulence. Although Loli welcomed us with great warmth, he couldn't provide a mat or a blanket for either of us to sleep on; our bed was to be the rough wooden floor in his quarters. There is no electricity at Long Leng; at night, the darkness is broken only by the glow of wood fires from cooking pits in the kitchens, which are at ground level behind each family's quarters. The rooms aren't much lighter during the day, because there are few windows; the Penan, who have lived in the darkness of the deep forest for centuries, seem comfortable in the dim light of the longhouse.

As we climbed to the veranda, children ran over to us, took one look at me, and raced to their mothers, shrieking in terror. I was later told that this was only the second time a Westerner had visited Long Leng. It had been a difficult journey, and I was hot and muddy enough to think about a bath in the nearby river, but the etiquette of the Borneo rain forest prescribes that a visitor must first sit on the floor of the headman's room, surrounded by anyone in the longhouse who is interested, and tell the story of his journey in elaborate detail. The Penan had no written language until Christian missionaries came, and they value such long accounts. Only when Jok had finished his story and answered questions did I leave for the river. The headman's son, Charley Loli, insisted on accompanying me, out of concern that I might meet up with a crocodile. Like many of the younger men at Long Leng, Charley, a tall man in his early twenties with a wispy mustache, wore shorts and a T-shirt instead of a loincloth. No one wore shoes; the Penan barefooted could master terrain that I found impossible in sneakers.

At Uma Bawang, I had had to attend the meetings at Jok's house to understand the difficulties that the natives faced. At Long Leng, the problems surrounded me, day and night. Within an hour of my arrival, I noticed a boy with a festering two-inch-long cut on his leg. I cleaned it with alcohol, then applied antibiotic ointment and a bandage. From that moment on, until I left the next day, people besieged me with requests for help with their medical problems. Two babies had been afflicted with diarrhea for several days, and one looked so weakened as to be in danger of dying; I could do nothing but recommend that they be taken to Marudi. Several people complained of toothaches, and when children crowded around me the smell of their breath was almost overpowering. Many of the Penan, including teenagers, had lost some or most of their teeth. At night, I heard the constant coughing and crying of children—a noise that penetrated the thin walls and traveled up and down the longhouse. Long Leng had a little two-room clinic, built by the government, but it contained no medicine and had no doctor. The shelves were bare except for many bottles of an orange-colored liquid, which I guessed was an antiseptic. I had heard about a government-sponsored flying-doctor service that visited longhouses by helicopter, but the people at Long Leng said they had never seen a doctor there. Later, in Kuching, a government official told me that the service didn't visit every community but announced by radio where it would be, so that people could come if they were within walking distance. The people at Long Leng, however, with no electricity and no money to buy batteries, hardly seemed to be in a position to benefit from that system.

Even government officials acknowledge that, of all the native groups, the Penan are suffering the most severely from the impact of logging. They are paying the price for their distinctive culture, with its complete dependence on the hunting of animals and the gathering of forest products for daily existence. Now that the wild game has been driven away by the logging operations, and many of the plants have been ground up by bulldozers, the Penan have found themselves incapable of making the quick changes needed for their survival. Most attempts at planting crops have failed, because the Penan have no sense of the passage of seasons that determine when the crops should be sown and harvested. They have had some success only with tapioca and bananas, since both can be harvested year-round.

In an interview, Wade Davis, the Canadian ethnobotanist, explained the problem: "The minute you have to plant things, it determines the notion of time, the patterns of settlement, and it totally transforms your relationship with nature. The Penan have no sense of time or season. If you ask a Penan whether his journey was long, a long journey will be one of hardship, or perhaps much exposure to the sun; a short journey is one in which there were many wild pigs to hunt. There is no traditional sense of the length of a journey, because of their nomadic past; they were constantly on the move, and there was no place to get to. Until five thousand years ago, this is what all of us were. These people represent what we were for most of our history." The Penan are doubly bedeviled: although it's important for them to switch to agriculture, they, unlike the other forest groups, have no traditional community farmland that they can claim. There is no question of compensation; the loggers can drive bulldozers to their door with impunity. And no Penan have taken logging jobs, for the skills needed are too removed from their culture. Nor have any of their young people chosen to settle in cities in the hope of earning money to send back to the longhouse; for them it would represent a far too alien existence.

Each year, the skills developed over the centuries by the Penan serve them less. "I spent three years all over Latin America studying the rain forests," Davis said. "I've been with at least twenty indigenous tribes in the Amazon and Latin America. But the knowledge of the forest by the Penan surpasses all of them. It's unbelievable." Those who have studied Penan feats of navigation through the rain forest are deeply impressed. The Penan chart their position in relation to rivers, knowing the size of each river and the angle at which it flows. They give names to various features along each trail—to a particular rock face, say—so that the features can be remembered and recognized. In the absence of a written language, the Penan developed an elaborate system of trail directions using whittled and notched sticks stuck in the ground, and they still use this system. As hunters, they are so skilled with the blowpipe that they can put two darts in it and blow out one at a time. They recognize more than a hundred fruiting trees and at least fifty medicinal plants. "There are plants that yield glue to trap birds, toxic latex for poison darts, rare resins and gums for trade, twine for baskets, leaves for shelter and sandpaper, wood to make blowpipes, boats, tools, and musical instruments," Davis writes. And combined with all these skills are a reverence for the forest and deep-seated traditions for preserving it. To maintain the population of wild pigs, they never cut or disturb trees that produce the fruits the pigs eat. They harvest sago—a starch from the trunk of a particular species of palm tree that serves as the basic carbohydrate in their diet—in a way that enhances the area's long-term sago growth, and they won't return to a depleted stand of sago palms for many years, so that it can regenerate. There is a word for cutting more sago than is needed—a deed that the Penan believe will incur the wrath of the supernatural.

Today, navigating through the rain forest consists of hitching a ride on a logging truck, since logging roads crisscross even the remotest reaches of the rain forest. What used to be a two-day walk from Long Leng to the nearest Kayan longhouse takes only an hour and a half by truck. Food is in desperately short supply; many of the stands of sago palms have been bulldozed by the logging operations. Much of the river water is polluted. In April 1990, Dr. Tatsuo Hayashi, a physician working with the Japan International Volunteer Center, spent two weeks examining Penan in the Baram region. "The lack of foods containing protein and vitamins was obvious," he reported. He found an "extremely high" rate of intestinal parasitic diseases and predicted a rapid rise in cases of amoebic dysentery and malnutrition.

The effects of logging magnified the problems that had already been created by the encroachment of modern civilization. Over the past several decades, all but a few hundred of Sarawak's nine thousand Penan abandoned their nomadic way of life and settled in longhouses—a difficult change for a people unschooled in the ways of agriculture and trade. The pressure for settlement had come from the government, starting in British colonial times; some officials found the idea of a nomadic tribe in the forest to be an embarrassment, and others genuinely wanted to provide the Penan with services. Pressure also came from the missionaries, who persuaded the Penan to discard a superstitious belief that required them to move on whenever a member of the community died. But adjustment to life in the longhouse was never easy. In February 1990, when a group of European and Asian foreign ministers held a meeting in Kuching, the Sarawak state government took them and some reporters to visit a showpiece longhouse that the state had opened for a group of Penan three months before, in Batu Bungan. Raphael Pura, who has covered the logging controversy extensively for the *Asian Wall Street Journal*, reported that, much to the chagrin of the Sarawak officials, the Penan used the occasion to complain about their conditions. "Logging has forced game to flee, polluted streams and generally made life as the Penan lead it unlivable," he wrote. "Bewildered about the present and uncertain about the future, the Penan appear dispirited."

The logging operations affected the lives of the Penan to such an extent that some of them turned to an activity that had no precedent in their culture: civil disobedience. Starting in March 1987, Penan families participated in erecting barricades on logging roads. In December 1988 and January 1989, a total of 128 Penan were arrested for manning the blockades, and many were kept in jail for several days, under what were later charged to be brutal conditions. In a statement to SAM's newspaper, one of the Penan said that during the first few days in the Marudi police station "over 70 of us were cooped up in two small cells with one toilet," and he added, "There wasn't a place to lie down, only to squat or sit the night through. Some of us had to lie on top of one another." As in the case of the Kayan arrested at Uma Bawang, none of the Penan were actually convicted. But handcuffing the men, dragging them from their families, and throwing them in jail under a system whose laws and language they didn't understand proved traumatic.

In their protests, the Penan gained an unlikely ally—a young, reclusive Swiss shepherd named Bruno Manser. Ultimately, he so alienated Malaysian officials that he had the unique distinction of being denounced simultaneously as a Communist, a Zionist, and a would-be Tarzan. Manser, who was fascinated by the indigenous people of the rain forest, had come to Sarawak in 1984 and lived with a group of nomadic Penan. He adopted the Penan life, wearing a loincloth, learning their language and hunting techniques, and giving up all material possessions except paper, a pen, and a flute. The pictures of Manser in the jungle, complete with ankle and leg bands and native circular haircut, are startling; he looks every inch a Penan except for a very European face with wire-rimmed glasses. In six years in the rain forest, Manser compiled a Penan-English dictionary, filled a number of journals with notes and sketches, and helped the Penan communicate with other native groups and with Western-ers about the difficulties caused by logging. It was this last activity that got him into trouble with the government, which seized upon his presence as proof that "outside agitators" were provoking the logging blockades. About two hundred soldiers searched the rain forest for him, and the government offered a $35,000 reward for his arrest. At one point, the soldiers caught him, but he escaped by diving off a police boat into a river. In 1990, Manser decided that he could do more good by leaving Borneo and publicizing the plight of the Penan, and he successfully slipped out of Sarawak.

Manser, a shy and introspective intellectual, bridles at the idea of being called a Tarzan or an Indiana Jones, and in interviews he will talk only about the Penan and not about himself. But Anja Light, an environmentalist who spent several days with him at Penan encampments in June 1989 and again in January 1990, told me about his life in the rain forest. Light's two trips to visit the nomadic Penan were themselves not without risk, since the police and soldiers looking for Manser had done their best to turn the rain forest into an armed camp. On her first visit, she had to walk a day and a half with a Penan guide to evade the troops searching for Manser; the second time, she hid under a tarpaulin in a Land Cruiser while her guide and her driver persuaded soldiers that they were out on a hunting expedition. "Bruno was treated by the Penan as one of their own," Light said. "They called him a *lakeh Penan*—a Penan person. They didn't want him to leave. A lot of his work was disseminating information among the tribes. He could write messages and help coordinate activities. Also, he talked to the Penan a lot about the methods of nonviolence; he was influenced strongly by Gandhi. He was a very solitary person; sometimes he went into the forest alone to do his studies. The Penan thought he was crazy when he would climb a ridge just so he could look out over the land, or when he caught snakes just to sketch them, and then let the snakes go. I liked Bruno from the start. I had my recorder, and we played flute and recorder duets together. He really seemed not to possess an ego; that was the Gandhian image in him. People who met him left feeling really touched." Light said that she visited Manser in Switzerland in September 1990. "Every day, he's speaking to groups," she said. "Every evening, he does writing about his experiences in the jungle. He has traveled all over the world on speaking tours, without a break, since he came out of the forest. He still looks like a Penan to me—his energy is like theirs."

I spoke with Manser by telephone in October 1990, when he stopped in Calgary in the course of a world tour that took him to another city every couple of days. "I don't like this life style," he said. "I will retire as soon as success is achieved."

I asked him why he was so dedicated to saving the Penan culture.

"What's being done is a violation of human rights," he replied. "It's more important than just an environmental disaster—there's a human rights issue. We are using their resources to promote our own way of life. They were a happy people, sharing everything with each other, with more than enough to eat. Their society had been in harmony with nature. 'Stay peaceful' is the law of the Penan. They don't take more from nature than they need. But look at our society. What are we leaving for future generations?"

Much of what I saw in Long Leng validated Manser's apprehensions. Long Leng's setting, in a bowl of hills and next to a fast-flowing river, is idyllic, but behind the ridgelines in every direction the loggers have already done their work. "Our longhouse is an island," Loli Mirai told me in one of several conversations we had. "The logging is all around. Before logging, you could hear the sounds of monkeys and other animals, but now the timber companies are surrounding us."

The first loggers arrived at Long Leng in 1981 and contributed building materials to the longhouse as a conciliatory gesture. But the good will did not last long, because it was followed by an act that the Penan considered a desecration. The very next year, the bulldozers plowed through the community's burial ground, a mile from the longhouse, and built a logging camp right on the grave sites. "We had put up a sign, but it did no good," a Penan named Seman Yang told me as I sat with a dozen Long Leng residents on the floor of Loli's room. "My mother and father were buried there."

The timber camp on the old burial ground was the site of one of the barricades that the Penan erected in 1987 and 1988. I asked the people at Long Leng whether any of them had been arrested in the protests. Many had been, I learned, and at one point four Long Leng residents had been kept in jail for two months. Joseph Lalong (some of the Penan bear Christian names, because of the influence of the missionaries) was one of the four. "There were so many mosquitoes I couldn't sleep," he said. "They wouldn't give me a mosquito net, and there was no soap the whole time. They wouldn't give us fresh water. They pointed to the pipe used to flush the latrine and said to drink from that pipe. During the two months, they allowed me only one visit by my wife, for five minutes. I was very worried about my wife and daughter. Three families lived in the same room; all the husbands were in jail, so my wife's father had to search for food for all of them. The day I was released, her father collapsed on the logging road and died. I think he starved to death."

I asked about the trial for bridge burning which I had attended in Marudi. Our conversation brought out the complete bewilderment that the Penan feel on being caught up in a swirl of political and economic forces that they barely understand. I pressed them about dates and chronology, but their responses were hopelessly contradictory, because none of them had learned to think about events in such a context. They had, however, heard the word "Communist"—a Communist, they knew, was someone bad— and when it came up in our conversation everyone laughed. "The government always calls us Communists," Loli said. "Actually, we feel the real Communists are the timber companies, because they are the destroyers."

The people of Long Leng had grasped little about the Marudi trial or about the significance of the magistrate's throwing out the confession of Aping Mirai, who was the one defendant who could sign his name. Aping was in the group speaking with me, and he told me how the whole affair had begun. "The police and timber-company officials came to the longhouse and asked us to come to the timber camp," he said. "The police officer they took me to see slapped me four times and said, 'You are a criminal.' I had no idea what this was about. I didn't know what was happening. Finally, they told us the timber company suspected us of burning the bridges. After they took us to Marudi and locked us up, we were so scared we agreed to what they said."

The dispute over logging wasn't all that was on the mind of the Penan of Long Leng. "The forest is empty," a man named Juling Deon told me. "There is no more food supply in the forest. Sometimes we don't have anything to cook. Sometimes our children are crying for food." That particular day, a hunting party had been out since dawn, and it returned as darkness fell. For a change, there had been some luck: one of the men had caught a mouse deer, an animal the size of a dog. But that would provide only one tiny bite of meat for each person in the longhouse. The hunters had walked for miles and had been without food for the entire day, but when I glanced at their faces

I saw more than hunger. A pall hung over them—the look of men who could no longer provide for their families. Charley Loli took me from kitchen to kitchen to visit all eighteen of the families. Some were stirring pots of tapioca paste, a substitute for sago; others, apparently having eaten all their tapioca flour earlier that day, were just sitting around their cooking fire talking in quiet voices. Loli's family of ten, whom I was joining for dinner, had the benefit of snack food I had brought for the trip. It wasn't much, but it supplemented the tapioca, and they plunged in eagerly. Then we sat on the floor in the darkness and talked, our conversation punctuated by the sound of rats skittering around the room.

My taxi driver in Kuching needed no address to find the house of Y. A. B. Datuk Patinggi Tan Sri Haji Abdul Taib bin Mahmud, the chief minister of Sarawak. Everyone knows where it is, for it is perhaps the most magnificent house in Sarawak, and, though I didn't have an invitation, I wanted at least to see it from the street. Situated on acres of land on a plain across the Sarawak River from central Kuching, the house has an unusual roof line, suggesting the turrets and the dome of the Taj Mahal. I later spoke with a Kuching resident who had been to the house many times, and she described the interior for me. "Have you seen a Hollywood set for the house of an eccentric Italian count?" she asked. "That's what it's like. It's stuffed full of antiques, and there are beautiful Oriental rugs. When there are official receptions, though, they take place outside the house, under canvas awnings. You can look through the windows, but you can't go in. Some people think that that's a bit much—they invite you to their house but they won't let you in." The house isn't the chief minister's only impressive possession. He drives a Rolls-Royce, and his office contains a fountain—because, one associate explains, "he is a religious man and it helps him meditate." In a country where politicians collect titles the way generals collect medals, his very name bespeaks status. Y. A. B., for Yang Amat Berhormat, is equivalent to "the Right Honorable." Datuk Patinggi is a title comparable to a British knighthood. Tan Sri translates as "lord." On official portraits, his name is followed by the initials of nine other honors, including one each from Thailand, Indonesia, Brunei, and South Korea.

While Taib is clearly a very wealthy man, his precise worth is a matter of speculation. It is masked by a complex web of financial transactions. The ITTO report on Sarawak neatly compresses what the organization calls the "concession hierarchy" into one sentence: "The licensee, i.e. the concession holder or concessionaire, sub-contracts his rights to a second party who in turn sub-contracts the [logging] operation to a third party who employs the people who actually do the logging on the basis of payment by output." At the top of the hierarchy is the minister of resource planning, who has sole discretion to give out logging concessions. Taib finds the time to hold this portfolio himself, along with that of chief minister. Under the law, he can grant concessions to anyone he wants: relatives, friends, political associates, or nominee shareholders—people who hold concessions on behalf of secret beneficiaries. The concessions are granted free of charge, and the holder isn't required to know the difference between a live tree and a telephone pole, since the actual logging can be subcontracted. Nor does the holder have to prove financial viability. "We've looked at their incorporation forms, and some say their paid-up capital is two dollars," Ngau told me. Occasionally, the chief minister is in a charitable mood, as was the case several years ago when he granted a concession to the Sarawak Football Association. But longhouse communities need not apply; all their efforts to gain concessions have been turned down.

The people of Sarawak got a peek behind the veil of secrecy in 1987, when a dispute erupted during Taib's campaign for re-election. His political opponent happened to be his uncle Abdul Rahman Yakub, who had been his predecessor as chief minister, and the two tried to make political capital out of revealing each other's timber holdings. Taib took the initiative, saying that he was revoking timber licenses for twenty-five concessions totalling 3 million acres held by friends and relatives of his uncle, and Rahman responded by giving the press the names of relatives, friends, and associates of Taib's who held almost 4 million acres. The lists of both candidates included wives and daughters and involved front companies and foreign bank accounts. The combined acreage of the two political opponents amounted to half the forest land in Sarawak that was then still available for logging. I had read an article putting the value of the logging concessions controlled by Taib at $4 billion, and in Penang I asked Thayalan, the SAM lawyer, whether such a thing was possible. He called the estimate "reasonable."

The politicians aren't the only people who profit. The timber merchants who do the actual logging—they are mostly Sarawaki-ans of Chinese descent—share in the proceeds. (There is a racial split throughout Malaysia, with politics dominated by the Malays and business by the ethnic Chinese. Taib is a Melanau, a member of a Muslim indigenous group in Sarawak closely allied with the Malays.) The most powerful of the timber merchants, Tiong Hiew King, is a man of considerable political influence, and he himself has been awarded logging concessions. A senator in the Malaysian Parliament, he runs a family timber company that does more than $185 million worth of business a year. Raphael Pura, of the *Asian Wall Street Journal*, investigated Sarawak landholdings in an article in February 1990 and reported, "Sen. Tiong's 800,000-hectare [1,970,000-acre] timber empire of concessions and logging contracts includes the forest that Uma Bawang's rebel farmers are struggling to retain. His partners in that concession: Tan Sri Taib's sister, the Sarawak government, a private Islamic foundation, and a second influen-

tial senator." How much the timber merchants pay the conces-
sionaires under the table to get the contracts for the logging
operations is unknown, but there is speculation that $20 million
to gain a single contract isn't unusual.

Of the vast amounts of revenue from logging, the system
provides a relative pittance to the government. The timber companies have to pay Malaysian income taxes, but their financial
statements often end up showing losses or only small profits. In
his 1990 article, Pura wrote about one such company, Rimbunan
Hijau, which operates in the Baram area. Between 1976 and
1987, it took in more than $750 million in revenues but paid the
federal government less than $2 million in taxes. The state
government collects a royalty on each ton of logs. That amounts
to only a percent or two of the timber's selling price, but so
extensive is the scale of logging that this revenue provides nearly
half of Sarawak's budget. Where does the rest of the logging
income go? Sarawak is rife with rumors of large-scale transfers
of capital overseas, of purchases of land and homes in Canada
and Australia, of bank accounts in Switzerland. "These people
are millionaires," Ngau says of Sarawak's politicians and timber
merchants. "They cannot spend the money in their lifetime."
One fact is certain: little money reaches the longhouses beyond
the wages of logging workers and whatever can be squeezed out
of the Sarawak government in the way of compensation for lost
lands. For the Penan, there is no money at all.

Everything about Sarawak's Ali Baba system of timber concessions places importance on getting as many logs as possible out
of the rain forest as quickly as possible. The politicians face an
election every five years, and if they lose, their successors could
revoke the concessions. The timber merchants get paid for each
ton cut, so a tree left unlogged represents money they cannot
claim. And hanging over all this is the specter of restrictions that
the government of Sarawak might someday be forced to impose
in order to make logging sustainable. That specter was renewed

again in March 1991, when the Malaysian government threatened to curb the export of raw logs in Sarawak, in an effort to spur the growth of wood-based industries. The result has been a feverish effort to cut down trees—an effort so intense that logs are being hauled away even in the middle of the night. "The truck drivers work until 11:00 p.m.," Ngau told me. "And then they're wakened by the foremen at 2:00 a.m. to work again. That's why the rate of accidents is so high." The government regulations that do exist are routinely ignored. State officials have never suspended or revoked a company's license for destructive logging practices. I asked a researcher who has spent some time in Sarawak about the impact of the concession system.

"The basic cause of the damage from logging is the economic system under which logging operates," he replied. "It's the policies that the government allows to prevail. The forest could have been harvested at a sustainable rate. The argument of the need for development is not an honest argument, because the amount being set aside for development is very low. You don't see alternative industries, new employment, improved housing, major gains in education, but all these things should have been possible in the way this resource has been converted into cash. Basically, the end result has been a massive transfer of wealth from the poor to the rich in the form of wood, which is being converted into cash and invested outside Sarawak."

I wanted to discuss this issue with Taib, but the chief minister had no interest in talking to me. His press secretary took my initial call and then refused to speak with me further, and never responded to my request for copies of Taib's speeches on logging. Some Sarawakian officials were more forthcoming, however. I met Leo Chai, the director of forests, in his office in the Sarawak Timber Industry Development Corporation Building, a twenty-story skyscraper that houses the government agencies concerned with forestry, as well as the Sarawak Timber Museum and the quasi-public STIDC. In an unfortunate flight of fancy, an architect had designed the building to look like an axed tree stump, with the roof flat in the center and slanting unevenly down to the vertical walls. The fact that the government agencies charged with protecting the rain forest are housed in a tree stump of sorts is a piece of symbolism not lost on opponents of logging. Chai declared that "there's no way we can finish logging the forest in eleven years," and he told me that the government had plans to reduce the annual logging cut by a third before 1995 to make sure that the logging was sustainable. "We will have a compromise with the timber companies," he said. "We will extend their licenses, and they, in turn, will reduce their annual cut." But Chai was less reassuring when I asked how such a provision could be enforced, since logging companies do pretty much as they please no matter what the regulations. "Their licenses can be suspended if they are found to do excessive damage," he said, but he conceded that in the first nine months of 1990 there had been only one suspension, and it was for logging in another company's area. Chai described himself as a professional forester and sidestepped questions on the concession system.

After my visit to Long Leng, I was curious about all the claims by state officials of government programs to aid the Penan. At Long Leng, except for a notice saying that the longhouse had been visited by a malaria-control officer, I could find no evidence of aid. I asked Jayl Langub, a Sarawakian government official who I had been informed had devised many of the Penan-assistance plans, what had happened to it. He told me of an idea proposed in 1988 as an alternative to uprooting the Penan and relocating them, which had been done at the unfortunate show-piece longhouse at Batu Bungan; instead, the government would establish service centers at centrally located Penan settlements, so that others could walk there. Each center would have a school, a clinic, and an agricultural station. "Our proposal was submitted in 1988," he said. "Now it's 1990, and not much has happened.

It has always been 'next year.' There is no lack of ideas, but we have a problem with implementation."

The most forceful advocate of the government's point of view is James Wong, the minister of the environment and tourism and also the head of a political party allied with Taib. Wong, who says of himself, "I am going to be famous for being infamous," happens to own a logging company and to operate a timber concession of 400,000 acres. In the anomalous world of Sarawakian politics, the fact that the environment minister moonlights as a logger doesn't raise an eyebrow. But it has drawn expressions of outrage from overseas, and Wong can't understand why; he points out that the trees he cuts down come under the jurisdiction of the Forestry Department, not his own. Other government officials might shy away from the press, but Wong relishes being interviewed. And in 1988, when the London *Sunday Times* printed an article he objected to, he responded by writing a five-part series called "Stumble in the Jungle" for a Sarawak newspaper. The series was illustrated with photographs of swidden agriculture, which Wong blames for the destruction of the forests. Captions included lines like "Not a single tree is spared" and "Soil erosion caused by shifting cultivation, which contributes to river pollution." The series included a poem Wong wrote about the Penan, beginning, "O Penan—Jungle wanderers of the Tree / What would the future hold for thee?" Referring to the wearing of loincloths, which are called *chawats*, the poem asks whether society "in good conscience" could "allow him"—a Penan—"to subsist in Blowpipes and clothed in *Chawats*."

On my last evening in Sarawak, I interviewed Datuk Amar Wong (Datuk Amar, like Taib's Datuk Patinggi, is a title equivalent to knighthood) just after he landed on a flight from Kuala Lumpur. In Malaysia, a high status in society provides you with many prerogatives, as well as with titles before your name. Wong arrived at a V.I.P. terminal next to Kuching airport's main terminal, and a large green Mercedes with flags on the front fenders waited outside for him. He was greeted by an entourage of family and associates, and then I went into a meeting room with him. The juxtaposition of his two jobs has made Wong easy to paint as the villain of the Sarawak logging tragedy, but in person he is difficult to dislike. Exuberant and intense, looking much younger than his age, which was sixty-eight, he raced from one subject to another; his volubility faded on only one subject. When I asked for an estimate of the worth of the timber holdings of Taib's family and associates, he simply said, "I can't answer that."

Wong feels maligned by the world's press. "Sarawak has 1.7 million people," he said. "There are twenty-four different native races, each with its own language and culture. The Penan are just one. And out of nine thousand Penan, only three hundred are real nomads. These are the ones Bruno Manser lived with. He got so much press, and he gave the impression we were ogres, having Penan for breakfast, lunch, and dinner. People don't understand that logging in Sarawak is selective logging, culling, leaving the balance to regenerate. Even our local papers made a hue and cry over logging. They say there's no more fish in the river and I say, 'Rubbish. I'll show you some fish. The fish are there; the forests are there.' After I showed the local reporters, they were converted. It would be nice if human beings could eat the egg without breaking the shell. Even the Greens live in houses, and those houses were built on land with trees on them. Will you please report factually? We love this country, we care."

Like Chai, Wong thinks that only a relatively modest reduction in logging is needed to make the timber supply in the Sarawak rain forest sustainable indefinitely. Environmentalists sharply disagree. A paper published by the National Wildlife Federation concluded that a reduction in Sarawak logging of at least 85 percent would be necessary. Other environmentalists question whether sustained-yield forestry can work under any set of circumstances in the tropics, because the soil is poor and might not support endless generations of newly planted trees. If Sarawakian officials are looking at the situation with undue optimism, it's easy to see why: the consequences of running out of logs are too grim for a politician to deal with before it happens. Native communities now dependent on income from logging jobs will be cut dry and will be unable to turn to the depleted forest for sustenance. Nor will the state, deprived of much of its revenues, be able to step in with support. "What's going to happen when the timber is gone?" asks Hong, the anthropologist. "Politicians will have made the money, and the natives will have lost their land and their society. They will be no better off than the aborigines in Australia. They'll drift to towns, become despondent, turn to alcohol. Drunkenness and violence are already increasing among the tribespeople who now live in the cities, and these are a people traditionally known for being peaceful."

A solution to the crisis of the Sarawak rain forest will not be easy to find. Some environmentalists want an international boycott of Malaysian timber, but others argue that if the trees are rendered valueless, vast areas of the forest will be bulldozed for agriculture, cattle ranches, and the like. Some rain forest advocates are also promoting a boycott against Mitsubishi products, since Mitsubishi is the most visible of the big Japanese conglomerates involved in the Borneo timber trade. Two long-term solutions make considerable sense. One is for the Sarawak government to ban the export of raw logs from Sarawak, since the milling process would create considerably more revenue and lessen the need to cut down so many trees; it's estimated that making a log into a piece of furniture, for instance, would increase the revenue yield seven times. The second is for the government to encourage tourism and the collection and sale of forest products to replace part of the income from logging; some experts feel that marketing pharmaceuticals from jungle plants represents a huge, largely untapped market. But either of these proposed solutions would require enormous international pressure to break the stranglehold of the politicians and timber merchants of Sarawak—a stranglehold that puts money in their pockets for every tree that is cut down.

What about the people of the rain forest? The issue is not whether change should come to the forest; as the color televisions in the wealthier longhouses illustrate, change is inevitable. The real question is who governs the change: those who live in the forest, or those who want to exploit the forest dwellers for the riches of their land? Several people I spoke with mentioned the Amish as an ideal model, since they have been free to choose for themselves what aspects of the modern world they want to accept. Rao, the United Nations forestry official, puts the problem this way: "Not all logging is ecologically destructive. We couldn't be where we are today without having created arable land. The question is: For whose benefit is the forest subject to attack? If this attack is happening to make a few rich men richer, it is repugnant to the values of society. If it benefits the life of the forest people—their health and education, their standard of living—then it's acceptable. There's one thing I can say categorically: the people who benefit should be the ones who have a vested interest in the resource for generations to come. The perceptions of outsiders should not be imposed on them. If they want change, if they feel the urgency of change, then you can't say that change will be for the worse."

Shibuya Station, in Tokyo, exceeds even that city's normal standards of congestion. With its rail and subway lines, it is always a sea of people, both inside and on a big plaza in front. In the plaza is a famous statue of a dog named Hachiko, who waited faithfully outside the station each day for ten years after his master died one day at work. One day in October 1990, a demonstration took place next to the statue to mark the opening of World Rain Forest Week. It was the first time Japanese environmentalists had participated in the worldwide activities, and about twenty members of the Japan Tropical Forest Action Network, or JATAN, passed out leaflets as a folksinger entertained. It was a warm, sunny day, and thousands of people passed by during the hour I was there. But only about thirty stopped to see what was going on, and about two-thirds of those were foreigners.

Clearly, the environmental movement has yet to penetrate, or even to dent, the Japanese consciousness, but activists are working hard to improve the situation. JATAN and several other environmental groups share a cramped apartment, piled to the ceiling with papers, in a run-down building with the grandly inappropriate name of Shibuya Mansion. Yoichi Kuroda, JATAN's coordinator, often sleeps on the floor there, because he is faced with too much work to allow him the luxury of going home at night. In a country of gray or blue suits for men and prim dresses for women, the uniform of both the male and the female environmentalists is blue jeans and a T-shirt. While the environmentalists haven't succeeded in spurring a mass movement, their frequent press conferences and demonstrations have caught the attention of Japanese companies. The companies have responded, but not by changing their practices. "They're very polite to me," Kuroda told me. "Corporations call our office and ask us to have lunch." In 1989, the Los Angeles *Times* reported, "Mitsubishi and 86 other members of the Japan Lumber Importers' Association have reacted to criticism by contributing to a $70,000 fund aimed at promoting environmental research. That represents a commitment of about $800 per company."

The voracious Japanese appetite for tropical hardwood has turned Sarawak into something resembling a Japanese plantation. The Japanese government sent foreign aid to build logging roads, justifying the move by arguing that the roads would be traveled by local people. Yet, as a National Wildlife Federation study of Japanese economic assistance pointed out, these people could use the road only by "hitchhiking rides on the many logging trucks, clinging dangerously to the back of speeding vehicles overloaded with logs." There are Japanese engineers directing the building of bridges and logging roads and Japanese companies supplying the heavy machinery. In 1989, Japanese imports of Sarawak logs jumped by 27 percent and represented 53 percent of Japan's total tropical-log import volume. That year, Sarawak sent almost half its logs to Japan; the remainder went mainly to eight other Asian countries.

I had come to Japan to learn about the final destination of so many of the trees taken from the Sarawak rain forest. I later realized that I carried an American's preconception—the idea that tropical hardwoods are put to the most artistic, craftsmanlike uses, like beautiful houses and finely carved furniture. But when the staff members of JATAN laid the statistics in front of me I saw something dramatically different. Three-quarters of the tropical hardwood coming into Japan ends up as plywood, mostly for the construction industry. Many of the new houses as well as commercial buildings going up in Japan today are of reinforced concrete, not wood. To pour the concrete walls, a mold is necessary, and the mold is almost always made of plywood. In the United States, plywood for this purpose comes from softwoods, often pine—a low-cost wood that can be grown on tree farms. But 96 percent of Japan's plywood is made from tropical hardwoods. On the average, the plywood molds can be used two or three times before they become heavily damaged. Then they are discarded—either buried in a landfill or (in areas with fewer air pollution problems than Tokyo) burned.

Sarawak's dipterocarps provide a beautiful, durable wood, resistant to warping, with a smooth, defect-free surface. Why use this wood for such a lowly purpose as plywood molding that quickly winds up on the scrap heap? The answer is price. In defiance of logic, it costs less to cut down a tree in Sarawak, ship it to Japan, mill it into thin sheets, and glue them together for plywood than to make plywood from an inferior softwood tree growing in Japan. Part of the explanation is labor; loggers and truck drivers in Japan earn far more than comparable workers in Sarawak. But a less obvious reason is that the Sarawak rain forests are free; no compensation for the use of the land is factored into the cost of the tree. The Sarawak government gives out the concessions instead of charging for them, and the forest people, whose land it has been for centuries, get nothing or a pittance. In the skewed system of politically motivated contracts and under-the-table payments, the actual worth of the raw material becomes irrelevant. The system allows, in effect, for the gold of the Sarawak rain forest to be minted into pennies.

The tropical plywood has become so much a part of the Japanese construction industry that building contractors wouldn't consider anything else. Richard Forrest, the eastern-Asia representative of the National Wildlife Federation—which is one of the groups that share the apartment in Shibuya Mansion—told me, "Plywood in the United States looks bad; there are knots, weak spots, and an uneven surface. In Japan, plywood has not a single knot, not a single defect. I spoke with an official of the Japan Lumber Importers' Association, and he said the Japanese construction industry would never accept what he called 'zebra plywood.' They're using a material far too good for many of its uses." Forrest said that some of this plywood also went to make cheap furniture—furniture so little valued that it's often discarded on the street when people move to a new home.

I asked Forrest to show me some of the plywood molding. We didn't have to walk far. The area around Shibuya Mansion was filled with construction sites, and sheets of the plywood were everywhere. At one building, the concrete had hardened, and the ripped-up plywood lay in a big heap, ready to be trucked off to the dump. In Shibuya Mansion itself, the elevator had sheets of the tropical hardwood taped to three of the walls, to keep the walls from being scratched when furniture was being moved, just as canvas is used for that purpose in the United States. I rubbed the palm of my hand across the plywood in a broad sweeping motion. I had always associated plywood with an uncomfortably rough surface and the possibility of a splinter, but here the wood had a completely smooth, almost velvety feel. As for the elevator walls that were being protected, they were made of plastic that unconvincingly imitated a wood-grain finish.

ACKNOWLEDGMENTS

The challenge of finding a good story in the jungles of Borneo and the mountains of Laos is not half as difficult as that of taking a long, impenetrable manuscript and whipping it into shape. A skilled editor is the rarest of talents in journalism, and I've had the great pleasure of working with five of them.

Bob Gottlieb, the former editor of *The New Yorker*, displayed unerring instincts again and again in handling my articles. Notwithstanding the endless pressures of a weekly magazine, he would usually read the manuscript the day it arrived, reacting with an uncanny ability to sense what was missing and what needed to be rearranged. Then Pat Crow would take over, with wisdom, a delightful dry wit, and the ability to remain unflappable against the onslaught of a writer's mania and paranoia.

Jon Segal, my editor at Knopf, painstakingly brought the pieces of this book together into a cohesive whole. Jeffrey Klein, the editor of *Mother Jones*, provided patience and skill in working with me on my manuscript on Burma; his advice made the articles that followed a much easier task. Above all, I want to thank Tom Goldstein, dean of the Graduate School of Journalism at the University of California, Berkeley, for his invaluable critiques and line editing; his sound judgment and his generous commitment of time left me with a debt I will never be able to repay.

INDEX